THE BIBLE CAME FROM SYRIA

JAMES RAPPAI

Published by Sagacity Books in 2014

For information regarding special discounts for bulk purchases, please contact Sagacity Books at: sagacitybooks@gmail.com

Manufactured in the United States of America

ISBN 978-81-906418-1-4

Subject classification: 1. Bible Evidence 2. Biblical Geography 3. Biblical Archaeology 4. Ancient Near Eastern Archaeology 5. Egyptology

To My Sweet Lord

T A B L E   O F   C O N T E N T S

Spoors Of A Predator

Now shall this company lick up all that are round about us, as the ox licketh up the grass of the field.... Behold, there is a people come out from Egypt: behold, they cover the face of the earth and they abide over against me: [Numbers 22.4&5]

The frightening specter of the Jewish army in repose across the River Jordan, after its first round of slaughter, draws incredible prose from Balak, the King of Moab. Note his inspired imagery: "this company lick up all... as ox licketh up the grass in the field... they cover the face of the earth." In modern parlance, it would translate to 'a veritable fighting machine capable of mowing down everything in its path.' The hapless king is out of his mind with fear. Tomorrow it is his kingdom's turn and his ill-equipped native army is no match for this professional army at his doorsteps.

One can well envision this unnerving sight documented in the Old Testament that heightened Balak's anxiety. Seen from atop the Mountains of Pisgah, this bird's eye view left nothing to imagination regarding the incredible strength and professionalism of the Jewish army. Balak was King of Moab, one of the principal kingdoms on the Plain of the Jordan and the professional army at its doorsteps, the one said to have 'come out of Egypt' was the Israelite army, the same that is associated with the Exodus episode. The Israelite army, purportedly a makeshift body of slaves totaling six hundred thousand odd, had dramatically exited out of Egypt in search of greener pastures. They had come here, to Canaan on the Plain of the Jordan, with intentions of capturing a native kingdom or two and gaining for themselves a 'readymade' homeland.

The presence of this rogue Jewish army in the region naturally caused all manners of defense mechanisms to go up amongst the kingdoms of the plain. Some, like the king of Jericho, preferred to initiate solid, time-tested practical solutions, such as shutting themselves up in their citadel with cauldrons of boiling tar, millstones and other heavy objects stockpiled atop the walls, to throw down at the enemy. Others had lined their borders with their respective armies to deter the Israelites from entering their fledgling kingdoms.

What strikes one as curious however, is the fact that most of the kingdoms of this region had seemingly abandoned conventional defense strategies and were instead coming up with innovative, desperate and even bizarre countermeasures. This unusual behavior suggests that the enemy at the doorsteps was in some way extraordinary. Midian, a kingdom of nomadic descent, for example, sent their women to mingle with the enemy soldiers, offer licentious sex and thus win their sympathies. It worked for a while, but eventually backfired. The Bible records with mirth, yet another indigent kingdom, the inhabitants of Gibeon and roundabouts, of having sent a delegation to meet the Israelite army, wearing dusty clothes, travel-worn shoes and carrying moldy bread in their pockets. Presenting themselves as allies they immediately set about doing menial tasks for the soldiers. When the bemused soldiers enquired who exactly they were, they pointed to their attire and moldy bread, and let it out that their kingdom was located very far away, not worth taking. Their ruse actually worked; their kingdom, which in fact was right around the corner, was spared! Still others had pinned their hopes on their God and god-men, like Balak here, whose bright idea it was to smite the Jews with curses. To that end and at great cost, he had hired the services of Balaam, a well-known seer from distant Mesopotamia, to 'hurl curses' from an elevated vantage point, upon the unsuspecting Israelite army below, firm in the belief that it was a 'weapon of mass destruction' as good as any!

Balaam, who incidentally came only after a great deal of persuasion, ended up blessing the Israelites instead! The spectacular sight of the orderly army below, in their neat arrays of tents spread out like a riverfront orchard, took the old seer's breath away. Impulsively, he breathed a blessing. "How goodly are thy tents, O Jacob and thy tabernacles, O Israel! As the valleys are they spread forth, as gardens by the river's side, as the trees of lign aloes which the LORD hath planted and as cedar trees beside the waters."[1]

Balaam's spontaneous outburst gives us yet another image of the thoroughly professional army at repose below. Eventually, after the exasperated king upbraided him, the reluctant prophet went into a wide-eyed trance and delivered his prophecy— more bad news for Balak, King of Moab—and yet another glimpse of reality for us. That army below, "shall eat up the nations his enemies and shall break their bones and pierce them through with his arrows" he said and added that he could not be persuaded "with all the gold and silver in Balak's kingdom" to say anything different.[2]

Clearly, there was something extraordinary about the Jewish army in their orderly tents across the River Jordan. They appear to have been powerful beyond the ordinary sense of the term. Indeed their prowess seems to have rendered futile the standard line of defense of the kingdoms of the plain. In fact, the whole scenario seems very much like a small country, opening its front door one bright morning, to find the US army, complete with war paint and state of the art weaponry, parked on their porch! You can sense the incredulity of such a happenstance in Balak's voice, in Balaam's spontaneity, in the foolhardiness of the countermeasures taken and in the overall flurry created by the presence of this high-profile 'Egypt trained' army in 'sleepy town' Canaan.

Incidentally, there is an abundance of evidence to suggest that the Israelites were professional mercenary soldiers right from the very beginning. That is to say, they were, very likely, a mercenary outfit of the Pharaoh's army and their 'exodus' from Egypt, an act of desertion, a foray for greener pastures. The Book of Numbers in the Bible, for instance, reads like a military report that was perhaps appended to it by mistake. The din that emanates from these pages is very 'veteran,' the familiarity and ease with which the Israelites go about reorganizing the army sounds very suspiciously like hardened soldiers—with a song in their heart—verily preparing for battle.

Consider for example, the manner in which these so-called slaves exited out of Egypt. It is, if anything, a dead give-away. There is palpable aggression in this episode and a 'bristling with arms' quality in their bearing. These indeed are the hallmarks of an unchallenged company of professional and belligerent soldiers.

But what really gives the game away is the fact that the Jews were able to walk out of Egypt without bloodshed. How could slaves possibly have done that, you wonder. Kings of the past were very rough customers. Aided by astute ministers, they were perfectly capable of evaluating a situation from all angles and if aggression was called for, more than happy to bring it to bear. Slaves, however many, would not have been allowed to walk out of Egypt without it turning into a bloodbath. An exodus of 'brick makers,' as far the kings of these times were concerned, were a soft target begging to be crucified all along the King's highway.

Sadly, even the concept of a 'Promised Land' rings in a 'soldiers of fortune' theme. The Old Testament recounts with unrepressed glee as to how the land was a 'ready-made paradise' with standing crops, vineyards, warm homes and wives. The Book of Joshua explicitly states, "And I have given you a land for which ye did not labor and cities which ye built not... vineyards and olive yards which ye planted not... "[3] How is one to interpret this? Frankly, if we set aside the spiritual shenanigans, this talk of 'gains without labor' begins to sound suspiciously like 'burglar talk,' the kind that signals a break-in, or in this case, a military coup—and a very easy one at that. One can almost hear the anticipatory licking of lips and discern the bravado of an easy victory in the above passage.

Now I have read my Bible and know very well the 'slaves metamorphosed to soldiers in the wilderness' theme. A second generation supposedly took over from the first and it was this resurgent army who were the professional soldiers and the ones who actually fought the war. But I am not buying that. To me, the 'slaves turned soldiers' storyline seems a later-date editing. There is no clear evidence of a second-generation and even the forty years spent in the wilderness is suspect. By the way, the veterans I described earlier, the ones we see 'whistling while whetting arrows' elaborated in the book of Numbers, is actually a glimpse of the army in their hapless slave mode!

We interpret with awe and Christian naivety, God of the Old Testament's promise to Abraham, " ...I will give unto thee and to thy seed after thee... all the land of Canaan, for an everlasting possession"[4] as his magnanimity, His love for the chosen people. However, the Promised Land was not handed over on a silver platter. It had to be taken; it had to be cleansed. There was this small matter of fighting the Canaanites, slaughtering their wives and children, before it could be had. Furthermore, the place was teaming with 'giants' and iron chariots, neither of them in a mood to make way for the Israelites, chosen or otherwise. All the above factors point to a military offensive.

Although the Bible strains to portray this army as a rabble of slaves, brick makers, masons and their like, the bewildering fact is that, we invariably catch glimpses of them in a diametrically opposite profile. These occasional 'unedited or unvarnished glimpses' starkly portray them as a powerful foe in full offensive mode, one that sent the indigent kingdoms of Canaan in a flurry. We see a professional 'Egypt trained' army, in a well-orchestrated military operation, systematically slaughter the ill-equipped natives. In short, at unguarded or 'unchristian' moments, it all sounds very much like a 'fox in a chicken coop' story that shocks our sensibilities and puts severely to test our intrinsic spiritualism.

A casual reader is likely to take to heart the 'freedom struggle' story the Bible shrewdly sells. However, if properly reevaluated, the entire Exodus episode, including the well-orchestrated offensive on the Plain of the Jordan, unequivocally points to a military operation. It points to a 'sitting duck' scenario, wherein a vastly superior rogue mercenary unit from Egypt, mows down a clutch of ill-equipped indigent kingdoms in adjoining Canaan, to make room for themselves.

Perhaps the Bible saga was re-engineered to deliver a theme that it originally was not designed to convey. Perhaps the original storyline was the straightforward history of an aggressive people, one that unabashedly documented their glorious and inglorious deeds, their conquests and their routing defeats. What attracted the world to this otherwise commonplace archive was the shining religious thread that ran throughout this saga; the commendable, even covetous faith in a God that the people in the narrative appear to have had. Why, one could even glean the supra-mundane theme of 'love of God' from this story![5] Their bloody deeds though, did somewhat mar this sublime theme. Wise men therefore judiciously edited this tangled story, discarded the unsavory bits to deliver a gleaming religious presentation.

Stripped clean of all spiritual overtones and later date editing, the overwhelming idea the Bible itself paints is, that the Jews who emerged from Egypt were a formidable force, perhaps a rogue mercenary army, who set about with ease, carving for themselves a choice portion of the very fertile and densely populated Plain of the Jordan in neighboring Canaan. The spoors are clearly that of a predator. Which is why Balak's words, "There is a people come out from Egypt: behold, they cover the face of the earth... Now shall this company lick up all that are round about us, as the ox licketh up the grass of the field..." struck me as singularly eloquent.

I find this unvarnished story eminently believable and a better fit with the textual potshards readily available in the Bible. However, what I find difficult to believe is the modern-day archaeologist's claim that this story has no historicity, archaeological evidence or textual corroboration. Indeed, I find it hard to believe that this fierce predator left no other track.

FATAL RECONSTRUCTION ERROR

Apart from its intrinsic religious content, for which no further evidence is required or asked for, the Bible offers the documented history of the Kingdom of ancient Israel from its nomadic days of wandering in antiquity (roughly 1800 BC), to its eventual destruction in 586 BC. This includes a golden period wherein Israel metamorphosed from a confederation of tribes, to a powerful kingdom ruled by dynasties of illustrious kings. The kingdom expanded rapidly, exponentially and for a brief spell is even said to have become a superpower of the Near-Eastern arena. Monuments, temples, palaces and cities were said to have been built. Battles were won and lost. In short, the Old Testament, to a large extent, doubles as the historical archive of the ancient Kingdom of Israel.

This archive, documented in exacting details, attracted an altogether different set of scholars—historians, biblical scholars and archaeologists—to the Bible. These scholars, crusaders of a different mien, simply could not wait to archaeologically 'resurrect' the fabled kingdom of Israel using the rich documented evidence available in the Bible.

To them it appeared a straightforward and very exciting proposal. Archaeology had come of age and excavations conducted at Babylonia, Assyria and Egypt had come up with some very satisfactory results. Indeed, this trio of so-called aggressors (from the biblical perspective), acquitted themselves admirably, although perhaps, the breath-taking grandeur of these heathen kingdoms was a bit disconcerting to the Christian scholars who breathed life into them.

Those were glorious days for the archaeologists and hopes were running feverishly high. Archaeologists were skipping from mound to mound, busily resurrecting lost kingdoms, magnificent palaces, cities and ziggurats with a minimum of effort. There was even a high-spirited British archaeologist who claimed to have found evidence of the epic biblical flood at Ur[1] and even the Garden of Eden, or paradise, was in danger of being broken into by these spade-wielding, gung-ho scholars, much to the consternation of God and aflutter of His angels!

It was thought therefore that finding ancient Israel would be a cakewalk. With a Bible tucked under one's armpit, one could stroll down the biblical arena, identify half-a-dozen key sites and be back home for lunch. Thus, there was a scramble, literally, to resurrect the Promised Land.

Unfortunately, things did not happen as expected. Archaeologists were bewildered at first and later, that is to say, after almost two centuries of trying every trick in their backpack, were disillusioned. The cause? For some unfathomable reason, the Bible adamantly refused to divulge its archaeological secrets. Bitterly cursed to oblivion by the fiery God of the Old Testament, the fabled kingdom of the Jews was not so easily to be had.

Fresh impetus was gained with the birth of modern Israel. Biblical archaeology became a national undertaking and the Israelis undertook renewed excavations on a war footing. There was a spate of discoveries under the aegis of Professor Yigael Yadin, a founder-father-turned-archaeologist of this new nation and others. However, upon closer examination by later-day scholars, these discoveries were found to be problematic.[2] Even so, these early-date discoveries that seemingly confirmed the Bible's historicity, continued to serve a section of society. Religious organizations, not wanting their sacred text to be tampered with, appropriated these discoveries and used them to firmly close the door on biblical archaeology. This is why the church, if asked, will stoically deliver the message that 'abundant archaeological evidence for the Bible has been found.' The opposite however, is closer to the truth.

The sad fact is, archaeological evidence for much of the Bible stories is yet to be found. Even more alarming is the fact that what little evidence is available rarely supports the Bible narrative in its details, chronology, or grandeur. On the contrary, it conspires to contradict the whole story. Another thing conspicuous by its absence is the nonexistence of written records. Unlike its neighbors, did Israel perhaps write on perishable papyrus rather than durable clay? Or this a case of having nothing at all to write about, and therefore what is available in the Bible is a later-date fabrication?[3]

Clearly, something was terribly wrong in the Biblical arena. Biblical archaeology, which by all counts, ought to have yielded rich dividends, seemed almost insistent on bankrupting its investors with little or no returns. And what is embarrassing about the whole episode is that the one and only time archaeologists actually possess detailed textual archives of an ancient kingdom, complete with elaborate triangulations, all diligently documented by the Bible, they miserably fail to find the archaeological evidence for the same. Indeed, the reversal has been so complete that most biblical archaeologists have given up or moved on. A few smart ones have restyled themselves as 'Levantine scholars,' having nimbly sidestepped to this overlapping field of study and continue to keep a wary eye on the biblical arena.

Biblical archaeology has become a near extinct field of study today. The remaining few biblical archaeologists have neither the grand optimism of the old guards nor the penchant to boldly trample into the territory of transcendentalists. This once close-knit and gung-ho community has split into two fractious halves, of maximalists and minimalists, and having set aside their spades, have taken to good old-fashioned mudslinging.

The biblical minimalists, brash, unhappy men of science, maintain that the Bible has no historic value whatsoever. They proclaim in a voice than rings clearer and louder than a church bell, that it is all runway fiction, a theme that the Jews very likely fine-tuned while in exile, between bouts of nostalgia and deep lamentation, possibly by the river of Babylon. 'If it had historicity, we would have seen archaeological evidence at least by now,' is their cornerstone argument. These scholars are willing only to concede to the barest minimum of the Bible narrative as having historicity. They prefer to be guided solely by archaeological evidence or the lack thereof. The minimalists feel that much of what is recorded in the Bible is distorted at best and some characters and events are entirely fictional. Most suspect that even Abraham, Isaac and Jacob, Judaism's traditional founders, never really existed. Many even doubt the tales of slavery in Egypt and the Exodus. There was no Moses, no crossing of the sea and no revelation on Mount Sinai. Even Joshua's conquest of Jericho and the rest of the Promised Land are not above suspicion.

The biblical maximalists on the other hand, like their Bible whole and literally believe in it from cover to cover. They are a decidedly thinner and not so vocal club of obdurate gentlemen scholars, unwilling to let go, and now increasingly comfortable with their obtuse stance. Although they are accused of basing their belief in the historicity of the Bible on their religious conviction, the reality is, they believe in the Bible because it reads like a convincing document. What underpins this simple stance is the conviction that the Bible stories contain innumerable 'micro-registers' or real-life 'background noises' that are scientifically verifiable. Indeed, by comparing biblical records with non-biblical or secular textual records of the same period, they have been of-late able to practically establish that the Bible literally hums with true and real-life background noises. Details from the Bible, such as the quoted price of slaves, the style of warfare, the laws of inheritance, etc., are all scientifically proven to be consistent with that available in contemporary secular textual sources.[4]

Be that as it may, excavations at prominent biblical sites such as Jericho and Ai continue to undermine the maximalist's optimistic stance. Indeed, it has now been established without a shade of doubt that the region in question was actually deserted from the beginning of the 15th century until the 11th century BC. Even the central hilly regions of this arena, which correspond to the territories of Judea and Samaria, that were considered biblical heartlands wherein all the 'action' took place, were entirely uninhabited during biblical times.

The minimalists extract maximum mileage from such seemingly rock-solid and scientifically proven arguments. Unfazed, the maximalists retaliate by attacking the very foundation of this argument. They suggest that no evidence exists, or that the hilly regions were uninhabited, because the places in question 'were located elsewhere' 3000 odd years ago.[5] In a like manner, they stoutly defend the Exodus story, which too is under concerted attack by the minimalists, by suggesting that no evidence has been found along the route of the Exodus for the simple reason that they probably 'went by a different route' than the one reconstructed by scholars.

The above, 'were located elsewhere' or 'went by a different route' appears to be the standard fall back argument of the maximalists and has the 'its-got-to-be-around-the-next-corner' desperate ring to it.

But what if it were true?

To elaborate, archaeologists, as would any manner of treasure hunters, require a map where 'x' marks the spot, in this case, a particular city or temple they wish to excavate. However, such a map was not readily available. Certainly, the Bible was not handed down to us with the map of Canaan drawn (by none other than Moses) on its endpapers! Biblical scholars had to painstakingly reconstruct this map from clues gleaned from the Bible and other related historical textual references. Needless to add, the whole thing was glued together with sizable dollops of educated guesses.

What if this speculatively reconstructed map was faulty? How was the map of the core biblical arena regenerated?

The American minister cum biblical scholar Edward Robinson is credited with having reconstructed much of what is accepted as biblical geography. He, along with his friend and student Eli Smith, who headed the Protestant Missionary at Beirut, had gone on two fact-finding missions (in 1838 and in 1852) through Ottoman Palestine, expressly to identify and redraw the map of the core biblical arena.[6] Together this duo was able to identify dozens of biblical sites by quizzing the locals and by intently studying the then existing Arabic place names. Others too have contributed to this field of study and bit by bit, over a period of many years, this map came into being. It is this map that serves to identify and excavate biblical sites. Indeed, it is this map, underpinned, I might add, by the knowledge of a handful of wide-eyed Bedouin herdsmen, which has now come around to bite and bitterly dispute the Bible's historicity.

While Edward Robinson is considered the first qualified biblical scholar in having studied the biblical arena's geography, the fact is, others before him had undertaken this very same exercise. For example, from 1095 to 1291, the crusaders had meticulously researched and redrawn the map of the core biblical arena. Numerous such maps are available at various libraries and museums around the world. Even before the crusaders, maps or at least geographical information of the core biblical area (Near-Eastern arena) was available in the writings of early historians such as Herodotus, Eratosthenes, Strabo, Ptolemy, Josephus and others. All these geographical presentations have a stake or say in the final version that is in rigorous use today. Is it not possible that at any one of these reconstructions stages—and not necessarily at the Edward Robinson-Bedouin herdsmen stage (although it does seem a very bright candidate)—a fatal error had crept in and is the root cause of the Bible's no show?

Getting back to the maximalist's 'were located elsewhere' or 'went by a different route' dug-in stance, we may now be certain that what they are obliquely referring to is a 'fatal reconstruction or mapping error.' What they are saying in not so many words is that the reconstructed scenario of the biblical region is 'faulty beyond repair,' 'radically different from the original.' In short, the maximalist's cornerstone argument really is a veiled and deadly one. Its cornered and seemingly desperate squeak, is in reality, a squeal, a voice threatening to blow the lid off a carefully preserved pretence.

Now in the 'fatal error scenario' we may right away exclude minor slip-ups. A little to right, a little to the left slip-ups that signal minor mapping discrepancies are at any rate factored in and caught on the field. What we seem to be dealing with here is a fundamental mapping error and one that would require us to go back to Robinson's drawing board or beyond. One would have to set aside all the archaeological finding (and their ingenious interpretations), and go back to reevaluating the textual clues that went into the reconstruction of the map of the core biblical arena, and if necessary, redraw the map of the core biblical arena. It is, without a doubt, a daunting task. Those afraid of upsetting the applecart of biblical archaeology might want to sit this one out. For this is, if anything, a call for planting new apple trees!

CHAPTER 1

TEXTUAL CORROBORATION

Is there a way to verify if the reconstructed core biblical arena suffers from a fatal mapping error?

Yes, there is. Theoretically at least, all one has to do is crosscheck the Bible's records with other ancient world secular sources from classical antiquity. If the Bible stories were true, mention of the more prominent historical events that underpin these stories should have found its way into these archives as well.

But do we have any independent ancient world secular historian who documented the Levant or parts thereof, with which we can compare the Bible's geography for similarities?

The answer to this question too is a fortunate yes. Inspired by Homer, Plato and others, quite a few enterprising Greek scholars were out there in the field, vying with each other to document world history, geography, politics and progress in general, including developments in new-fangled sciences. There was a market for such literary productions and enterprising Greeks scholars were already cashing in on it.

Of course, ancient world scholars in general are shown to be 'not overly trusted' when it comes to documenting the truth, by their modern-day counterparts, the modern-day scholars. This blanket suspicion may perhaps have something to do with the superior technology available today and the empowering conceit it seems to bestow. Ancient world scholars, poor valiant souls, could not help but be tainted by the shadowy beliefs of their times. Often they inadvertently borrow from the untenable pages of mythology and prevalent beliefs, to supplement their histories, never even suspecting for a moment that this simple act constitutes the ultimate faux pas in the eyes of their modern-day counterparts. Even the sciences during their times, were in their infancy.

Geography for example, was barely complete and most of these gentlemen stumbled about with the grand notion that the world was, well, flat. The bottom line is, modern-day scholars, view with suspicion—perhaps unfairly so—everything that ancient world secular scholars have to say. Historians especially were thought to be gullible fools who spruced up their history to satisfy the tyrannical rulers of their times. Even so, ancient world secular scholars are a rich textual source of historic information and if cautiously used, ought to be able to deliver a recognizable framework of Levantine geography, with which we can compare the reconstructed one.

HERODOTUS

One such an ancient world secular scholar is Herodotus. The Greek historian Herodotus (484 BC - 425 BC) was born in Halicarnassus, now in Turkey. Exiled from Halicarnassus for conspiring against Persian rule, this maverick scholar traveled throughout Asia Minor, Babylonia, Egypt and Greece and accumulated valuable firsthand knowledge of virtually the entire Ancient Near East. This serves as the foundation of his epic work entitled 'The History of Herodotus.' Herodotus eventually went to Athens, the centre and focus of culture in the Greek world and there his weighty tome won him the admiration of the most illustrious men of Greece, including the great Athenian political leader Pericles and his consort, the able Aspasia. Indeed, his contribution to history won him the appellation 'father of history.' In later years, Herodotus moved to Thurii in southern Italy and devoted the remainder of his days in refining his work.

Not all is well with Herodotus today though. There was a time when he reigned supreme, when his documentation on Egypt was pretty much all the knowledge we had of this ancient land. All that changed once archaeologists stumbled upon the ruins of Egypt and began to draw their own picture of Egypt through the vast archives recorded in hieroglyphics, carved profusely on the walls and preserved in pristine condition by the dry desert air. Naturally, the deciphering of these archives did not happen overnight. But when it finally did in 1822, thanks to the efforts of a Frenchman named Jean Francois Champollion,[1] and scholars were able to literally read the hieroglyphics off the walls, a very curious fact came to light. Herodotus and his hugely popular 'The History of Herodotus,' which until that point was praised to no end for the author's keen sense of observation and high fidelity, begged to differ. It soon became apparent that Herodotus' Egypt seemed radically different from that of the modern-day Egyptologists.

Herodotus presents information about ancient Egypt that is disquieting to say the least. He differs in a number of crucial topographical and political details; indeed his version of ancient Egypt is radically different from the accepted archaeologically resurrected version. If that was not blasphemous enough, he goes on to systematically and scientifically anchor his version with a number of recognizable landmarks. To complicate matters, Herodotus is positively earnest and his documentation sounds annoyingly transparent. Nor indeed can one peremptorily dismiss his credentials. During his days, he was welcomed into the folds of the powerful and elite Greek academia that orbited around Aspasia, thanks to this very same production, his 'The History of Herodotus,' his life's work. What is more, Egypt needed no rediscovering. It was very much around and still at the center of world attention. Thus, Herodotus' description of Egypt cannot have differed from the real thing even by a hair's breadth.

Now ordinarily, while reconstructing a region from potshards and such like, a marked disagreement with an ancient world textual source ought to have set off all sorts of alarm bells ringing. Ancient world sources, some of them at least, had literally walked down the streets of the kingdom they so painstakingly describe. It would be very unwise therefore for reconstruction scholars to ignore discordance with ancient world textual sources. However, 'who needs inept ancient world historians' was the prevailing mood. And, going by the modern fare, all glossily presented, with only niggling 'what they (mummies) had for lunch' questions continuing to engage native Egyptologists, Herodotus' documentation does come across as the prattle of a blundering tourist, amateurishly capturing quaint tales and idiosyncratic anecdotes, in an geographical scenario that was pathetically quixotic. Today, the sad fact is that modern scholars cannot mention Herodotus' name without a show of annoyance.

Even so, Herodotus continues to humbly serve. Indeed, he serves as an excellent doormat if you please. His anecdotes that exude an ancient world charm are generously used to set the mood for handsomely bound coffee table publications on Egypt by modern-day 'no-nonsense' scholars. His 'thesis' on embalming, considered the pièce de résistance, is morbidly fascinating and has unfailingly added that borrowed sparkle to many a vapid modern-day publication.

Also, haunted by the daunting prospect of marketing their indescribably drab productions, starchy modern scholars are beginning to come around to Herodotus' ways. Who will sit late into the night pouring over their work if it were not spiced up a little? A thunderous battle here, a spill of blood and gore there, the titillating flash of bare breasts, stories of flying serpents and gold digging ants and other colorful tales as Herodotus had expertly used to spice up his history, they realize, is perhaps the way to go after all.

Like the scarab beetle of Egyptian fame, Herodotus appears to have gotten right under the skin of the modern-day scholars. They appear not to know whether to love him or hate him. His annoying transparency and detailed documentation makes it difficult for them to call his bluff and effectively quarantine him.

It is this very quality that caught my attention. The fact that Herodotus digs in his heels and stoically begs to differ with modern scholars, puts him in league with the Bible, the other ancient world secular textual source, that modern-day scholars are having a spot of trouble in swallowing whole. It is also interesting to note that both these sources seem transparent, and their only sin seems to be to innocently reveal a markedly different picture of the Levant region.

Now, two ancient world witnesses reporting significantly different pictures of the Levant would still not accomplish anything. But what if they were to concurrently report a noticeably different picture of the Levant? What if they delivered a remarkably similar, 'landmark for landmark' tallied picture of the Levant (or at least the core biblical arena) that is markedly different from the current reconstructed scenario? Then we would most certainly have a rock solid case. Indeed, the beauty of corroboration is, it is scientifically impossible for two independent ancient world secular sources that have not proliferated from each other, and are separated by time and space, to deliver a concurrent scenario, unless and until both reverently present the truth. Let us see therefore if the Bible, in conjunction with secular ancient world historians, can deliver a concurrent picture of the Levant.

CHAPTER 2

A TANTALIZING LEAD

The one thing that strikes as unusual on reading ancient world secular histories that pertain to the Levant region is the fascination these historians had for the kingdom called 'Ethiopia.' For some reason, Ethiopia enthralled ancient world secular historians to such an extent that they almost invariably included a study of it in their histories. Thus, we have Strabo (64 BC—24 AD), the Greek historian cum geographer, Eratosthenes (276 BC—194 BC), the Greek mathematician, geographer and astronomer, Flavius Josephus (37 AD—100 AD), the Jewish historian, Herodotus (484 BC—425 BC), and a host of other ancient world secular scholars, gladly pitching in with all the information that one would ever need about this seemingly insignificant kingdom.

Ethiopia was Egypt's immediate neighbor to the south. Although it was not considered a progressive nation on par with Egypt, it nonetheless attracted considerable attention of the Greek scholars, possibly because of its tangy 'barbaric' flavor. In fact, 'Ethiopia' was not even the kingdom's proper name. The name 'Ethiopia' is a derogatory generic term that the Greeks freely used, to refer to the 'dark-skinned and barbaric' denizens of this region.

So what of Ethiopia of the ancient world Greek scholars?

It is just this. Egypt's immediate neighbor to the south, according to the Bible was not Ethiopia. It was Canaan. That is right. Canaan and not Ethiopia is consistently referred to in the Bible as Egypt's southern neighbor. Remember, how the Jewish patriarchs, including Joseph and his band of brothers, kept bouncing back and forth between Egypt and Canaan, making it seem like an over-night camel ride? Here, take a look:

> *And they told him all the words of Joseph, which he had said unto them: and when he saw the wagons which Joseph had sent to carry him, the spirit of Jacob their father revived. [Genesis 45:27]*

> *And Joseph went up to bury his father (in Canaan): and with him went up all the servants of Pharaoh, the elders of his house and all the elders of the land of Egypt. [Genesis 50:7]*

From the above extracts, it appears that Egypt and Canaan were next-door neighbors and possibly, there even was a road connecting these two kingdoms. Wagons were constantly shuttling back and forth between Egypt and Canaan, suggesting that the distance involved could not have been very great; say not more than 50-odd miles. The fact that Canaan was the 'south country,' meaning, situated south of Egypt, too is consistently documented. Here are a few extracts:

> *And Abraham journeyed from thence toward the south country and dwelled between Kadesh and Shur and sojourned in Gerar [Genesis 20.1]*

> *So Joshua took all that land, the hills and all the south country and all the land of Goshen and the valley and the plain and the mountain of Israel and the valley of the same; [Joshua 11.16]*

> *In the mountains and in the valleys and in the plains and in the springs and in the wilderness and in the south country; the Hittites, the Amorites and the Canaanites, the Perizzites, the Hivites and the Jebusites: [Joshua 12.8]*

'South country' used here appears to have been the then used generic term to refer to the confederation of indigent kingdoms south of Egypt. The people themselves were collectively called 'Amorites' or 'Canaanites.' In reality, they were Canaanites, Hittites, Amorites, Perizzites, Hivites and others. In short, the south country or 'Canaan' (which is the generic term currently in use in place of 'south country') of the Bible appeared to have occupied the exact same spot as generic Ethiopia of the Greek scholars.

This raises a fascinating and very real possibility. Could this 'generic' Ethiopia of the Greek scholars have been the 'generic' Canaan of the Bible? Could the generic 'Ethiopian' have been the generic 'Amorites,' the inhabitants of Canaan? It is a simple equation really. Both lay claims to have been Egypt's southern neighbor. Both histories use a generic term to refer to the citizenry of this region that appears to identify a 'barbaric' or 'backward,' possibly a dark-skinned and distinctly different people.

To reiterate, on the one hand, we are having serious trouble with the current reconstruction of the Levant and have more or less zeroed in on a fatal reconstruction or mapping error as being the root cause. On the other, we have a tantalizing lead, a hint of duplication, with the assurance of serious anomalies, if instead of one kingdom, two were inadvertently created. Modern-day scholars have after all reconstructed two separate kingdoms. Canaan in the Ancient Near Eastern arena, following the dictates of the Bible, and Ethiopia has been reconstructed south of modern-day Egypt, based on clues offered by ancient world secular historians such as Herodotus and Strabo.

Could this inadvertent duplication in the Levantine arena, if indeed there is one, be the fatal reconstruction error we are looking for? It seems likely and what is more, quite easy to settle. All we have to do is compare the description given of Canaan in the Bible with that of Ethiopia proffered by the ancient world secular scholars and see if they match.

THE CANAAN ETHIOPIA DUPLICATION

CHAPTER 3

HISTORY SIMILARITIES

The journey was becoming increasingly hazardous and Herodotus was having second thoughts about continuing his voyage. He had reached the southern-most Egyptian city called Elephantine, located in the mountains and wanted very much to continue, finish the voyage, sail gloriously down into Ethiopia... but it no longer was safe. He writes, "...as one advance beyond Elephantine, the land rises. Hence, it is necessary in this part of the river to attach a rope to the boat on each side, as men harness an ox and so proceed on the journey. If the rope snaps, the vessel is borne away downstream by the force of the current." The ride back to Elephantine was guaranteed to be swift and dangerous. This tumbling scenario perhaps flashed across the intrepid historian's mind and reluctantly, he discontinued his voyage. However, he was not about give up his precious documentation. Hopping out of the boat, he quickly established an interview stand by the river. He was now ready to glean information about Ethiopia by interrogating weary travelers who emerged from this dark region.

Ancient Egypt and the Nile clearly enamored Herodotus. Egypt perhaps for her stateliness, her cosmopolitan vibrancy and bustling commerce and the Nile for its myriad mysteries. With the aplomb of a master storyteller, he weaved the history of ancient Egypt as a voyage down the Nile. The Nile truly engaged him and we find our glib historian spinning off one convolute theory after another, flitting from soil mechanics to astrophysics, trying his hand at all branches of science, attempting to explain some unusual phenomena or the other. Why did it flood off-season? Where was its source? Why were the banks so high? This then is Herodotus at his engaging best, unafraid to crank up a theory or throw in a quirky anecdote or two, to keep you from nodding off.

So there he stood, like a seasoned angler at the outpost called Elephantine, trapping weary travelers who emerged from Ethiopia, to pummel them for information of their unknown country. Ethiopians were considered barbarians, flesh eaters and cannibals and they in turn were precious fodder for the haughty Greek academia, who loved to marvel at their culture or the lack thereof. Possibly Herodotus was here to gather juicy tit-bits to spice up his history. With his ears already ringing with the sweet exclamations of the ladies of the academy (a remarkable feat indeed, considering that the Nile deafeningly crashed through the rocks no more than a few yards away) and his mind-eye discerning the indulgent smiles of approval of the intelligentsia of the academy, our diligent little scholar excitedly documented his information in a systematic manner. The icthyophagis or fish eaters on one page, the lotophagis or lotus-eaters on another and the androphagis, the friendly neighborhood cannibals, the ones who would eat him if they could, on yet another, though perhaps in a bold or a red font.

Now, applying arbitrary appellations is never a good idea even in the best of times. A 'Thomas' who was also called 'Jude' may unwittingly assume separate identities in the unsuspecting hands of a later-date researcher.[1] In other words, the generic-named kingdom 'Ethiopia' could easily find itself resurrected alongside its proper-named counterpart. There is a risk here for an inadvertent duplication to take place.

At any rate, it is here, at his makeshift interview stand, that Herodotus hears the faded narrative of the Deserters. The settlement appears to have long since disappeared and what still flickered about was merely a legend, presumably the most memorable deeds of this people. The dying tale of the Deserters appealed to the quintessential historian and he did not fail it. Gently, ever so carefully, Herodotus rescued this lone voice, possibly of millions, and enshrined it in his history, giving it a precious life-extension. He liked quaint tales; they added romance and color to his history. And, as he gazed into the tumbling river before him, lost in reverie by what he had just done, he perhaps felt a strange sense of premonition. Possibly, he saw the glimmer of destiny in his actions. He was merely reporting of course, doing what historians do best. But who can tell, some intrepid future explorer might just be able to make sense of it, use this very documentation to anchor something truly extraordinary.[2]

Little else is recorded of the Deserters. What was the original name of the kingdom, who were their illustrious kings, their conquests, their defeats... details with which we can identify them, were already devoured by inexorable time.

Regarding the Deserters, Herodotus writes:

On leaving this city and again mounting the stream, in the same space of time, which it took you to reach the capital from Elephantine, you come to the Deserters, who bear the name of Asmach. This word, translated into our language, means "the men who stand on the left hand of the king." These Deserters are Egyptians of the warrior caste, who, to the number of two hundred and forty thousand, went over to the Ethiopians in the reign of King Psammetichus. Now, it happened, that on one occasion the garrisons were not relieved during the space of three years; the soldiers, therefore, at the end of that time, consulted together and having determined by common consent to revolt, marched

*away towards Ethiopia. Psammetichus informed of the
movement, set out in pursuit and coming up with them,
besought them with many words not to desert the gods
of their country, nor abandon their wives and children.
[Herodotus 2.30]*

'The Deserters' refers to a non-indigenous settlement on the
banks of the Nile in Ethiopia. As the appellation implies, they
were soldiers who had deserted their king, Psammetichus and
country, Egypt, to establish a settlement in Ethiopia. A
sizeable company was involved: three garrisons, totaling two
hundred and forty thousand soldiers. The cause of desertion
was political harassment. Apparently, these soldiers were
neglected by the king, shunted off to border postings and not
relieved for long stretches—in this particular instance for
three years. Clearly and deliberately harassed, the soldiers
concurred amongst themselves and decided to seek fresh
pastures. The king made a half-hearted attempt to stop this
veritable exodus with sweet words, but failed.

Before I go on, I would like to make it clear that this is not
a stray or solitary documentation. Other ancient world secular
sources too offer almost the exact same fare, giving the
distinct impression that the historians concerned were all
documenting a very familiar topic. For example, Strabo, the
64 BC Greek scholar, who independently recorded the above
fragment of history in his book, titled 'Geography,' wrote:

*Above the confluence of the Astaboras and the Nile, he
says, at a distance of seven hundred stadia, lies Meroe,
a city bearing the same name as the island; and there
is another island above Meroe, which is held by the
Aegyptian fugitives who revolted in the time of
Psammitichus, and are called "Sembritae," meaning
"foreigners." [Strabo, Geography 17.1.2]*

Notice here that Herodotus' Deserters are referred to as
'Aegyptian fugitives' and called 'Semebritae' or 'foreigners' by

Strabo. Both the terms are, everyone would readily agree, nearly synonymous to and unambiguously present the 'deserters' theme. The Egyptian king mentioned here too is Psammetichus. The contextual topographical and political settings (discussed in forthcoming chapters) too are consistent with that of Herodotus' version. Although documented later than Herodotus' 'History,' this one is clearly an independent presentation. Strabo, according to his own admission, picked it up from Eratosthenes, the 276 BC Greek mathematician, geographer cum astronomer.

Reverting to Herodotus' version, the given meaning of the term, 'Asmach' is 'the men who stand on the left hand of the king.' This indicates that perhaps the Asmach were elite warriors who served as the king's personal guards. As is generally the case, foreign mercenaries usually fill this role. Mercenaries help a strongman become king and for their troubles, they are given a share of the spoils. This often translated to lavish land grants and other concessions, including perhaps the elite 'Asmach' status.

Be that as it may, Psammetichus did not much care for his Asmach warriors, for here he is, contriving to drive them off. The plausible explanation could be that Psammetichus 'inherited' this lot of mercenaries. Possibly, the Asmach belonged to a former king and they became Psammetichus' along with the rest of the retinue when he ascended the throne. This would well explain the Asmach predicament. Indeed, having lived off the fat of the land possibly for generations, "and multiplied and waxed mighty," this corpulent body was a scourge on the land and was probably right at the very top of Psammetichus' 'get rid of them' list.

Being thus harassed, these soldiers took matters in their own hands and voluntarily moved out, or deserted their king and kingdom in search of fresh pastures. After journeying for months, presumably avoiding unnecessary confrontation en-route, 'slinking through the wilderness' so to speak, this veritable exodus of elite soldiers eventually reached Ethiopia.

I should tell here and now that there is in fact no record of them 'slinking through the wilderness.' Herodotus does not report it. But the point is, how else would a rogue army of deserters move through a neighborhood on high alert? Minor kingdoms along the way would most certainly have kept a watchful eye on them. They would very likely have had their armies lining their respective borders to ensure that the deserters did not enter or even pass through their territories. Even from the rogue army's point of view, it would make eminent sense to avoid unnecessary confrontation and therefore 'slinking through the wilderness' would be the textbook way to go.

At any rate, they could not have reached Ethiopia at a better time, for a wonderful stroke of luck awaited them. On seeing this wayward army of deserters, a quick-thinking Ethiopian king of the region promptly engaged them for a military mission. Herodotus writes, "Arrived in Ethiopia, they (the Deserters) placed themselves at the disposal of the king. In return, he made them a present of a tract of land, which belonged to certain Ethiopians with whom he was at feud, bidding them expel the inhabitants and take possession of their territory." [Herodotus 2.30]

The Ethiopian king invited the Deserters to evict a minor king who had usurped a portion of his land. In return for their assistance, which they smartly executed, he allowed them to retain that very same tract of land. The Deserters could not have hoped for a better deal. Readymade homes, standing crops, livestock and vineyards were handed to them on a platter. Indeed, they had inherited a promised land!

To recapitulate a story that is getting increasingly familiar: we see an elite class of warriors, possibly foreign mercenaries, who had served Egypt with their life-blood in some manner. In turn, they were given grand concessions and presumably 'lived off the fat' of the land for generations. Eventually, a new Egyptian king, a native Egyptian and representing a new lineage, Pharaoh Psammetichus, harassed these foreign mercenaries, in the hope of evicting them. Fed up with the king's shamefaced political maneuverings, the mercenaries deserted Egypt. Their departure is notably without bloodshed. To avoid unnecessary confrontation with minor neighboring kingdoms, this rogue army slinked through the wilderness and eventually reached Ethiopia, Egypt's southern neighbor. Here they were engaged by an Ethiopian king to expel his enemies from a certain tract of land. The Deserters did as bid and were invited to take possession of that very same tract. The Deserters could not have asked for more. They inherited a ready-made paradise, complete with standing crops, cattle, vineyards and what not. In case you have forgotten, this is from Herodotus and Strabo.

The likeness between the story of the Deserters of Herodotus or Sembritae of Strabo, with that of the Exodus of Jews as recounted by the Bible, is indeed hard to miss. The two versions are uncannily similar. However, they are by no means exact copies of each other, thereby betraying proliferation from a single source. Intrinsic differences exist between the two, suggesting that they are independent perspectives and that too from opposite camps. In fact, the two versions are very like the opposite sides of a coin. The biblical version is the Jewish side of the story, whereas Herodotus-Strabo version is actually the Egyptian side of the story. Even the word 'Deserters' used, echoes the marked difference of mood in the Egyptian camp. Derogatory and implicating, it conveys a sense of outrage, which starkly contrasts with the triumph and exhilaration associated with the Bible version.

Is the ancient world secular historian's version the long sought Egyptian record of the Exodus? Were the Deserters of Herodotus, or Sembritae of Strabo, the Jews of the Bible? Could the revolt-desertion described by these historians, be a fleeting glimpse of the Exodus? After many days of pondering, the questions disquietingly coalesced into a single but seemingly silly one. 'Had Thomas, who was also called Jude, assumed separate identities in the unsuspecting hands of later-date researchers?' Deciphered of course, there was nothing remotely silly about it. For it asked, 'Have modern-day scholars inadvertently recreated a separate Ethiopia and a separate Canaan when in reality they were one?' If true, it points to an unthinkable archaeological reconstruction error of gargantuan proportions.

A complete list of history similarities are given below. Those that require elaboration are dealt with in forthcoming chapters.	
HISTORY SIMILARITIES	
ETHIOPIA	CANAAN
Elite Asmach soldiers desert from Egypt	Jews footmen or men of war desert from Egypt
The Asmach were harassed by a new king	The Jews were harassed by a new king
The Asmach were professional mercenary soldiers	The Jews too were clearly 'men of war'

The king makes a last minute effort to make them stay	The Egyptian king negotiates with Moses and Arnon to stop them from going
Bloodless exit	The Jews exit out of Egypt without reprisal or bloodshed
A large number of Asmach soldiers (250,000) deserted	Large numbers of Jews soldiers (603,550) are said to have deserted
Went to Ethiopia, Egypt's immediate southern neighbor.	Went to Canaan, Egypt's immediate southern neighbor.
The Asmach were engaged by an Ethiopian king to expel his enemies from a certain tract of land (which belonged to him)	The Jews were (apparently) engaged by Moab to get rid of Sihon and Og who clearly were usurpers of Moab's territories
The Ethiopian king allows them to retain the very same stretch of land that the Asmach help win back	The Jews are seen to retain the territories of Sihon and Og which they won in battle
The desertion, attack and gaining of territories all hint at a secret alliance the Asmach had with the Ethiopian king in question	The Exodus from Egypt, attack and gaining of territories, all speak of a secret alliance the Jews, especially Moses had with the Canaanite king in question. Moses, is even said to have married 'Tharbis' daughter of the said king
The Asmach gains a 'promised land,' one that was promised to them, and one that was a ready-made paradise with standing crop and all	The Deserters gain the 'Promised Land,' which was a ready-made paradise, and one that was perhaps promised to them by the Canaanite king with whom they had a secret alliance

The Asmach abandoned their families in Egypt	The Jews too had clearly abandoned their families in Egypt and their first order of business in their new kingdom was to find replacement wives in Canaan
Psammetichus was the Egyptian king in question	The new king mentioned was called Pharaoh King of Egypt and even 'Palmanothes,' both of which refer to Psammetichus

'MEN OF WAR'

"They are entangled in the land! The wilderness hath shut them in!" All Egypt was abuzz as these cries rent the air. Just the day before they had witnessed a rare and historic event. They had seen the Exodus assemblage ponderously go from Rameses to Succoth and finally to Etham situated at the edge of the wilderness. But now they were back!

The Pharaoh's elegant face creased with worry. Something was not right. What was Moses up to now? Had he not had enough trouble with him already? He wanted the Jews to go, but now he was not so sure if it was a good idea. Moses, with his magic and maneuverings had forced his hand. Now they were back... but why? As he pondered on their latest move, absolute intelligence dawned; the picture became crystal-clear. Seething with rage, the Pharaoh King of Egypt made a snap decision. He chose six hundred of his quickest chariots and pursued the children of Israel.

Over at the other camp, Moses impatiently waited for this very news. "The Egyptians are coming!" Then his spies uttered the magic words, "in chariots!" A sense of tremendous relief surged through Moses. He had of course expected it, counted on it and in fact, engineered it. It was he after all who led the Jews to the edge of the wilderness. The ponderous Egyptian infantry had of course followed, and now, they were stranded there, and he and the Jews were back here, at the edge of the sea. It was a tight maneuver and had gained him a window of opportunity of no more than a few hours. It was all he could do and hopefully it would serve. By now of course, the Pharaoh King of Egypt would have guessed his game plan, and possibly even his escape route.

Instinctively, Moses turned and cast a feverish glance at the sea—his escape route—for reassurance. The tall papyrus reeds that choked the Sea of Reeds (Red Sea) serenely undulated and gently blew a breeze of reassurance upon his tortured face.

The plan itself was not a novel one. The Sea of Reeds had always been a favorite get-away route and hiding place for Egyptian fugitives. Anybody who wanted to make a quick getaway, just disappeared into the reeds, waded through the shallow waters and either crossed over or stayed put on the numerous marsh islands in its midst.[1]

Moses planned to do the same. However, taking the whole assemblage through it was definitely a first and therefore unsuspected. On land, they would be visible for days, tracked and harassed, to an inevitable and terrible end. But here, in the reeds, they could be out of sight in a matter of hours. This was what attracted him to this route in the first place. But of course, the best part was—chariots could not follow; they would be stuck in the oozing mud and it would take them far too long to circumvent this sea!

With the bulk of the Egyptian army tangled in the wilderness, Moses had just the fast moving chariots to contend with, for which of course he was more than prepared. Everything had fallen in place, or rather, everything had been perfectly orchestrated. It was now time for the final act. And, even as he raised his staff to give the signal, he could see in the distance, the advancing dust storm raised by the Pharaoh's swift moving chariots. Down came his shaft. The Israelites rose as a body and surged forth through the Sea of

Reeds—leaving in their wake, a broad avenue of trampled reeds, well defined by standing reeds on either side. To those who looked behind, it almost appeared as if the sea had been miraculously cleaved!

Okay, quick question. What just happened here? No, miracle is not the answer I am looking for, but yes, someone just organized and executed a picture-perfect military subterfuge! But who could have pulled off this fancy footwork? Evasive action that is hinged on deception and stop-clock synchronized maneuverings can only mean one thing. A veteran army, who understood the elements of military deception and indeed was capable of moving as one, could alone have possibly executed this grand subterfuge.

Have you recently watched Animal Planet; the one that shamefacedly cashes in on the mind-numbing drama of death enacted by prey and predator in the animal world? Go ahead and watch it, but for a change, keep your eyes glued on the prey and watch with awe the scintillating evasive action it takes. It has, you will find, an unimaginable repertoire of elusive tactics up its camouflaged sleeves! The uncanny ability to hide in the predator's blind spots or blend into shadow or change color—or indeed, wriggle through the unlikeliest of escape routes!

The point is, evasive action, especially the one hinged on deception—the kind evident in the Exodus subterfuge—takes great finesse to plan and greater dexterity to execute. What is more, this manner of fancy footwork would take years of military training for men to emulate. Yes, I can see a disciplined company of veteran soldiers like Herodotus' Asmach do it in a flash. They were, after all, elite corps—the very best of the best. Indeed, Herodotus, who has no axe to grind, gets full marks for his company. The Bible however bombs with its mob. I cannot see a barely-in-control rabble of brick makers and slaves, burdened with families, livestock, loot and unleavened bread, pulling off the Sea of Reeds stunt!

Here lies a minor enigma. While the ancient world secular sources emphatically say 'soldiers,' the Bible mulishly takes an ambiguous stance and vacillates between a slave and professional soldier profile. Whenever the opportunity presents itself, the Bible promptly grabs it and paints the Jews as oppressed slaves. However, the slave profile seems contrived, for ever so often the mask slips, revealing the diametrically opposite profile of professional soldiers. The professional soldier profile is also the one better mated with the unfolding storyline of unremitting aggression that the Bible reveals.

Let us begin our comparative study by resolving this minor ambiguity.

Oppression

Although Herodotus speaks of elite soldiers of Egypt, this too is a story of oppression. However, how can professional soldiers be oppressed, you wonder. This is easily explained. The harassment was inflicted by a politician, the king, with an ulterior motive. The king wanted the Asmach to leave and therefore he engineered their exit. Politicians, kings, and their like, do know very well how to make even a company of seasoned soldiers squirm.

Biblical Concurrence

The Bible's version is similar. The Jews too were oppressed in Egypt by a king. A new king, possibly one who ushered in a new lineage, is said to have contrived to drive them out.

Both histories speak of organized professional armies. Herodotus speaks of three garrisons of elite Asmach soldiers. Three garrisons were maintained at that time in Egypt. One in the city of Elephantine against the Ethiopians, another in the Pelusiac Daphnae against the Syrians and Arabians and a third, against the Libyans in Marea.[2] All three garrisons were involved in this act of desertion. Herodotus puts the number down at 240,000 soldiers. Let us see if the Bible agrees with all this garrison talk and has the numbers to match.

Biblical Concurrence

Actually, the Bible does even better. The Book of Numbers gives us a peek into a military camp and gives us a detailed description as to how these professional soldiers reorganized themselves into a 12-division army in a very professional manner. Indeed, the individual strengths of the 12-division Jewish army that reorganized under family banners in the wilderness of Kadesh, is meticulously recorded in the Bible. The total count of soldiers given is 603,550.

Now admittedly, the activities mentioned in the book of Numbers, does give the impression of a fledgling makeshift army being hastily assembled together. Indeed, that is how the Bible presents it. Able-bodied men between the age of twenty and sixty were conscripted to form a provisional army.

It is possible however, to interpret the above-mentioned flurry of activities as a restructuring of a professional army. The argument is as such. If the Jews were indeed professional soldiers while in Egypt, then clearly, their first priority at camp Horeb would be to reorganize back into cohesive fighting units. Teamwork is essential in warfare. This is why, after every battle, the first order of business always is to rearrange or reconstitute the soldiers back to cohesive fighting units.

Now, even if the garrisons in question had deserted en bloc from Egypt as Herodotus reports, there still would be need to reorganize the soldiers into say, smaller units, or, reshuffle them in accordance with the new management's policies. These may well have included a plan to group the soldiers under family banners to facilitating a future resettlement program.

Given the above arguments, it is very likely that the hustle and bustle that we read of in the Book of Numbers, could well have been former Egyptian mercenaries realigning themselves into a twelve-division army (under family banners), to befit or better serve their brand new status, as the first army of independent Israel. Indeed, the more you look at this ideology, the more feasible it sounds. For example, it might now strike you, why would untrained men for any reason engage in such marked regimentation. In the real world, who other than professional soldiers reconnoiter, reshuffle, or restructure?

SECOND GENERATION ARMY

Here is another issue that needs to be resolved. The Bible talks of two generations of Exodus soldiers. A first generation of slave-turned-to makeshift-soldiers who stumbled out of Egypt and a second generation of professional soldiers that rose like a phoenix in the wilderness during the forty-year halt.

The second generation, instead of learning the gentle art of baking bread or bricks, learnt instead the art of warfare, which clearly was the need of the hour. And, it was this resurgent second-generation army of professional soldiers that Joshua used with brilliant effect, to carve a sizable portion of Canaan.

However, closer examination reveals discernable discrepancies. Was there actually a second-generation army? Was there really a forty-year halt? These are some of the doubts that come to mind, especially if you are willing to ask a few pertinent questions such as, what happened to the first generation army of 603,550 slaves? The terse answer given in the Bible is, they perished to the last man during the forty-year period, leaving just two persons, Joshua and a crusty individual by the name of Caleb. Apparently, the Eschol Valley debacle put the God of the Old Testament in such a foul mood that he cursed the entire first-generation army to die in the wilderness.

Okay, we can accept that. But now the question is, what about the all-important textual potshards to support the demise of 603,550 slaves? In addition, where is the textual evidence to support the emergence of the new generation? It is not there, at least not in sufficient detail. The first-generation army, it is said, fell to diseases; a sizable lot was done in by a devastating fire; and the rest defeated by inglorious old age and attendant death. Indeed, the original army of 603,550 strong is vanquished almost to the last man, in a couple of brief sentences.

While there are complete chapters in the Bible devoted to reorganizing and so on, there is nothing to bid adieu to this 603,550 army of brave-hearts, who had broken the 420-year yoke of subjugation. These men were heroes and yet not an extra sentence or stone is spared to mark their graves. This is incongruous and especially so for a people who commemorate every event, every circumcision with much fanfare.

Same is the case with the second-generation army as well. Here again there is no textual evidence. One minute the Bible is talking about the first generation army and in the next, it is the second. It all happens in a sentence or two, requiring us to reread the paragraph just to spot the swap. Where are the pages that record their training? Why do we not hear the echo of their voices of frustration reverberating in the wilderness? Surely, they would have been yet another handful for the God of the Old Testament, who in turn would have suffered them with much histrionics. Where are these precious pages gone?

The brevity and the sleight of hand manner in which the swapping of sizable armies is done, in my opinion, reveals the hand of man rather than that of the God. The forty-year period woven into the text, appears to be the crucial facilitator for this editorial exercise. The thinking here appears to be, 'anything can be accommodated if given adequate time.'

Biblical scholars, for once are in agreement with me. They too are of the opinion that the 40-year duration mentioned is figurative—worked into the text to strengthen the hands of the God of the Old Testament, to give more bite to his curse.[3] I feel that it has been cleverly incorporated to effect the swapping of the armies. For some reason, the Bible wishes its readers to think that the first generation who broke out of captivity were hapless slaves and it was a second generation, need-of-the-hour professional soldiers, trained in the wilderness, that won them their battles at Canaan. Rewritten as such, the story becomes palatable, wins our sympathies and generally sits better with the quasi-spiritual theme the Bible strains to impart.

Moving on, both histories record a negotiation of sorts with the Pharaoh King of Egypt, concerning their imminent departure. Herodotus records the king futilely begging the soldiers not to leave. His version is fairly straightforward and believable. When the king's own mercenaries decide to desert for whatever reason, there is little that he can do other than to plead. Hence, the king actively negotiating from a disadvantageous position is actually a perfectly acceptable scenario.

Biblical Concurrence

Even in the Bible, the Pharaoh King of Egypt is seen patiently hearing out the Moses-Aaron team. He even accommodates their veiled threats and magic with patience and exemplary tolerance. Contrary to popular belief and despite the fact that he had misgivings, the Pharaoh King of Egypt, when asked, readily gave permission to the Jews to go and worship in the desert. Forewarned by his ministers that something was afoot, he is seen here at his diplomatic best.[4]

How is it that the slaves were so well organized and in a position to negotiate terms with the world's most powerful ruler, the Pharaoh King of Egypt, you wonder? It simply does not add up. Nevertheless, as a concurrence it does tot up very nicely indeed. Both histories record protracted negotiation with the Pharaoh King of Egypt and in both instances, the king is seen to take a less aggressive 'almost on his knees' stance.

BLOODLESS EXIT

Both histories are emphatic that this desertion-exodus occurred without the loss of life. The scenario painted by Herodotus clearly says so. The soldiers marched off without hindrance or reprisal. The king initiated no military action to stop them. From Herodotus we hear a believable story. A combat-ready army of mercenaries does somewhat dampen one's enthusiasm for confrontation. Best let them pass; allow them to take what they want on their way out.

Biblical Concurrence

The story the Bible offers is remarkably similar. The Jews too went out of Egypt without bloodshed. The only difference is, they were slaves and they managed their exit with God at the wheels and miracles spewing from the tailpipe!

Indeed, an avalanche of miracles is described. Ten plagues are laid out back to back, after which the sea is cleaved. Still not content, two pillars, one of clouds the other of fire, are whirled in. In all, thirteen separate feats of miracles are presented end-to-end, leaving us wondering, why is there such an over kill at this juncture.

It is not that I am unwilling to concede to a miracle or two. The Bible, after all, strains to convey a spiritual import and I would be only too glad to allow the standard allowance of miracles. The problem here however is of plenitude. There are far too many miracles happening at this particular juncture. In fact, it is only here, at this juncture, that the Old Testament resorts to or reports miracles. Miracles, by the way, are strictly a New Testament phenomenon, a Jesus thing, where they are proclaimed straight-faced at every turn of page. The Old Testament, on the other hand, regardless of its old world eccentricities and eye-for-an-eye dictum, is a down-to-earth presentation that ordinarily steers clear of miracles.

Why then were miracles used so inexpertly now, you wonder. The only answer that comes to mind is that it is a desperate remedy, an attempt to fix a hemorrhaging wound. Someone had surgically excised out 'belligerent and bristling-with-arms mercenaries' from the original storyline and replaced them with 'broken-backed and browbeaten brick-makers.' Unfortunately, this editorial exercise—a glaring inconsistency if ever there was one—did not mate well with the unfolding storyline of unprecedented slaughter. Sheep, after all, cannot be expected to leave the spoor of a mountain lion. What came immediately under the glaring arc light of disbelief is the 'no-bloodshed' exit from Egypt. Who would believe that slaves could waltz out of Egypt without it becoming a bloodbath? I for one cannot see it happening. Luckily, the men who were straining to rewrite this story too were unable to figure this one out. However, not knowing how to fix it, in sheer desperation, this august body of well-meaning Bible editors, bandaged the whole thing with yards and yards of miracles, and surreptitiously tied the end to the God of the Old Testament's coattail!

LOOTING

Ah, here is something that fits in well with the mercenary soldier theme. I am of course referring to the looting carried out by the Jews on the eve of departure. It clearly indicates that the Jews were armed and dangerous. The Bible documents, "And the children of Israel did according to the word of Moses; and they borrowed of the Egyptians jewels of silver and jewels of gold and raiment... " [Exodus 12.35]

Once again, I find it hard to believe that the ancient world's super power stood by, as if bewitched, when the Jews blithely filled their war chest. The Bible shrewdly uses the term 'borrowing' in an effort to blunt this clear act of aggression. After the long-drawn negotiation drama with the Pharaoh, the plagues and all, are we to assume that the city and its citizens, was oblivious as to what was going on? When the news of this event had spread like a forest fire to the neighboring city-states, when all roads were being monitored and every city-state for hundreds of miles in every direction had sealed their respective borders, are we to accept that the Egyptians alone were oblivious to the event unfolding under their noses and naively lent their hard-earned wealth to the Jews? I think not. An unbiased view of the incident would be that of belligerent soldiers systematically looting the cities at spear point before exiting.

Secular Source Concurrence

Herodotus does not document the Deserters going on a looting spree before departing from Egypt. He does however document the fact that they were elite mercenaries of Egypt and even the Pharaoh King of Egypt who tried to stop them had to resort to begging. It is therefore conceivable that such an outfit may well have helped themselves to some 'gold and raiment' to help them along on the way. But yes, it is not documented. Then again, why record something so crassly predictable may well have been the thinking here.

What we need to take home from this incident is the fact that the looting spree recorded in the Bible is a better fit with the Deserter's aggressive profile than with that of the Exodus slaves.

Similarities apart, if the two exoduses were separate occurrences, as scholars currently believe, it would mean that Egypt, the superpower of the ancient world, was incapable of stemming devastating loss of work force—twice. No kingdom can afford such a loss. It would have had exhausting economic repercussions in Egypt as well as in the neighboring kingdoms. Also, the influx of such a large company into adjoining regions would have created a separate wave of economic and territorial tension. Considering the scale of the events and its attendant repercussions, the chances that they occurred twice in Egypt are very slim indeed.

To conclude, strong evidence suggests that the Exodus Jews were in fact professional, 'Egypt-trained' mercenaries, just like the Deserters of Herodotus or the Sembritae of Strabo. The Exodus did take place, for we now have two ancient world historians corroborating this fact in great detail.

Modern-day scholars who currently deny its occurrence and are willing to charitably concede to just a handful of Jews having slinked away from Egypt, six hundred being their best take-or-leave-it offer, will not be so darned pleased.

THE 'PROMISED' LAND

"Welcome my friend, welcome!" greeted the king, as Moses silently stepped out from the shadows. Much later, that is, after he had taken care of his guest in the elaborate customary fashion avidly observed in these parts, the king gently broached the subject that he intuitively knew was on Moses' mind. He asked, "So, are you still interested in the proposal we discussed earlier? Moses found no reason to comment. "Ah, but I can see that you are!" continued the king. "Very well then, the offer still stands. You get rid of that upstart Og and his fiend friend who sits in Bashan and in return, you can keep that very tract of land. It is a win-win situation. I will get my revenge and you will get a readymade kingdom, complete with vineyards, standing crops and all!"

The Jewish historian, Flavius Josephus from antiquity, provides the facts for the above dramatization. Josephus offers an intriguing bit of evidence that appears to ring true. According to him, Moses was formerly a general in the Pharaoh's army, whose area of operation was Ethiopia and he married Tharbis the daughter of an Ethiopian king. Furthermore, under a secret agreement, this king allowed Moses to subdue Ethiopia (possibly an errant kingdom or two) by his Egyptian army.[1]

Now, if Ethiopia was indeed Canaan, then it would mean, Moses, according to Josephus, did indeed have a secret alliance with a certain Canaanite king, wherein he was required to subdue a portion of Ethiopia, in return for something.

Does the Bible concur? Never shy to reveal the truth, the Bible tells the same story, although not in so much detail. It states that Moses was an Egyptian prince and adds that he married an Ethiopian woman. By these admissions, it gives tacit support to Josephus' secret alliance story.

But wait, there is more. Slinking through the wilderness, passing by numerous kingdoms en-route, the Jewish army appears intent on reaching a predestined rendezvous point. On two occasions, they even sought permission from the kings whose kingdoms lay en-route, to allow them to cut thought their territory, with the assurance that they would not even drink water or pluck a stalk of grain while doing so. Unfortunately, these kings were in no mood to take their word for it. In the end, after taking a circuitous route, we see the Jewish army arrive at Canaan and right away attack and capture the minor kingdoms of the Amorite kings of Sihon and Og.

One could well ask, why did they avoid fighting with the kingdoms en-route? If a tract of land was all they were after, an opportunistic mercenary army could well have engaged any and everyone in their path. Instead, we see them go single-mindedly after the territories of Sihon and Og.

Were these Amorite kingdoms the predetermined targets from the very beginning?

As if on cue, the Bible drops a hint. While recounting this tale, which it does often enough, it never fails to add, that the said territory which the Jews did take from Sihon and Og, originally belonged to the King of Moab. Apparently, Sihon and his oversized friend Og, had snatched it from Moab some time earlier. Here it is now:

*For Heshbon was the city of Sihon the king of the
Amorites, who had fought against the former king of
Moab and taken all his land out of his hand, even unto
Arnon. [Numbers 21.26]*

Originally, the primary target did belong to someone else.
Sihon and Og had usurped the territory from Moab. Is it
possible that the King of Moab extracted his revenge by
arranging with the Jewish army that had had emerged from
Egypt, to get rid of these Amorite kings? It seems very likely,
for rather strangely, not an inch of Moab's territory was
annexed by the Jews in their initial series of attacks. It is
therefore quite probable that some manner of secret alliance
existed between the King of Moab and the Jews.

But here is the main argument. As explained earlier, the
'Promised Land' with all its talks of a 'ready-made paradise,'
reveals it to have been a military mission. However, a military
operation is inherently fraught with danger. So the question
is, why would anyone append the term 'promised' to such a
mission? Was perhaps victory in some way guaranteed? Does
it hint of a secret alliance? Was this land perhaps 'promised'
to Moses by the Ethiopian king for a service to be rendered as
Josephus plainly states?

An unsuspecting reader of the Bible would accept the
freedom struggle story the Bible slyly sells. The carefully
wrought scenes are of an enslaved people overthrowing their
shackles and carving a small and well-deserved piece of land
from the heathens. However, if we are willing to look afresh,
then like in a holographic sticker, we are rewarded with an
entirely different scenario. Glimpses of a disciplined army
stealthily moving through the wilderness can be seen. Military
strategists can be observed busy planning subterfuges and
offensives. Spies, guides, scouts can be discerned busy at their
various posts. Now, we also have clear-cut evidence of a

secret alliance. Thus, the unmistakable impression that this was indeed a pre-planned military operation and undertaken by a company of seasoned mercenary soldiers can very easily be gained.

The Bible chooses to rewrite this conquest as a triumph of good over evil, a subduing or slaughtering of pagans even, to set the scene for the religious theme it presents. Originally perhaps it was no more that a sordid tale of conquest by a vastly superior 'Egypt trained' fighting force, who had a secret alliance with one of the kings on the Plain of Canaan.

However, we are here merely to seek corroboration. Let us see if our friend Herodotus was able to gain a whiff of this conspiracy theory to color his history of Ethiopia.

Secular Source Concurrence

From Herodotus we learn that the roving army of Deserters, no doubt under able leadership, sojourned through the wilderness and eventually reached Ethiopia. Here a perfect opportunity to gain territory in this lush region presented itself. An Ethiopian king of the region had earlier lost a portion of his territory to another king. The Deserters therefore "...placed themselves at the disposal of the king. In return, he made them a present of a tract of land which belonged to certain Ethiopians with whom he was at feud, bidding them expel the inhabitants and take possession of their territory." [Herodotus 2.30]

It is the exact same story here as well! A certain Ethiopian king had actually invited the Deserters to fight for him and dispose off his enemy. In return for this service, the king suggested that they take possession of the disposed king's tract of land. The Deserters were only too glad to oblige and smartly stepped into what by all counts was a readymade paradise, a promised land.

The convenience, the incredible ease and not to mention luck, with which a perfect opportunity to gain territory presents itself to the Deserters, leads one to suspect a secret alliance. Perhaps the whole plan was laid out long before the Deserters took a single step out of Egypt. Very likely, it was on the strength of this commitment that the soldiers confidently deserted the service of King Psammetichus and stumbled through the wilderness, as if on an uncharted adventure.

To conclude, both, the Jews of the Bible narrative and the Deserters of Herodotus' history, had a well laid out plan that included a secret alliance with a king of Canaan-Ethiopia, in the event that the new Pharaoh King of Egypt connived to eject them out of Egypt. Thanks to this secret alliance, they were able to step out of Egypt and right into another kingdom, a readymade paradise if you please, in the neighboring southerly kingdom of 'Canaan-Ethiopia.'

WOMEN & CHILDREN ABANDONED

Have ye saved all the women alive? [Numbers 31.15]

"Nay, but," said one of the Deserters with an unseemly gesture, "wherever we go, we are sure enough of finding wives and children." [Herodotus 2.30] Famous last words these. They were spat out in reply to Psammetichus, the Pharaoh King of Egypt, who when informed of the desertion, had hastened to meet the soldiers and to beg them not to desert their gods and country, or indeed abandon their wives and children. So records Herodotus.

The above detail accurately reflects the devil-may-care attitude of the Deserters and is congruent with the unfolding storyline. Hardened frontline mercenary soldiers, who presumably had little contact with their families to begin with, would not find it hard to abandon them. Besides, as far as they were concerned, they were going out on a dangerous mission and there really was no scope of taking their families along. They probably were relatively safe in Egypt and if need be, could well be called for at a later date once things were settled in the new location.

Note that the above is a specific 'detail' of the Deserter's story. And, in the business of finding concurrency, there is nothing more valuable than such precious little nuggets. Obscure details are indeed the 'micro-registers' of truth, for these are usually small enough to pass though without notice or censure, and at the same time big enough to establish the truth. Indeed, these are not unlike DNA fingerprints.

So, the question is, do we see the same DNA fingerprint in the Exodus story of the Bible? Did the Jews also abandon their wives and their little ones in Egypt?

Biblical Concurrence

Although the Bible mentions in places that the Exodus group consisted of families as well as livestock, the emphasis is always on footmen or men-of-war. Women and children are in fact rarely mentioned. Nonetheless, let us look for concrete evidence of abandonment.

Let us begin by going to the negotiation table where the Moses-Aaron team tried to thrash out a deal with the Pharaoh King of Egypt, on behalf of the Jewish community, for going out on a short prayer expedition in the wilderness. This was of course a ruse; we now know that they did not intend to come back. The book of Exodus documents:

> *And he said unto them, Let the LORD be so with you, as I will let you go and your little ones: look to it; for evil is before you. Not so: go now ye that are men and serve the LORD; for that ye did desire. [Exodus 10.11]*

The Pharaoh King of Egypt too, it would seem, knew what was afoot, and is seen here playing his card well. He is seen here parrying with Moses, "...go now ye that are men and serve the Lord..." The Pharaoh King of Egypt readily gave the men permission to leave, but disallowed them from taking their families along. He argued that men alone carry out the worship; women and children were in any case not allowed to participate.

Note that here the 'men only' theme is being energetically bandied about. The Pharaoh King of Egypt, who appeared to know that something was afoot, is seen here artfully using this theme to stall an exodus. Indeed, he very readily gave the men permission to go, but put up resistance and reluctance to let them take their families along as well.

Actually, it only became a tussle when the Moses-Aaron team insisted that they be allowed to take their women and children along. In short, not only was the subject of taking or not taking the families along on this prayer expedition discussed, the negotiations actually broke down because of this very issue. We cannot say exactly what actually transpired after this point, for the Bible chooses to trot off into miracle country at this very juncture. It is very likely therefore that an unsavory truth is buried here and perhaps that unsavory truth is, that the Jews were mercenary soldiers and that they did in fact abandon their wives and children in Egypt and set off on their own.

SEX IN THE CAMP

Here is an action-packed scene that vigorously supports the 'families were abandoned in Egypt' theme. As soon as the Jews encountered the Canaanite kingdom of Moab, they began to behave exactly as an army starved of female company. Large-scale sexual association with Midianite women is said to have totally disrupted camp life.[1] Perhaps the elders had initially turned a blind eye towards these escapades, allowing the battle-fatigued men to indulge in some worldly pleasures. But evidently, it got right out of hand. Excluding perhaps the pin-studded invasion map on Moses' table, men were seen doing it everywhere!

Now ordinarily, this is to be expected. A battle fatigued army helping itself to some well-deserved rest and recreation. But then we are told that this particular army was not ordinary. It purportedly had its rest and recreation—meaning its womenfolk—in tow. So, why the frenzy? Why did the sex become such an issue? Why did Phinehas, the grandson of Aaron the priest, who went after such a frenzied couple with a javelin "and thrust both of them through, the man of Israel and the woman through her belly"[2] and why is it said that it ended the plague? What plague? Of unrestrained sex? It all points to one thing. Women, their own, they did not have in the camp.

HARVESTING VIRGINS

All the above arguments pale into insignificance, when you consider that there is ample evidence in the Bible of how the Jewish soldiers raced to get themselves new wives—almost in fulfillment of Herodotus' soldier's airy prediction, "wherever we go, we are sure enough of finding wives and children."[3]

Two verses from the Bible prove our point without a shade of doubt. Here the patriarch Moses himself is giving specific instructions to capture unwed girls and women. The Bible documents in the book of Numbers, Moses eagerly enquiring, "Have ye saved all the women alive?" [Numbers 31.15] A sentence or two later, the same idea is reiterated. The Bible records Moses calmly instructing, "Now therefore kill every male among the little ones and kill every woman that hath known man by lying with him. But all the women children, that have not known a man by lying with him, keep alive for yourselves." [Numbers 31.17]

These are the set of instructions given by Moses to the Jewish army concerning the capturing of prisoners from Midian. The attack had a two-pronged intent. Midian was specifically attacked to pay back for their having disrupted the camp earlier by sending in their women. The second reason was to capture virgin girls. All the males, children and married women were slaughtered. Only the unwed girls were kept.

You can see right away that the virgin girls were specifically harvested, 'keep alive for yourselves,' for marriage, no doubt to replace the wives the soldiers presumably abandoned in Egypt.

Nehemiah Episode

If the idea of abandoning women and children in Egypt seems too harsh for your Christian sensibilities, then perhaps you should read the book of Nehemiah. This second incidence occurred hundreds of years later, but here again, another set of wives and children were similarly abandoned.

Having organized the rebuilding of the destroyed and abandoned city of Jerusalem, Nehemiah after much weeping and fasting, cajoling and threatening, was able to bring back the scattered Jews from neighboring areas to come and settle in the abandoned walled-city of Jerusalem. All was going well according to plan until one day Nehemiah heard the children speak. His keen ears pick up a garble of local languages. The children "spake half in the speech of Ashdod," and "could not speak in the Jews' language!" [Nehemiah 13.24] Generations of interbreeding with the outsiders had effectively polluted the chosen race and made obsolete their sacred language.

Nehemiah did not like it; he did not like it at all.

Prophets see in the innocent faces of children the sins of their parents. Earlier, I had read how Elisha had vanquished forty children in his wrath and now here was Nehemiah in a paroxysm triggered by another pack of laughing, playing children. He stalked off, called an emergency meeting of the chosen ones, "cursed them and smote certain of them and plucked off their hair and made them swear by God" [Nehemiah 13.25] never to intermarry again. After much histrionics, he convinced the Jews to purge themselves of their foreign wives and children. There was some reluctance no doubt, but at the end of the day, all the foreign wives and the children were abandoned outside the newly set gates of Jerusalem. Perhaps the strength for this second round of purging was borne by the first.

To conclude, the Jews were unable or unwilling to take their wives and children with them when they exited out of Egypt. And, amongst the first thing they did after they established themselves in Canaan, was to replace the wives they had left behind, possibly in Egypt, just as Herodotus reports.

The Bible stories are painstakingly true. They have to be. Otherwise, our friend, the indomitable Herodotus, would not have been able to extract this very same story down to the last detail from travel weary Ethiopians, standing there at his windswept interview stand, high up in the mountains beyond Elephantine.

'PHARAOH'

*Now there arose a new king over Egypt, which knew
not Joseph. [Exodus 1.8]*

Any discussion about the kings of Egypt is incomplete without
propitiating the chronologists, the current high priests of
Egyptology. Indeed, their enthusiasm and mastery of the
subject seems to match that of the early Egyptian priests, who
had a similar penchant for this field of study. Yet, dating the
ancient kings has proved to be a tricky waltz in the vaults for
their modern counterparts. Here are a series of arguments
that unambiguously identifies the Pharaoh of the Exodus.

NEW KING

"Now there arose a new king over Egypt, which knew not
Joseph..." [Exodus 1.8] is all that the Bible is willing to reveal
about the upheaval that eventually led to the Exodus of the
Jews from Egypt. They were in Egypt for a total of 430 years
without being harassed. A new king, it appears, changed that
overnight. The new Pharaoh, whoever he was, had certainly
put the brakes on the Jewish community's hereto-
unchallenged freedom to 'multiply unlimitedly and wax
mightily' in cosmopolitan comfort and ushered in a period of
wandering and uncertainty.

But why is the Bible, which appears to otherwise have no
compunction about admitting graphic, gory, petty and
insignificant details to its runaway narrative, be so unnaturally
closed-mouthed about this most disastrous blow?

Are we perhaps missing something here? Let us take that single terse statement and see what we can make of it.

Perhaps the phrase "a new king... which knew not Joseph" carries with it a deadly import that we do not fully comprehend today. Allow me to explain. Remember, King David's deathbed instructions to Solomon which went something like, 'Son, I owe 'x,' 'y,' and 'z.' Take good care of them. I owe 'w' as well, but that debt expires with me. Promise me that you will bring down w's 'hoar head to the grave with blood' the minute I close my eyes.'[1] The son would follow these instructions to the letter, and no doubt would pass on similar deathbed instructions to his son and so on. Kings of old took the phrase 'keep your friends close, and your enemies closer' very seriously. A particular dynasty's inner circle of well-wishers were diligently allowed to live off the 'fat of the land,' and they in turn would leave no stone unturned to ensure that the king and his lineage continued undisturbed. Joseph was indeed a name favorably whispered at the deathbeds of several kings until finally, after 430 long years, it no longer was. This represents an unthinkable breach, one that promised upheaval and death to many. Although we may have difficulty in discerning its deadly import, be assured that this terse sentence would have stopped an ancient world citizen dead in his tracks. The fact that the name was no longer passed down can only mean that the dynastic link was broken. In other words, the dynasty that favored Joseph and his descendents had ceased to exist. The 'new' in the 'new king' mentioned in the Bible without a doubt represented a new dynasty. Let us see if the ancient world secular scholars have anything to contribute on this subject. What we are looking for is an Egyptian dynasty that ruled for 430 odd years and had some reason to be favorable to the Jews. It had to be followed by a new dynasty with its first king documented to have engineered an exodus of sorts, of a sizable number of people, seconds after he took over.

Secular Source Concurrence

With the death of Sethos, Egypt shrugged off its long-standing foreign ruler and in the spirit of freedom and nationalism, divided its regions into twelve sectors and elected as many native kings that included Psammetichus, to rule the kingdom. This experiment lasted for a brief period. Eventually, Psammetichus emerged as sole monarch and ushered in a pro-Egypt rule. All this is diligently documented by Herodotus in his history.

Pharaoh Psammetichus represented a new lineage that had emerged after a 300-year reign by foreign kings known as Priest of Vulcan kings. Now, usually a change in reign has a dominoes effect and we see a change of guard in almost every field of governance. Amongst the exiting parties, we see the Asmach soldiers—very likely a corpulent body of pampered soldiers patronized by the earlier dynasty—exit out of Egypt. Right away, we can see that this does indeed sit well with the Bible's 'new king' and Exodus upheaval story.

But wait, there is more. Interestingly, modern-day scholars identify the old Priest of Vulcan kings regime as the Hyksos or shepherd kings. Now, the terms 'foreign' in conjunction with the term 'shepherd' used to describe the earlier dynasty, suggests a Semitic race. In other words, Egypt, it would appear, was ruled for considerable period by kings of Semitic origin. That being the case, their patronizing the Jews for the full extent of their dynastic rule would be an acceptable scenario. The argument here is, a foreign regime would prefer to keep their own kind to serve as personal bodyguards or protective corps. Thus, by default we get that the Asmach too were of Semitic descent and Psammetichus the new native

Egyptian King, who ushered in the replacement dynasty, and who lost no time in engineering the exit of the Asmach soldiers out of Egypt, was the 'Pharaoh of the Exodus.'

THE LABYRINTH ARGUMENT

Here is a brand new and exciting argument that identifies Psammetichus as the Pharaoh of the Exodus.

The Bible, we assume, is too paralyzed with fear to say anything more than "a new king on the block who knew not Joseph," declining even to name the Egyptian king in question. Not true. It does indeed unambiguously name the king; however, biblical scholars are too preoccupied in 'promoting Ramesses' to discern it.

Consider the following argument. The Bible, we assume referred to the Egyptian kings by the title 'Pharaoh' and very rarely used their proper names such as Shishak, Neco and Hophra, which on rare occasions inadvertently slip out. Once again, not true. If we study the Bible closely, it will be seen that the 'Pharaoh' title is only used in the five books of Moses, and here the Egyptian king is consistently referred to by the curious and full title 'Pharaoh King of Egypt.' Scholars have assumed that it merely is an appellation that meant 'great king' and promptly disregarded it.

Even the Quran registers this change in title during this period. Only during the Moses period does the Quran repeatedly call the King of Egypt 'Firawn,' or Pharaoh. Otherwise, during Joseph's days for instance, he is consistently referred to and addressed by the term 'Malik' meaning king.[2] We can therefore tentatively conclude that the title 'Pharaoh' specifically referred to a particular king who ruled during Moses' times.

The famous English Egyptologist, Sir Alan Gardiner agrees to the above argument, for he states that the title 'Pharaoh' was first applied to the king at about 950 BC. He also mentions that the term 'Pharaoh' actually meant a 'great house.'[3]

Now, a 'great house' title may be taken to represent a great lineage, in which case, it has nothing to offer. If on the other hand, if it were an 'associative name,' one that linked a specific king to a specific monument or edifice that he erected, then we may well have something to go by. Perhaps the king in question commissioned a 'great house' of significance and was therefore referred to as 'the king who built the great house.' Presumably, over the years this title was abbreviated to just 'great house' or 'Pharaoh.' This should not be difficult for us to imagine, living as we are amidst a plethora of products that brandish the original inventor's name.

Now, the great house in question had to be significantly different from the ordinary. But what? Rather than speculate our way into woods here, I suggest that we try to pick up the threads of this interesting story from Herodotus' documentation.

Secular Source Concurrence

A quick reference to Herodotus' history greets us with a pleasant surprise. In his section on the man-made wonders of Egypt, the historian appears quite taken in by a curious edifice he calls the 'Labyrinth.' As the name implies, the Labyrinth was a great sprawling house. It was built specifically to commemorate a momentous event in Egypt's history. After the 300-hundred year rule by the foreign Priests of Vulcan kings, Egypt was splintered and ruled by twelve local kings. Eventually, these kings, in a bid to re-unite Egypt, formed a pact to rule Egypt collectively. The Labyrinth palace was specifically built to commemorate this accord.

Herodotus waxes eloquently on the Labyrinth and with rare enthusiasm. "It has twelve courts, all of them roofed, with gates exactly opposite one another, six looking to the north and six to the south. A single wall surrounds the entire building. There are two different sorts of chambers throughout—half underground, half above ground... the whole number of these chambers is three thousand, fifteen hundred of each kind... the roof was throughout of stone, like the walls; and the walls were carved all over with figures; every court was surrounded with a colonnade which was built of white stones exquisitely fitted together." But what is truly astounding is that he reports that the Labyrinth surpassed even the pyramids in grandeur! He says, "The pyramids likewise surpass description and are severally equal to a number of the greatest works of the Greeks, but the Labyrinth surpasses the pyramids."[Herodotus 2.148]

So, is the labyrinth of Herodotus the 'great house' or 'pharaoh' being referred to in the Bible? It is quite feasible, actually. The much-admired labyrinth of Herodotus was in all probability the 'great house' mentioned in the Bible. And possibly the king who built it was the one originally called the 'Pharaoh.'

But who was the king associated with the labyrinth? Why, it was Psammetichus of course! Psammetichus was indeed the architect of the labyrinth accord and it was he who became the monarch shortly thereafter. If anyone deserved to be called 'the king who built the Pharaoh' or the great house, it is Psammetichus. Since the title Pharaoh came into use during Moses' time, it would indicate that Psammetichus was indeed the king then and therefore he was the Pharaoh of the Exodus.

Incredibly, the truth about Psammetichus is confirmed by the Jewish historian, Artapanus. According to the historian, Pharaoh during the time of Moses was called 'Palmanothes.' He also reveals that 'at that time there were many kings of Egypt.'[4] Surely, is not 'Palmanothes' the corrupt version of 'Psammetichus' or vice versa? **Psa-mme-ti-chus=Pal-mano-t-hes**, of that there is little doubt. The second reference to the 'many kings' during this time too fits in well with the twelve kings of the Labyrinth Accord scenario. This too therefore unambiguously indicates Psammetichus. Indeed, what we have here is an independent documentation that directly links Psammetichus with Moses and the Exodus!

CHRONOLOGICAL CONFIRMATION

Modern-day chronologists have compiled a composite list of the Egyptian kings, which is loosely based on two versions (that of Josephus and Eusebius) of the fragmented list originally compiled by Manetho, a 3rd century BC Egyptian priest. This has been further tweaked using cross-references from various sources including those available in the Bible, the Turin papyrus, Abydos tablet, the Saqqarah tablet and the wall list of Karnak and anything else that remotely resembles a list.

Lest there be a grocery list inadvertently included in the above, conscientious Egyptologists, caution us that these lists are only provisional and that there is a great deal of confusion on this subject amongst scholars. For example, Champollion gives the date 5867 BC for the beginning of the first Dynasty, while J. G. Wilkinson dates it at 2320 BC.[5] Thus, two prominent schools of thought exist in this field of study, sharing between them an unresolved discrepancy of 3547-years. Such being the case, modern chronologists, lesser mortals by all counts and not wanting to upset the apple cart, quietly tiptoe along an irrelevant and entirely irreverent mid-path between the two masters!

Modern-day 'revisionist' chronologists have therefore taken the bold step to reveal the bits of strings and spittle that bond Egyptian chronology. Prominent amongst them is David Rohl. According to him, three of the four main mainstays of Egyptian chronology are unsound. The Shishak=Shoshenk synchronism, originally indicated by Champollion himself, is historically untenable. Shishak of the Bible is not the Shoshenk of the Manetho. Many respected Egyptologists question the reliability of the Ebers Sothic calendar as well, which is yet another mainstay of Egypt's chronology. The store-city Raamses (Pithom and Raamses) mentioned in the Bible, which was made to synchronize with Ramesses of Manetho list by means of the Ebers formula, and considered the third mainstay of Egypt's chronology, too tumbles down along with the Ebers formula, in a domino effect. Thus, of the four chronological mainstays of Egypt's chronology, only one pillar—the sacking of Thebes by the Assyrians—is sound according to revisionist chronologists.[6]

Incidentally, the date of the sacking of Thebes by the Assyrians under Ashurbanipal in Egyptian chronology is based on Neo-Babylonian chronology. It also is the anchor for the reign of Psammetichus (Psamtek I) in Egyptian chronology, who is thought to have taken over Egypt immediately thereafter. In other words, the year 664 BC derived for the Egyptian Psammetichus, is wholly based on Neo-Babylonian chronology with not even a nod to conventional Egyptian chronology. Thanks to this bit of borrowing, we find Psammetichus shunted to the 664 BC - 610 BC slot on the timeline. This rearrangement blatantly ignores the fact that Herodotus and other ancient world scholars, place Psammetichus immediately after Sethos who ruled from 1294 BC to 1279 BC. Sethos is not moved; he is allowed to retain his slot. The end result is, Psammetichus now finds himself separated from Sethos by a full 615 years. This when compared to ancient world textual sources, is a blatant discrepancy and is unacceptable. Psammetichus taking over from Sethos represents a crucial changeover. The dynasty changes, the rulers change from foreign (Priest of Vulcan kings) to native rulers after a 300 odd years, etc. Egypt is in a delirious flux, experimenting with multiple kings... why, it is almost as if the country gained its independence! How can one ignore all this?

What seems to be evident here in all this protracted wheeling and dealing is the fact that the slot that comes after Sethos is very special. What was so special about this particular slot? Who is the person so assiduously being promoted, you wonder. A scant search reveals the sordid story and its child-like logic. Apparently, the slot in question was the one occupied by the Pharaoh of the Exodus. The king being so assiduously promoted is one Ramesses. Thanks wholly to the mention in passing in the Bible of the 'store cities Pithom and Raamses,' chronologists were bending over backwards to accommodate an errant Ramesses. Poor Psammetichus, the rightful occupant, was unceremoniously evicted! If we merely revert to the original chronology as suggested by the ancient world scholars, Psammetichus will automatically be the Pharaoh of the oppression and Exodus.[7] To conclude, the Sethos-Psammetichus epochal changeover is indeed the one that is enshrined in the cryptic biblical verse, "Now there arose a new king over Egypt" and the term 'Pharaoh King of Egypt' used in the Bible specifically referred to Psammetichus.

CHAPTER 8

THE JOSEPH LEGACY

Engaging a superior fighting force of foreign mercenaries whose loyalty is ensured by better pay has been a standard practice that appealed to rulers of yore. Dazed 'brazen men' (soldiers swathed in full-bodied bronze armor) were landing on the East Mediterranean coast by the shiploads and the Egyptian kings were only too glad to put them to good use. Psammetichus too, had need for mercenaries. He is said to have engaged some of these Ionian and Carian mercenaries to fight the eleven kings who had banished him into the swamps. After gaining the throne, Psammetichus is said to have rewarded his mercenaries by firmly ensconcing them in Egypt in enviable comfort. Record has it that Psammetichus' mercenaries, the Ionian and Carian, lived undisturbed in grand style in the region known as the 'the camps,' located in a choice portion of Egypt for three generations, until finally Amasis eventually shunted them to another location. [Herodotus 2.154]

So the question is, if Psammetichus had his Ionians and Carians, whose mercenaries were the Asmach?

As mentioned before, the obvious answer to this question is that Psammetichus probably inherited the Asmach. Now, we know that Psammetichus represented a new regime that replaced the long lineage of 'Priests of Vulcan' kings who had ruled Egypt for a considerable time. Sethos was the last of these kings and surprisingly, even Sethos, it appears, had a spot of trouble with rebellious mercenaries. Indeed, the unfortunate Sethos was abandoned by his mercenaries and had to face the Assyrian King Sennacherib with ordinary citizens posing as soldiers. [Herodotus 2.141] Is it possible that the rebellious mercenaries referred to here, were the very same Asmach? If so, then clearly, he too had inherited these notorious soldiers from his predecessor. Looks like we will have to go further back in time to find the original king to whom the Asmach owed their allegiance and he in turn set them up in Egypt in choice lands.

Searching through the fragmentary chronology provided by the historian Herodotus, Sesostris, the original Priest of Vulcan King, who undertook a campaign to expand his kingdom, caught my attention. Sesostris it is said "collected a vast armament and made progress by land across the continent, conquering every people which fell in his way." It is also mentioned that he was "accompanied by vast multitudes of the people whose countries he had subdued." [Herodotus 2.102]

Is it possible that it was this rag-tag army of foreign mercenaries, who had bled for Sesostris in this campaign, and whom he presumably set up in Egypt in great comfort, was the redoubtable Asmach? It is and what is interesting to note here is that the region that Sesostris passed through was the Near Eastern arena, and therefore it is more than likely that the mercenaries in question were of Semitic descend.

Incidentally, Sesostris is also credited to have re-distributed land in Egypt and collected rent. Consider the following extract from 'The History of Herodotus' by Herodotus.

Sesostris also, they declared, made a division of the soil of Egypt among the inhabitants, assigning square plots of ground of equal size to all and obtaining his chief

*revenue from the rent, which the holders were required
to pay him year by year. [Herodotus 2.109]*

Added to that, Sesostris was the only Egyptian king who is said
to have ruled over both Egypt and Ethiopia.

*Sesostris was king not only of Egypt, but also of
Ethiopia. He was the only Egyptian monarch who ever
ruled over the latter country. [Herodotus 2.110]*

Now, according to my hypothesis Ethiopia was Canaan. For
this argument, let us assume that it indeed was. Then it would
mean that Sesostris was the only Egyptian king who ruled
over both Egypt and Canaan.

To reiterate, Sesostris undertook a major land campaign in
which he was aided by a huge army of foreign mercenaries of
Semitic stock and paid back his dues by settling these foreign
mercenaries of Near Eastern descent, in enviable comfort in
Egypt. Sesostris was the only Egyptian King who ruled both
Egypt and Canaan-Ethiopia. Furthermore, Sesostris is also
documented to have divided all the land that he had in his
custody into square parcels, gave it to the citizens and
obtained his chief revenue by collecting rent.

Let us see now see if the Bible has anything similar to
report.

Biblical Concurrence

Propitiously my Bible falls open at a page that reveals a
terrible famine that raged over both Egypt and Canaan for a
long period. I am of course referring to the 'seven fat cows
and seven thin cows' dream-turned-reality, documented here.
The spotlight here is of course on Joseph the Jew, the
dreamer, the new vizier of all Egypt.

Joseph is credited with three important achievements.
One, during the seven years of plentitude, Joseph is said to

have purchased all the corn in the land at a throwaway price. Then, during the famine that followed, he sold the corn back to the farmers in return for their money, cattle and land, thereby making the King of Egypt the owner of all the land in Egypt. At a later date, that is to say, during the years of famine, he redistributed seed and the land back again to the farmers and required them to give a fifth of the harvest to the King of Egypt as rent. Now, I am not making all this up, for here indeed is proof:

> *And Joseph bought all the land of Egypt for Pharaoh; for the Egyptians sold every man his field... so the land became Pharaoh's. Then Joseph said... Behold, I have bought you this day and your land for Pharaoh: lo, here is seed for you, and ye shall sow the land.... ye shall give the fifth part unto Pharaoh, and four parts shall be your own. [Genesis 47.20, 22, 23, 24]*

Two, not one to be stopped by boundaries, Joseph had made his moves in Canaan as well, which too was reeling under the effects of the drought. Thanks to Joseph, the King of Egypt was able to similarly buy up all the tillable land in adjoining Canaan and thereby become the ruler of Canaan as well. All the money, followed by all the cattle and finally all the land of Canaan too was procured by Joseph for the King of Egypt, in exchange for corn.

> *And Joseph gathered up all the money that was found in the land of Egypt, and in the land of Canaan, for the corn which they bought [Genesis 47.14]*

Three, it was also during this period that, the Jews were able to settle in Egypt, purportedly by the good office of Joseph.

In an effort to trace the genesis of the Asmach, we scour Herodotus' history and find a reference to a rabid campaign undertaken by Sesostris to expand the kingdom. He was "accompanied by vast multitudes of the people whose countries he had subdued." We wondered if this rag-tag mercenary army, which he eventually resettled in enviable comfort in Egypt, is indeed an early glimpse of the Asmach. Then we learn that Sesostris was the only Egyptian king who ruled both Egypt and adjoining Ethiopia. Added to that, we learn that he was credited with having divided the land and collected rent. This is about when we stop and exclaim in utter bewilderment, 'Hey, wait a minute, is this not the story of Joseph the quintessential Jew, who played tic-tac-toe with the farmers and usurped all the land in Egypt and Canaan? Is he not that shrewd vizier of all Egypt, who purchased all the land in Egypt and Canaan for the Pharaoh King of Egypt and later collected rent for the same?' How in the world did Sesostris' story get so inextricably enmeshed with that of Joseph's?

So, was Joseph perhaps the vizier of Sesostris? Probably yes, considering the very high level of concurrencies. The Sesostris-Joseph team was in rare form; indeed the Bible's portrayal of Joseph as having been the de-facto king of Egypt was true! Incredibly, the two storylines come together exactly as two broken halves seamlessly joined back! Even the manner in which the business was conducted, betrays the all too well known Jewish hand for such things!

But what about the 'Asmach' ... or 'the rag-tag army of Sesostris Jewish soldiers' theme?

The Bible documents the fact that the Jews were indeed accommodated in Goshen during this period but gives all the credit to Joseph who was at the palace, wheeling and dealing to accommodate them. While this is a perfectly acceptable story, can we not see the Jews as shepherd-soldiers come in on their own?

We naively assume that the Jews were meek nomadic shepherds and fail to give adequate weight to the word 'nomadic' associated with it. Perhaps the true operative word here is indeed 'nomadic.' Now, nomadic shepherds were no ordinary shepherds. They in fact served a dual function. They tended to their flock all right, but their real business was as guards or soldiers. When all your wealth is out in the open, you really need a veritable army of soldiers, who can also double as shepherds, to keep an eye on things. Ask Abram, Isaac or Jacob all of whom were powerful nomadic princes, who maintained sizable armies of this unique brand of shepherd-soldiers to safeguard their wealth. In fact, the Bible begins off its saga with exactly such a tale. Abram, the patriarch, reportedly lent his army of 300-odd shepherd-soldiers to recover the wealth of regular kings of the plain! To be sure, the minor kings of the region had a healthy respect for these wandering nomadic princes and always allowed them safe harbor—and with alacrity—whenever they suddenly appeared like a nemesis on their outskirts. Actually, nomads, gypsies and their like, manage to elicit pretty much the same response the world over. They are fearless and have always inspired a nameless fear in the hearts of walled-city mortals!

Having established that the Jews were soldier-shepherds of the most dreaded kind, and that there must have been a veritable army of such nomadic Jewish soldiers-shepherds, I ask, what happened to them? Where did they disappear? It is suggested that they probably signed up in droves to join Sesostris' army and helped him expand his kingdom. Sesostris, the first priest of Vulcan kings, who ruled Egypt for 300-years and presumably of Semitic descent himself, paid back in kind. He invited the Jewish soldier-shepherds to settle in Egypt, which they did, and went down in history as the infamous Asmach.

History Similarities

GIANTS

Here is an interesting similarity. The Ethiopians were "the tallest" race in the whole world," pronounces the exacting Herodotus. Still not satisfied, he throws in "and handsomest men" as well. But this does not tell us much. However, what he says next catches my attention. Apparently, the Ethiopians chose the tallest and strongest amongst them to be their king. "In their customs they differ greatly from the rest of mankind," says Herodotus and adds, "particularly in the way they choose their kings; for they find out the man who is the tallest of all the citizens and of strength equal to his height and appoint him to rule over them." [Herodotus 3.20]

For the man from Greece, where the state was run by philosophers and thinkers, and the air was thick with new-fangled ideas like democracy and such like, this practice of choosing the tallest and strongest as king, seriously rankled, giving even the barbarians a bad name. Herodotus thus scrambled to record this most aberrant behavior of the barbarians, no doubt to win brownie points at the beautiful Aspasia's elite gatherings. The Ethiopians, records Herodotus with a rolling of his eyes, "choose the tallest amongst them to be their king."

We of the twenty-first century, with our marked preference for actors, are of course not in the least bit perturbed. Our only query here is, 'Does the Bible concur; does it have a similar idiosyncrasy to report?'

Incredibly, even in such small details, the Bible concurs. It too mentions that the Amorites of Canaan were exceedingly tall and often refers to them as "giants." In fact, the Amorite's unusual stature purportedly resulted in a forty-year setback in the Israelite conquest plans. The twelve spies sent to the Eschol valley to evaluate this enemy, left nothing to imagination. Their ill-fated 'Grasshopper' report, "...we saw men of great stature... we saw giants... we were in our own sight as grasshoppers... " entirely demoralized the Jewish army.

Now, any reference to giants instantly resets our imagination to that of a four-year old. Yet, the Jews did not see 'giants' as Jack of the beanstalk fame presumably did. They 'saw men of great stature' as the Bible itself later admits. Perhaps the average height of the enemy was over six feet and compared to the Jew's average stature, they indeed did look like giants.

But it certainly did make a lasting impression on the Jews. For, the Bible skid-stops in its miracle spewing tracks, to record in awe the Amorite King's "thirteen feet by six feet" iron bedstead. Og's king-size iron bedstead so besotted the Jews, that they reportedly dragged it to Rabbath, where it was presumably kept on permanent display to be gawked at, by generations of diminutive Jews down the ages.

And a good thing too. For, this inordinately large item of furniture now comes to the aid of this beleaguered people. It confirms Herodotus' own observation of the Ethiopians. While Herodotus informs us that the Ethiopians were exceedingly tall and choose the tallest and strongest man amongst them to be their king, the Bible emphatically confirms it and goes a step further by producing a fine specimen—Og—complete with his custom-made, seen-to-be-believed, gigantic cot for inspection!

Comment

Modern-day scholars have all along wondered why is it that the Exodus, a cataclysmic event in every sense of the word, is not reflected in the annals of Egyptian history. Ironically, all the while it has been there, enshrined in the writings of the most popular historian of our times. Herodotus' version is distilled; nonetheless he manages to capture the essence of Israel's most dramatic event, the Exodus, thanks wholly to his predilection for including legends and idiosyncratic tales in his book—an act, alas, that has only gained him ill-repute until now.

TOPOGRAPHICAL SIMILARITIES

The wilderness detours the Exodus was obliged to slink through, gives us the distinct impression that Canaan was in and accessible only through uninhabited wilderness. To complicate matters, it would seem that the Bible has not a sentence to spare to document the topography of the region, being understandably overburdened by the task of conveying religious import.

In truth however, the Exodus trail gives us a 'slow train view' of the changing topography of the region, beginning from Egypt and leading all the way to Canaan. Indeed, it faithfully records every bump and pothole on the trail, so much so that one could, as Edison would say, 'run the apparatus backwards'[1] and playback the trail.

After much study of the terrain, I am inclined to break it up into the following well-defined tracts.

1. Reed (Red) Sea Tract
2. The Wilderness Tract
3. The Horeb Detour
4. The Canaan Plain

THE REED (RED) SEA TRACT

The Reed Sea dominates this segment of the trail. We see the Exodus assemblage camp on one side of the sea, cut across the sea, camp on the other side, and so on. Now most of you may not have discerned it, however, this very sea bewilderingly appears on the Exodus trail yet again, after many months of wandering in the wilderness.

The sea is described as a marshy one, choked with tall reeds. Since the reed association is strong (the term used in the Bible is 'Yum Suph,' which translates to Reed Sea), it is likely that the Reed Sea was in fact a large marshy, freshwater lake.

Everything is straightforward here, except of course the curious second sighting. The Exodus assemblage comes upon the sea yet again after many months of wandering. What could this mean? Was this a very large lake, or merely a long one? Of course, the Exodus did retrace a segment of their route, and this may well be the reason for this second sighting.

THE WILDERNESS TRACT

This tract too is not without mystery. After crossing the Reed Sea, we see the Exodus assemblage ducking into one wilderness tract after another, such as, Wilderness of Etham, Wilderness of Elim, Wilderness of Sin, and so on. Now, we assume that the wilderness tracts defined barren or desert tracts. However, I am not so sure. I think that forest tracts better fit the description. This is supported by the fact that for a considerable stretch through these tracts the Exodus Jews ate manna, a forest produce, which in all likelihood was the sweet resinous exudate that come out as drops on the bark of the Tamarisk mannifera tree. There is no mystery at all associated with manna. But yes, the Jews were unfamiliar with this forest produce and furthermore, it came in extremely handy under extreme circumstances, and therefore they considered it a miracle food. Manna is still available today in Turkish bazaars. It is called *Kudrethelvası* and the way to collect is to lay a bed-sheet under the tree and give the tree a good shake. Alternatively, you could let it fall overnight.

Apart from the manna indicator, the manner in which the Jews entered into one wilderness patch after another, suggests that these were indeed forest tracts. The exodus assemblage used the forest tracts as cover. Essentially, they 'ducked' into one wilderness after another. One cannot very well 'duck into' barren tracts. Besides, they would be considerably exposed, were the tracts in question devoid of vegetative cover.

Also, I suspect that the wilderness tracts were probably contiguous. The different names for different segments may be chalked down to the 'not fully thought through' manner in which old world denizens assigned names. 'That is 'Sin,' and that is 'Zin'' they would say, seemingly pointing to one forest clump with maybe a barely perceptible shift of the head, and wonder why you cannot seem to get it. Thus, what we have on hand appears to be a long continuous tract of forest, which began from Egypt and led all the way into the Canaan Plain.

What would form such a long and continuous tract of forest? The answer to this question is obvious. A river of course. A river usually forms a greenbelt all along its course.

But was there a river in the scenario; does the Bible mention a river? Of course there is, and yes, the Bible does very well mention a river. It shows up at Kadesh and is called the River of Wilderness. Therefore, all the Exodus assemblage really did was to go upstream alongside a river and happily reach Canaan.

Now I know that this is radically different from the current model and thinking on this subject. However, be assured that much of that model's coloring has been derived from the reconstructed terrain the Exodus trail is thought to have passed through. Their trail passes through the Sinai Peninsula, which is a terrible desert tract. This alone is why biblical scholars render terms such as 'wilderness', to deliver the 'barren desert tract theme.'

If you are still having trouble accepting my reconstructed model, look at it from another perspective. Would not a water source all along the Exodus trail be a prerequisite? Surely, 603,550 soldiers would need a great quantity of water. At say, roughly one gallon per person per day, the assemblage would require 603,550 gallons per day. In fact, we do not hear of too many water related woes along the route, except for one unfortunate incident. Indeed, at that particular instance, the situation had gone so out of hand that Moses had to pay for it with his life. What does that tell us? Just this: water was far too explosive an issue to be trifled with. Consider all the above points, I doubt if the Exodus assemblage was ever more than a few steps away from a plentiful water source all along the way.

Here is yet another argument in support of my reconstruction. Surely, there was a straightforward route from Egypt to the Canaan Plain. This is but reasonable thinking. After all, the countries were next-door neighbors. Possibly, even a well-used pathway, one that is frequently referred to in the Bible by the term 'King's highway,' did connect Canaan to Egypt.

THE HOREB DETOUR & THE SHORTCUT

The straightforward route to Canaan is of course obscured by the confusion created by the Horeb detour. The Horeb dash was clearly a detour, a secret spot to regroup. What is more, this could well have been a dash through a desert tract. The idea was to hightail to Horeb, and wait until things cooled off a bit. It was indeed a perfect hideout and what is more, Moses had a Midianite connection there.

Mt. Horeb was almost certainly a volcano. In fact, the stratospheric ash-stack of this volcano, which was visible from vast distances both day and night (when it reflected the red-hot lava at its base), played an important role. The Bible reports that a pillar of cloud and another of fire 'twisted' about in front of the assemblage, and led the way, as one would suppose, a tornado could do. No, no, no! What really transpired was, the instruction to 'keep that ash-stack always in front, walk towards it, use it as a beacon to lead the way' was given in no uncertain terms. To be sure, no better advice than this could be had or given while fleeing across a featureless desert landscape, especially so if the ash-spewing volcano in question was actually the destination. A beacon that was visible for miles was exactly what the Exodus assemblage needed and very likely, the place of rendezvous was chosen because of it. I mean, when you are on the run, it is imperative that you designate a secret but highly visible place to regroup.

After things cooled off, the Exodus army took a short cut from Horeb to get on to the regular route, catch it halfway. This involved crossing over a mountain range. Possibly, the shortcut brought them on the outer side of the mountain range. Spies were sent across, to gauge the feasibility of the move and they brought back a negative report. The army decided to go ahead anyway. The plan backfired. They were repulsed by the mountains-dwellers, the Edomites, and not allowed to crossover. Thus, they were forced to look for an alternative point of entry by which to catch the regular route. Since a mountain range intervened, this meant circumnavigating it. It meant backtracking almost halfway back to Egypt.

Eventually they reached the Canaan Plain from the regular route. On the way in, they passed the point where they tried to cut-in by crossing over the mountains. This time however, the Edomites were unconcerned and merely glared down at them, reports the Bible.

In the Canaan Plain, one can sense a change in terrain. The land is flat and fertile. There are marshes and rivers here aplenty. Fields are growing on either side and the land is teaming with unfriendly people. Presumably, this is that stretch supposedly flowing with milk and honey. Fascinatingly, a 'Sea of the Plain,' possibly, yet another large lake is mentioned.

To reiterate, the topographical features that one sees between Egypt and Canaan by studying the Exodus trail are as such: A straightforward trail that followed the course of a river, led from Egypt to Canaan. Somewhere along the way, there were mountains. The Canaan Plain was a fertile and well-watered tract. A large lake seems to be a landmark feature of this plain.

But the real question is, did Herodotus manage to document a topography that is anything like the above? Do we see any of the above terrain features reflected in Herodotus' approach route from Egypt to Ethiopia, via the Elephantine route?

The only way to find out is to start once again from Elephantine. This time around, instead of looking for legends and quirky tales, let us keep our eyes open for topographical similarities.

As one advances beyond Elephantine, the land rises. Hence it is necessary in this part of the river to attach a rope to the boat on each side, as men harness an ox

"As one advances beyond Elephantine the land rises," writes Herodotus. He goes on to explain how "it is necessary in this part of the river to attach a rope to the boat on each side, as men harness an ox. If the rope snaps, the vessel is borne away downstream by the force of the current."

"The navigation continues the same for four days, the river winding greatly, like the Maeander," continues the historian. "And, after traversed a distance amounting to twelve schoenes, you come upon a smooth and level plain, where the Nile flows in two branches, round an island called Tachompso." Herodotus goes on to inform us "the Ethiopians, possess one-half of this island, the Egyptians occupying the other." We may assume that the island was possibly divided into two by some form of natural boundary. After or "above the island, there is a great lake; after passing it, you come again to the stream of the Nile, which runs into the lake."

From here onwards, the river is not navigable. "Sharp peaks" he says "jut out from the water" and "the sunken rocks which abound in that part of the stream" leave you no recourse but to walk alongside the banks "for forty days." After you pass this portion of the river, "you go on board another boat and proceed by water for twelve days more, at the end of which time you reach a great city called Meroe, which is said to be the capital of the other Ethiopians."

Lastly, Herodotus adds, "On leaving this city and again mounting the stream, in the same space of time which it took you to reach the capital from Elephantine, you come to the Deserters, who bear the name of Asmach."

Right away, it can be seen that a river, the Nile that is, defined the route from Egypt to Ethiopia. In addition, there were mountains on the path for, above Elephantine, the land is said to rise, and the river to meander for four days. Eventually, a smooth and level plain, the Plain of Ethiopia is reached. On the plain, there is a river island, followed by a great lake. In short, the topographical features presented by Herodotus in the above extract are promising. Furthermore, an exhaustive study of Ethiopia's topography gleaned from various secular ancient world historians reveals it to be an exact copy of Canaan's terrain as presented by the Bible.

A complete list of topographical similarities between Ethiopia and Canaan is given below. Those that require elaboration are discussed in detail in the following chapters.

TOPOGRAPHICAL SIMILARITIES

ETHIOPIA	CANAAN
Red Sea	Reed Sea
Mountains	Seir Mountains
Plain of Ethiopia	Plain of the Jordan
The Nile leading to Ethiopia	The 'River of Egypt' leading to Canaan
The tributaries were Astapus and Astaboras	The tributaries were Arnon and Jabbok
An island, Tachompso	The land amidst the river, Tahtimhodshi
A great lake	The Sea of the Plain

CHAPTER 11

Topographical Similarities

THE PLAIN OF THE JORDAN

And Lot lifted up his eyes and beheld all the plain of Jordan, that it was well watered everywhere, before the LORD destroyed Sodom and Gomorrah, even as the garden of the LORD, like the land of Egypt, as thou comest unto Zoar. [Genesis 13.10]

Ah, Sodom and Gomorrah, the cities of the plain, where even the archangels of the Lord feared to tread! Viewed from the mountains, they burned brightly, portending all manners of evil. However, it was not the cities that attracted the patriarch, Abraham, brooding in his mountaintop lair. It was the rich fertile plain, on which they lewdly stood, that positively riveted him. Like a true prince, wise in the ways of the world, he, as did Lot, liked what he saw. Choice lands, ideal to grow into, maybe spawn a kingdom or two.

The verdant plain below, with the Jordan meandering through it in numerous branches, was a truly magnificent sight to behold. With reluctance, the old shepherd prince looked up at the skies above and let out a deep sigh. He could not decide which was better. The starry skies above, the vast real estate he inherited from his nomadic ancestors, or the misty plain below. Of course, a true nomad would sooner gorge his eyes out than make such an odious comparison. However, what was to be done. The nomadic way of existence was fast being edged out. Perhaps he was a renegade, or he was of mixed blood. He was a fallen angel, he decided, for the paradise below, this land that flowed with milk and honey... oh how it had smitten him!

A little bit of history would help here. Abraham and Lot were nomad princes who and had recently migrated from Ur of the Chaldees and double-parked their caravans in the mountains that fringed the Plain of the Jordan. They had sizable holdings of livestock and an equally large entourage of family members. The shepherds and their families, including three hundred and eighteen fighting men, pushed the total of humans alone to two-thousand or more. In short, they were like mobile townships and far too ponderous for the nomadic way of life.

This is why they eventually decided to split. "Separate thyself, I pray thee, from me: if thou wilt take the left hand, then I will go to the right... " [Genesis 13:9]. Lot, having set his eyes on the plains, moved into the fringe regions amidst the cities of the plain. Abraham chose to remain in the mountains. But that did not dim his lust for the Plain of the Jordan, that glimmered like a jewel from his mountaintop lair. On the contrary, it multiplied, as did his descendants, the Jews.

In and around the mountains that fringed the Plain of the Jordan, the Jews lived nomadically, making no mark or laying no claim on the land. Famines eventually forced them to migrate to Egypt, where they lived for many generations.

Four hundred and thirty odd years later, the Jews returned, not as footloose nomads, but as an organized army, determined to carve for themselves a homeland. And as they quietly gazed down at the Plain of the Jordan below, from almost the exact spot where their ancestor Abraham had done before, they too were smitten. The Jordan shimmered and very easily aroused a powerful lust for the land in their embittered hearts. The land—their land—they noted, was worth dying for and wished their patriarch Abraham had had the sense to move in alongside Lot. For indeed, Sodom and Gomorrah were long gone, in its place were Edom, Moab, Ammon and Midian, all descendants of crafty Lot, his dreams[2] long since realized, and now, just as firmly entrenched.

It is this extraordinarily covetous Plain of the Jordan, the so-called Promised Land, which is at the heart of the Bible saga. From the general topographical information available, one gets the impression that the plain was extensive, large enough to hold two or three sizeable kingdoms. It was "…well watered everywhere" and exceedingly fertile and enchanting "even as the garden of the Lord… " and this region was located somewhere south of Egypt.

Let us see if our friend, the indomitable Herodotus, has anything to report on it. He did find us the Deserters after all. Perhaps he stumbled upon the Promised Land as well and like a good little historian, tucked it away in his bric-a-brac history among other oddities!

Secular Source Concurrence

> *As one advances beyond Elephantine, the land rises.*
> *Hence it is necessary in this part of the river to attach a*
> *rope. The navigation continues the same for four days,*
> *the river winding greatly. Here you come upon a*
> *smooth and level plain. [Herodotus 2.29]*

Here is that key paragraph which describes the topography of Ethiopia and its relative position in relation to Egypt. The basic topographical setting was as such: Both Egypt and Ethiopia were river valley civilizations and shared the same river, which was the Nile. While Egypt was situated in a cloistered valley between two parallel mountains, through which the river presumably flowed, Ethiopia was situated higher up-stream but on a plain, again presumably through which the river flowed. The extract also fills us in about a four-day stretch, which appears to have been a patch of highland through which the river meandered greatly.

In other words, after ascending up-river beyond Elephantine, the last outpost of Egypt and taking in four days of meandering upon the river (the Nile), one would suddenly come upon the smooth and level Plain of Ethiopia.

Hold on. Are we not in search of a plain? Then here, in the heart of Ethiopia was a magnificent one. Was the Plain of Ethiopia, the very same Plain of the Jordan? Well, we cannot be sure as of now, but certainly as a similarity between Canaan and Ethiopia, plain for a plain, we can definitely put it in the bag.

The River Of Egypt

*And now what hast thou to do in the way of Egypt, to
drink the waters of Sihor? or what hast thou to do in
the way of Assyria, to drink the waters of the river?
[Book of Jeremiah 2.18]*

Prophet Jeremiah was in despair. He realized that raving and
ranting, which he was very good at and happy to deliver, had
lost its considerable bite. Thus, he pleaded, even begged and
was not ashamed to put his heart into it. Wooden faced Jews,
fed up with the concept of a Promised Land and migrating in
droves to other kingdoms, were however in no mood to
listen.

Earlier, powerful kings used to send their troops to
fledgling neighboring kingdoms, raid them, and deport the
people. Later they realized that it was enough to stand
outside their gates and merely shake their spears. Petty kings
sulked, then obediently scraped the beaten gold off their
palace walls—originally put there with much labor—and
handed it across the wall. Newer political ideology helped
further refine the aggressor's modus operandi. Indeed, it
finally dawned upon these barbarians, that enterprising
people represented the true wealth of a nation. What is more,
this kind of asset could be made to jump across the wall all of
their own accord. All one had to do was provide safe haven
and offer an improved quality of life. Wealth on two legs from
the world over would come a-skipping to roost. No need to
send troops, or even shake spears. 'Diaspora' as this

phenomenon came to be known, became fashionable, much to the chagrin of prophets stuck-in-time.

This is why Jeremiah is now intently pleading. "Why hath thou to do by way of Egypt? To drink the water of the Shihor?"

Now, tangling with the Prophet is the last thing on my mind. I am merely here looking for topographical clues. And, in Jeremiah's line of enquiry, I see the glimmer of one. Indeed, his query does seem to establish a clear proximity between Egypt and the River Shihor. It is like equating the River Ganges to India. The prophet equates the waters of the Shihor to Egypt. Clearly, the River Shihor had to be intrinsically Egyptian for him to have framed his question in such a querulous manner.

Here is another verse from the Bible that refers to the Shihor:

And by great waters the seed of Sihor, the harvest of the river, is her revenue; and she is a mart of nations. [Isaiah 23.3]

Perhaps Shihor was the name of a grain-producing province, but eventually even the river that watered this region and carried its produce to the marts, came to be known by this name. The 'seed of Shihor,' the 'harvest of the river' clearly indicates that the Shihor was watering a major grain bowl. Tyre, the mart of the nation, it appears, grew wealthy by shipping the produce of this river. Imagine, thus, the significance of this river. Going by the above verse in the Bible, one would have no choice but to allocate a full-bodied perennial river for Shihor. But alas, rivers are in such short supply in the biblical region. Given that, biblical scholars have allocated a miserable *wadi* on the extreme north of biblical Israel to represent the mighty Shihor.

Moving on, another mystery river surreptitiously flowed through the Biblical Land as well. And oddly enough, this one was called 'the River of Egypt.' Consider the following verses:

And the border shall fetch a compass from Azmon unto the river of Egypt and the goings out of it shall be at the sea. [Numbers 34.5]

Ashdod with her towns and her villages, Gaza with her towns and her villages, unto the river of Egypt and the great sea and the border thereof: [Joshua 15.47]

It appears that this river, called the River of Egypt, formed a segment of Israel's border. The said river emptied into a great sea, conceivably the Mediterranean Sea, before passing by the Philistine coastal settlements of Gaza and Ashdod. Since the river is called the 'River of Egypt,' it is very likely that it was intrinsically connected to Egypt.

Now we have two rivers described in the Bible that are intrinsically Egyptian. One was the Shihor and the other the River of Egypt. Were they perhaps the same? I mean, is it not likely that they are merely two different names (that emerged during different times) for the same river? Let us see if we can establish this.

Consider the following verses:

So David gathered all Israel together, from Shihor of Egypt even unto the entering of Hemath, to bring the ark of God from Kirjathjearim. [1 Chronicles 13.5]

Also at the same time Solomon kept the feast seven days and all Israel with him, a very great congregation, from the entering in of Hamath unto the river of Egypt. [2 Chronicles 7.8]

The above two verses refer to the 'entering of Hamath' and a river. In the first verse, the entering of Hamath, which appears to have been a mountain pass, is associated with the Shihor of Egypt, from 'the entering of Hamath' to the 'Shihor of Egypt.'

David, after much indecisiveness, brings the Ark of the Covenant to Israel. He commemorates the event with a seven-day feast for which he gathers all the people of Israel, from the Hamath Pass to the River Shihor. Evidently, these two natural boundaries represented the borders (say, north and south) of Israel during that time.

The second verse describes a similar event, which also happens to be related to the one described above. David is long gone; however, his son, King Solomon fulfils the promise made by him and builds a temple to house the Ark of the Covenant. He too commemorates the consecration of the temple with a seven-day feast, similar to the one held earlier by David. Thus, once again all the people of Israel from 'the entering of Hamath to the River of Egypt' gather to celebrate the event.

As before, our interest is merely in finding topographical clues. Sure enough, a shred of information has been trampled in, enshrined for posterity, by all this celebratory cavorting. We find that while describing David's celebration, the Bible records that the people gathered from the 'Hamath pass to the Shihor of Egypt.' However, in the second event, the records say, that the people gathered from the 'Hamath pass to the River of Egypt.' This can mean only one thing. The 'River of Egypt' was without doubt the 'Shihor of Egypt.'

But ah, the mystery does not end here. Consider the following verse:

> *But, behold, I will raise up against you a nation, O house of Israel, saith the LORD the God of hosts; and they shall afflict you from the entering in of Hemath unto the river of the wilderness. [Amos 16.14]*

Here the entering of Hamath is associated with a river called 'the river of the wilderness.' This confirms that 'the River of

Egypt' or 'the Shihor' apparently flowed through the wilderness and as such, was occasionally known as 'the River of Wilderness' as well. Combining all the above information, a fuller picture of a mysterious river, known in the Bible by different names, emerges. A mighty river that was intrinsically connected to Egypt, perhaps the Nile itself, flowed into the core biblical arena. The Bible called it by various names such as 'the River of Egypt,' 'the Shihor,' 'the River of the Wilderness,' and so on.

The Bible has grudgingly revealed this mystery. However, to make up for its reluctance, it offers one solid piece of evidence. It is a verse from antiquity, which without ambiguity, supports this single river concept:

> *And the name of the second river is Gihon: the same is it that compasseth the whole land of Ethiopia. [Genesis 2.13]*

The Gihon flowed through the whole land of Ethiopia. Now, if we apply our Ethiopia equals Canaan theory to the above information, it will yield: A single river named Gihon compasseth the whole land of Canaan. The Gihon, presumably yet another name from antiquity for the Shihor, thus stoutly supports our theory. Coming to think of it, even the name Gihon sounds somewhat similar to Shihor. G-**iho**-n=Sh-**iho**-r. Gihon probably became Shihon and later Shihor.

However, the real question is, does Herodotus, our ancient world friend, have such a mighty river on his plate?

Secular Source Concurrence

He calls it the Nile, for indeed, it was the Nile, the same upon which he had made his journey up to Elephantine and beyond (seen of course through the eyes of his Ethiopian sources) deep into Ethiopia. Clearly, the Nile flowed through Canaan-Ethiopia as well. Herodotus, Strabo and all the other ancient world secular sources are in agreement concerning this issue. The concurrence derived by this exercise is, The River of Egypt=The Nile. It may be noted here that the term 'River of Egypt' from a straightforward point of view, is almost synonymous to the Nile. The above information may seem a little difficult to digest for now, but that is because of our familiarity with the present day erroneous reconstruction. The fact that the Nile flowed through the Holy land is what the ancient world textual sources concurrently and unambiguously reveal.

Comment

Biblical scholars, having not the patience to unravel such mysteries, have gone ahead and recreated two separate rivers in their reconstruction. As far as they are concerned, the River of Egypt was different from the Shihor, or for that matter, from the River of the Wilderness. Not content with this faux pas, they have gone ahead and located these rivers at the opposite extremes of their reconstructed Israel. While, the River of Egypt is on Israel's southern border, almost in the Sinai desert, trying to get as close to Egypt as possible, in keeping with its name, the Shihor is placed in the extreme north, trying to be as close as possible to Tyre. Not that there are rivers here on the ground. Bone dried *wadis* had to be found to represent this perennial river or rivers. With such obvious reconstruction flaws, it is hardly surprising that biblical archaeologists have yet to find a shred of evidence in support of biblical history.

Chapter 13

Land Amidst The River Arnon

Another topographical feature described in Herodotus' history is the island Tachompso situated on the Plain of Ethiopia.

> *As one advances beyond Elephantine, the land rises.... The navigation continues the same for four days, the river winding greatly, like the Maeander and the distance traversed amounting to twelve schoenes. Here you come upon a smooth and level plain, where the Nile flows in two branches, round an island called Tachompso. [Herodotus 2.29]*

The river Nile, after meandering for a distance of four days, enters into the Plain of Ethiopia. Here, it splits into two tributaries and flows around this landmass, cordoning it off in its midst. In other words, Tachompso is a 'river island.'

River islands were not in the 'middle of the river' sandbars. They essentially were tracts of land that were cordoned off by rivers and its tributaries. Such islands were much prized by ancient world military strategists and even historians made a very big deal of them, for the simple reason that they were ideally situated from a security point of view.

Incidentally, Strabo describes the island Tachompso in great detail. Here, take a look:

> *The island is said to be like an oblong shield in shape. Its size has perhaps been exaggerated: about three thousand stadia in length and one thousand in breadth. The island has both numerous mountains and large thickets; it is inhabited partly by nomads, partly*

by hunters, and partly by farmers; and it has mines of copper, iron, gold, and different kinds of precious stones. It is bounded on the Libyan side by large sand-dunes, and on the Arabian side by continuous precipices, and above, on the south, by the confluence of the three rivers—the Astaboras, and the Astapus and the Astasobas [Strabo, Geography 17.2.2]

The island was apparently in the shape of an oblong shield and had both mountains and large thickets. It was bound on the Libyan side by large sand dunes, on the Arabian side by continuous precipices and on the south by the confluence of three rivers. The extract also mentions that the river tributaries in the scenario were called Astaboras, Astapus, and Astasobas. This detail too is pertinent; however, it would be premature to discuss it at this point. You will find this topic satisfactorily covered in a later chapter.

Let us see if the Bible has anything to report of this nature.

Biblical Concurrence

The Bible unfortunately has nothing immediately discernable as an island in its arena. However, it does go on and on about 'city in the midst' of the River Arnon. Now a number of references in the Bible clearly establish Arnon as a river, yet modern-day editions, taking their cue from the archaeologists, now refer to it as a gorge. If you compare your Bible with an older version, you would immediately discern this anomaly. While the older and some of the conservative later editions would refer to Arnon as a river, the newer, brought-up-to-speed contemporary editions will have you know that it was a gorge.

The reason for this distortion can be traced to the fact that River Arnon seems to have had a 'city in its midst.' Here are three references from the King James Version, which continues to call the Arnon a river, and makes mention of a city in its midst:

> *From Aroer, that is upon the bank of the river Arnon and the city that is in the midst of the river and all the plain of Medeba unto Dibon and all the plain by Medeba. [Joshua 13.9]*

> *And their coast was from Aroer, that is on the bank of the river Arnon and the city that is in the midst of the river. [Joshua 13.16]*

> *And they passed over Jordan and pitched in Aroer, on the right side of the city that lieth in the midst of the river of Gad and toward Jazer: [2 Samuel 24.5]*

A consistent reference to 'a city that is in the midst of the river' has puzzled biblical scholars for a long time. What did it mean? Had the river in question, the Arnon, dried up or changed course and a lissome little city promptly jumped in and occupied its vacated bed? Was Arnon a gorge? This line of thinking of course meant doing away with the River Arnon, which incidentally is otherwise unambiguously described as a perennial river. However, since finding perennial rivers in their reconstructed biblical arena was thinning hair on far too many heads, the gorge interpretation was welcomed with rare solidarity. Today, as I mentioned earlier, most modern Bible translations depict the River Arnon as a gorge without even an apologetic footnote.

Now, the consistent reference to land midst the river in the Bible might indicate just that: land amidst the river, which possibly was a tract of land that was cordoned off by a determined river that flowed on both sides, creating a river island. Frankly, this is the more straightforward explanation of the term 'land amidst the river.' Why twist it, turn it into a gorge?

Fortunately, we do not have to rely entirely on speculation here. Josephus, in his 'Antiquities of the Jews,' confirms the above interpretation and offers an unambiguous picture of an island in the core biblical arena. Here is the extract:

> *Hereupon the Hebrews took possession of their land, which is a country situated between three rivers and naturally resembled an island: the river Arnon being its southern; the river Jabbok determining its northern side, which running into Jordan loses its own name and takes the other; while Jordan itself runs along by it, on its western coast. [Flavius Josephus, Antiquities of the Jews, 4.5]*

The above is an extract from Josephus' commentary on the biblical landscape. Note here that the river-island is cordoned off by three rivers, the Arnon, Jabbok and the Jordan is unambiguously described. We now know for certain that a river island certainly existed in the core biblical arena.

Showing a remarkable consistency, accuracy and a scientific bent of mind, the Bible presents the 'land amidst the river,' which I must add, is a technically purer description of the landmass in question, than the term 'island' used by Herodotus. What is more, this exactly matches the description of the river island on the Plain of Ethiopia, described by Herodotus. We may therefore chalk this down as yet another topographical similarity.

Ironically, what the Bible has so responsibly delivered intact across a three-thousand year time span, modern-day scholars have nearly obliterated in thirty by their 'gorge' interpretation.

CHAPTER 14

Topographical Similarities

EAST JORDAN, WEST JORDAN

The Jewish people's obvious love for history is evident in the descriptive names they use. And, such is the sterling quality of their descriptive names assigned to people, places, and so on, that they reveal the history of a place or the lineage of a person in the blink of an eye. Indeed, the Jews revel in associative names.

Perhaps it is thus that no one thinks twice about the omniscient 'identification tag' prefixed to the name Jordan. The River Jordan is almost always qualified with a lengthy identification tag. It is never plain Jordan, but is always, 'this side Jordan,' 'other side Jordan,' 'Jordan by Jericho,' 'Jordan in the Arabah,' 'this Jordan,' 'yonder Jordan,' 'forward Jordan,' 'Jordan eastwards towards the sun rising' or 'in the land of Moab' or 'in the wilderness' or 'in the valley over against Bethpeor,' etc.

Biblical scholars too had noticed this peculiarity and accepted it as an attempt to identify the bank (east or west) of the river. Indeed, it is this bit of biblical interpretation that has given birth to the interesting tract called the 'West Bank' in this region. But in truth, the identification tags appear almost mandatory and much too specific for something as simple as that.

If on the other hand, the Jordan had split into two on the plain, presumably to flow around an obstructing landmass or so, only to combine again after a short distance, then to identify the two separate tributaries, identification tags would be the preferred way to go. In other words, if for a short distance one river became two, it is unlikely to attract or warrant different names. Indeed, different names in such situations can only add to the confusion and can turn nightmarish during documentation. Directional prefixes like 'north,' as in North Dakota, or 'west' as in West Virginia, etc. is all it really needs.

This is perhaps why we find the river Jordan festooned with such directional prefixes and suffixes. A computer check reveals that there are fourteen references in the Bible of 'this side Jordan' and sixteen references of 'other side Jordan' besides, of course a host of other descriptive names. Conceivably, they were the two tributaries of the Jordan.

The other names used such as the 'Jordan by Jericho,' 'Jordan in the Arabah,' etc., were probably alternative names for these two tributaries and presumably came into being over the ages, possibly to accommodate 'directionally challenged' individuals. Here are a few samples:

> *And they brought the captives and the prey and the spoil, unto Moses and Eleazar the priest and unto the congregation of the children of Israel, unto the camp at the plains of Moab, which are by Jordan near Jericho. [Numbers 31.12]*

> *Are they not on the other side Jordan, by the way where the sun goeth down, in the land of the Canaanites, which dwell in the champaign over against Gilgal, beside the plains of Moreh? [Deuteronomy 11.30]*

In the first, the tributary in question is the 'Jordan by Jericho.' In the second, it is the 'Other Side Jordan' towards the west. As can be seen, inordinate care has been exercised to properly identify the tributaries in question.

Here is another verse that mentions the river and also refers to a specific bank. This should dispel the 'opposite banks' theory:

And on the other side Jordan by Jericho, on the east side of Jordan, were given them out of the tribe of Reuben, Bezer in the wilderness with her suburbs and Jahzah with her suburbs. [1 Chronicles 6.78]

In the above verse, the Jordan mentioned is the 'Other Side Jordan,' which is the same as 'Jordan by Jericho.' What is more, here a bank of the river, the east bank, is specifically mentioned. This clearly indicates that we are indeed dealing with separate rivers, rather than opposite banks of a river.

Finally, in the verse below, both the tributaries are being referred to in the same sentence:

For we will not inherit with them on yonder side Jordan, or forward; because our inheritance is fallen to us on this side Jordan eastward. [Numbers 32.19]

Here 'yonder side Jordan' is further qualified with the word 'forward.' It clearly indicates the second tributary that lies further west, while 'this side Jordan eastward' refers to the first tributary. Without a doubt, two rivers are being referred to here.

Given that the Jordan is almost never without identification tags and two separate tributaries can be readily identified, we can tentatively surmise that the Jordan did split into two on the plain and flowed as two separate rivers for a short distance.

Given the complicity of the issue (two rivers with same names), the Bible has, by the judicious use of qualifying nametags, made a valiant attempt to create order out of an otherwise chaotic situation. Unfortunately, it is still open to mischievous misinterpretation. But the reality is, if one is indeed in search for the truth here, the River Jordan was in fact two rivers—the East Jordan and the West Jordan.

Secular Source Concurrence

Ancient world secular scholars are happy to concur on this issue. Herodotus informs us that on the cloistered fertile Plain of Ethiopia, the river (the Nile) is said to have flowed in two branches, around the island called Tachompso. Here is a portion of that extract for ready reference:

> *Here you come upon a smooth and level plain, where the Nile flows in two branches, round an island called Tachompso. [Herodotus 2.29]*

We may tentatively conclude that the twin tributaries mentioned by ancient world textual sources are referred to as the East Jordan and West Jordan in the Bible narrative.

JABBOK & ARNON

Continuing with the theme of the earlier chapter, while Herodotus does not name the two tributaries of the Nile on the Plain of Ethiopia, Strabo does. He calls them Astaboras and the Astapus. Here, look:

The island is said to be like an oblong shield in shape. Its size has perhaps been exaggerated…. It is bounded on the Libyan side by large sand dunes, and on the Arabian side by continuous precipices, and above, on the south, by the confluence of the three rivers—the Astaboras, and the Astapus and the Astasobas. [Strabo, Geography 17.2.2]

Two rivers empty into it, which flow from some lakes on the east and enclose Meroe, a rather large island. One of these rivers, which flows on the eastern side of the island, is called Astaboras and the other is called Astapus, though some call it Astasobas. [Strabo, Geography 17.1.2]

What we have here is a large shield shaped island formed by two rivers. The rivers are referred to as the Astaboras and the Astapus. This reflects the exact same scenario as that of Herodotus on the Plain of Ethiopia. We can therefore tentatively conclude that the Astaboras and Astapus were the two tributaries of the Nile that formed the island. The third river, the Astasobas mentioned here, may well have contributed in some manner in the formation of the island.

Incredibly, Flavius Josephus too offers the very same scenario, complete with names and other pertinent details. Here too the tributaries are called Astaboras and Astapus.

> *At length they retired to Saba, which was a royal city of Ethiopia, which Cambyses afterwards named Mero, after the name of his own sister. The place was to be besieged with very great difficulty, since it was both encompassed by the Nile quite round and the other rivers, Astapus and Astaboras, made it a very difficult thing for such as attempted to pass over them; for the city was situate in a retired place and was inhabited after the manner of an island, being encompassed with a strong wall and having the rivers to guard them from their enemies and having great ramparts between the wall and the rivers . [Josephus, Antiquities of the Jews 2.10]*

The ancient world sources are clearly in harmony here. The exact same scenario painted by Strabo is reflected in Josephus' text as well. The two tributaries that formed the island were indeed the Astaboras and the Astapus. The Astasobas, the third river, in Strabo's version is replaced by the Nile in Josephus' scenario. It is possible therefore that all three rivers formed the island. Thus, we conclude that on the Plain of Ethiopia, the Nile, the main river, let out two tributaries and these two tributaries, called the Astaboras and Astapus formed a river island.

Let us take this scenario to the Bible and see what it has to reveal.

Biblical Concurrence

Now, we already have the East Jordan and West Jordan concept to fall back on. However, that is old news now. Let us therefore roll up our sleeves and dig assiduously for some fresh evidence. Unfortunately, the Bible has no more to give on this subject, but the flamboyant Flavius Josephus, the

Jewish historian from antiquity, steps in to bat for the Bible. Josephus incredibly offers the very same scenario with one very astounding change. Instead of the strange Greek names, he offers up the exact same scenario with biblical names for the tributaries! It is an extract from his 'Antiquities of the Jews,' from the section, which covers the core biblical arena. Here, take a look:

> *Hereupon the Hebrews took possession of their land, which is a country situated between three rivers and naturally resembled an island: the river Arnon being its southern; the river Jabbok determining its northern side, which running into Jordan loses its own name and takes the other; while Jordan itself runs along by it, on its western coast. [Josephus, Antiquities of the Jews, 4.5]*

Josephus' commentary on the biblical landscape mentions the Rivers Arnon, the Jabbok as well as the Jordan, as having circumscribed an island on the plain of Jordan. From this extract, it becomes apparent that the Arnon and the Jabbok were the tributaries, for, one of them, it is said, eventually lost its identity, having merged with the main river that was called the Jordan. As can be seen, the topographical scenario of two tributaries (the Arnon and the Jabbok), forming a river island on the Plain of the Jordan is strikingly similar to the scenario of the two tributaries (the Astapus and the Astaboras) forming a river island on the Plain of Ethiopia! Clearly, they refer to the same scenario.

This got me thinking. Were perhaps Astaboras and the Astapus the Greek derivatives of the biblical names, Jabbok and Arnon? Actually, if compelled, I will admit on seeing a slight similarity between the names 'Jabbok' and the 'tabor' in As-tabor-as. J-**abbo**-k=T-**abo**-r. The 'as' at both the ends of 'tabor' are harmless inflections that denotes gender, tense, etc., that invariably get added on when converted to Greek.

What then of East Jordan and West Jordan? Were they possibly earlier names or alternate names for the Arnon and Jabbok? Well, it would certainly seem so. For, here is an extract that suggests that Arnon was in fact one of the Jordan tributaries:

> *Wherefore it is said in the Book of the wars of the LORD, What he did in the Red sea and in the brooks of Arnon and at the stream of the brooks that goeth down to the dwelling of Ar and lieth upon the border of Moab. [Numbers 21.13]*

The above extract refers to the miraculous cleaving of water bodies by the God of the Old Testament. Now we all know that it was the Jordan 'that flowed by Jericho' that was cleaved (in connection with the Jericho siege) exactly as the Red Sea. However, in the above verse, it is the 'brooks of Arnon,' which are said to have been cleaved, and not Jordan. This seems to suggest that the Jordan 'that flowed by Jericho' was the same as the Arnon.

To sum up, the picture that the ancient world historians and the Bible concurrently provide of the island on the Canaan-Ethiopia plain was as such: The main river, the Nile referred to in biblical text by the generic term 'Jordan,' split into two tributaries and formed an oblong shield-shaped river island. The tributaries were called the Jabbok and Arnon. Astaboras and Astapus are merely Greek derivative of these very names.

On reading the above similarities, biblical scholars and Egyptologists must surely be bewildered. They had, after all, firmly set the rivers Astaboras, Astapus and the Astasobas as the Atbara, the White Nile and the Blue Nile, deep in the African continent, with much fanfare. Indeed, even as I write, there are dank towns complete with dark mayors, all portly and pretentious, considering with newfound gravity, how to commemorate or keep clean these rivers that misguided archaeologists had so munificently bequeathed them. Is it not remarkable that all the rivers that modern-day scholars have strewn over two continents, I have managed to squeeze onto the Plain of Canaan?

Note

Incidentally, I wonder how many of you noticed that Josephus mentions the river-island in both the Ethiopian as well as the biblical contexts. He documents it as Saba the Ethiopian island, captured by Cambyses, in part two of his 'Antiquities of the Jews,' and later, in the same book, in part four, which contains a commentary on the Bible, the same island resurfaces in the biblical context as the 'country situated between three rivers' or indeed the 'land amidst the river.' The first reference goes as such:

> *At length they retired to Saba, which was a royal city of Ethiopia, which Cambyses afterwards named Mero, after the name of his own sister. The place was to be besieged with very great difficulty, since it was both encompassed by the Nile quite round and the other rivers, Astapus and Astaboras, made it a very difficult thing for such as attempted to pass over them; for the city was situate in a retired place and was inhabited after the manner of an island, being encompassed with a strong wall and having the rivers to guard them from their enemies and having great ramparts between the wall and the rivers. [Josephus, Antiquities of the Jews 2.10]*

In the second, Josephus writes:

> *Hereupon the Hebrews took possession of their land, which is a country situated between three rivers and naturally resembled an island: the river Arnon being its southern; the river Jabbok determining its northern side, which running into Jordan loses its own name and takes the other; while Jordan itself runs along by it, on*

Both extracts, offer detailed descriptions of the river-island formed by three rivers and can be easily recognized as the same topographical setting. What is astonishing is the fact that Josephus does not appear to know this fact! But then again, this is to be expected and easily explained. First, hundreds of years separate the two histories in question and therefore the co-relation is not that obvious. Second, to historians, it is more important to document than to decipher. They are happy just to pickle and preserve for posterity and leave all the deciphering to armchair explorers like me!

THE SEA OF THE PLAIN

After the island formation, the next topographical feature documented by Herodotus on the Plain of Ethiopia was a great lake. Presumably, it was a fresh water lake for the river Nile is said to have fed it.

> *Above the island there is a great lake, the shores of which are inhabited by Ethiopian nomads; after passing it, you come again to the stream of the Nile, which runs into the lake. [Herodotus 2.29]*

The same scenario is reflected in Strabo's documentation as well. Here is the extract:

> *Above Meroe is Psebo, a large lake, containing a well-inhabited island. As the Libyans occupy the western bank of the Nile, and the Ethiopians the country on the other side of the river, they thus dispute by turns the possession of the islands and the banks of the river, one party repulsing the other, or yielding to the superiority of its opponent. [Strabo, Geography 17.2.3]*

From Strabo's Geography, we learn that the large lake was called 'Psebo.' Other similarities mentioned, such as the island that was 'jointly occupied by Ethiopians and Libyans' confirms that this is indeed the same region that Herodotus speaks of. A great lake therefore can be counted as a well-documented landmark on the Plain of Ethiopia. If anyone entertains doubts regarding the extracts cited, they are welcome to read them in context from the source books directly.

Let us see if the Bible concurs with this scenario.

The Bible consistently refers to a sea called 'the Sea of the Plain' that was situated centrally within the core biblical arena. From the name itself, it is evident that the Sea of the Plain was a very large, inland body of water that was situated on the Plain of the Jordan.

Consider the following verses:

The plain also and Jordan and the coast thereof, from Chinnereth even unto the sea of the plain, even the salt sea, under Ashdothpisgah eastward. [Deuteronomy 3.17]

And all the plain on this side Jordan eastward, even unto the sea of the plain, under the springs of Pisgah. [Deuteronomy 4.49]

Without much fuss, the Bible admits to the fact that a large water body existed on the Plain of the Jordan. Herodotus mention a large inland lake, the Bible concurs with a large inland sea and calls it 'The Sea of the Plain.' Thus, this is yet another similarity between Ethiopia and Canaan and won with considerable ease.

Comment

Biblical scholars too have the Sea of the Plain in their reconstruction scenario. However, operating on an entirely different reconstruction model, they have identified the Sea of the Plain as the Dead Sea.

The Dead Sea is an erroneous and unfortunate choice. It is highly salty and was considered very poisonous during ancient times. Birds were never seen flying across it and it was assumed that the ones that inadvertently did, fell down dead midway, poisoned by the noxious vapors rising from this sea. Such being the case, I doubt that people during ancient times even ventured near the Dead Sea, let alone lived around it.

Even from the modern scientific point of view, the Dead Sea and its shores are considered unfit for permanent inhabitation. Nearly seven times saltier than the regular sea, the Dead Sea contains at a depth of 305 m (1000 ft) some twenty-seven percent solid substances: sodium chloride (common salt), magnesium chloride, calcium chloride, potassium chloride, magnesium bromide and many other dangerous chemicals. Because of the density of solids in the water, the human body easily floats on the surface.[1]

Needless to add, the Dead Sea contains no life forms at all. Except for rare varieties of microbes that can tolerate very high concentrations of chemicals, nothing can survive in its noxious waters. Regular sea fish introduced into its noxious waters quickly die. Rocks on its shores are thickly coated with crystalline salts and unambiguously forewarn of the Dead Sea's deadly content.

Another fact that rules out this region is its high temperature. The Dead Sea region, holds, I believe, the record for being one of the hottest places on the earth. From all this, we can safely conclude that the Dead Sea was certainly not the Sea of the Plain that is mentioned in the Bible.

Admittedly, at first glance, the Dead Sea, being an inland sea, having a river flowing into it and generally corresponding to what is said about it in the textual sources, does seem eminently suitable for the role of the Sea of the Plain. Very likely, this fact made a considerable impression upon Biblical scholars, who then, it would appear, decided to ignore its negative scientific verdict and go ahead and misleadingly use this deadly sea as a sheet anchor for their core biblical area.

POLITICAL SIMILARITIES

The political scenario of Canaan discernable from the Bible was perhaps as such: A cluster of city-states that included Edom, Midian, Ammon and Moab, co-existed in a cloistered valley south of Egypt that was generically referred to as 'south country' or 'Canaan.' Canaan was backward in development, nowhere near Egypt, its immediate neighbor to the north. Indeed, it appears to have established a synergy with Egypt, met its requirements in manpower, farm and forest produce, etc., in much the same manner that say, Mexico relates and serves the United States.

A highway called the 'King's highway' is said to have connected Canaan to Egypt, no doubt to facilitate this commerce. And, while Israel slinked through the wilderness to freedom and independence, life in the above-mentioned kingdoms was actually hurtling down this very highway at full throttle. This then is the workable political picture of Canaan.

Do any of the secular ancient world historians report such a land south of Egypt? Do we see a conglomerate of lesser kingdoms assiduously serving this commercial hub? Do we see glimpses of the Edomites, the Ammonites, the Midianites and the Moabites, in Herodotus' history, or Strabo's geography, as we plainly see in the Bible?

Reverting to Herodotus and his Nile expedition, in all likelihood, it was perhaps besides this very King's highway that Herodotus waited for weary travelers to emerge from Ethiopia, so as to quiz them about their dark kingdom. Having voyaged all the way up to Elephantine, a border town in

Upper Egypt, Herodotus continued to gather facts for his book by these means. You recollect this of course. The historian stood by the Nile, possibly on the King's highway, patiently waiting to plunder travelers for information about Canaan-Ethiopia. And a good thing too, for it is this bit of second-hand information gathering that will help us resolve the mystery of the Promised Land. Indeed, the highway mentioned here, possibly no more than a simple country road that hazardously meandered through the mountains, actually leads to the religious capital of the modern world—one that we have inadvertently lost!

Now, we already have had considerable luck with history and topographical similarities between Ethiopia and Canaan. Let us see if our luck holds for political similarities as well. Here once again, is that key passage from Herodotus that enshrines all the information that we need:

The country above Elephantine is inhabited by the Ethiopians, who possess one-half of this island, the Egyptians occupying the other. Above the island there is a great lake, the shores of which are inhabited by Ethiopian nomads; after passing it, you come again to the stream of the Nile, which runs into the lake. Here you land and travel for forty days along the banks of the river, since it is impossible to proceed further in a boat on account of the sharp peaks which jut out from the water and the sunken rocks which abound in that part of the stream. When you have passed this portion of the river in the space of forty days, you go on board another boat and proceed by water for twelve days more, at the end of which time you reach a great city called Meroe, which is said to be the capital of the other Ethiopians. The only gods worshipped by the inhabitants are Jupiter and Bacchus, to whom great honours are paid. There is an oracle of Jupiter in the city, which directs the warlike expeditions of the Ethiopians; when it commands they go to war and in whatever direction it bids them march, thither straightway they carry their arms.

On leaving this city and again mounting the stream, in the same space of time, which it took you to reach the capital from Elephantine, you come to the Deserters, who bear the name of Asmach. [Herodotus 2.29&30]

In the above passage, Herodotus mentions four distinct groups of Ethiopians. They appear segregated and possibly represent four separate Ethiopian kingdoms. To this, we can add a fifth—the settlement of the Deserters—as revealed in the last paragraph. A famous oracle of Jupiter too is mentioned. This is a good pointer, for oracles were quite popular and we are sure to find mention of them in other contemporaneous textual sources as well. In all, it appears that a confederation of five kingdoms, along with a prominent seat of an oracle co-existed in this region, increasingly known to us as Canaan-Ethiopia.

A quick comparison of the political scenario of Herodotus' Ethiopia as delineated above, with that of Canaan as described in the Bible, seems promising. As in Herodotus' Ethiopia, Canaan too had five prominent kingdoms. There is an overwhelming reference to an oracle of Jupiter in this region as well.

A complete list of political similarities is given below. Those that require elaboration are dealt with in the

following chapters.	
POLITICAL SIMILARITIES	
ETHIOPIA	CANAAN
Mountain dwelling Ethiopians	Possibly Edomites of the Bible who lived on the Seir Mountains
Ammon	Ammon
Tachompso	Tahtimhodshi
Saba	Rabbah
Aethiopia Media	Midian
Meroe	Aroer(Moab ?)
Deserter from Egypt	The Exodus assemblage from Egypt (Ancient Israel)
Oracle of Jupiter	Oracle of Baal

CHAPTER 18

Political Similarities

EDOM

After a two-year halt at Horeb, the Israelites were ready for battle. Thus, they moved to Kadesh situated outside the Mountains of the Amorites (Seir). From this base camp, spies were sent out. They cut across the mountains, entered the valley and eventually came back with a report of a fine valley inhabited by giants with iron chariots. This unfortunate report did somewhat dampen the Israelite army's enthusiasm. Even so, they went ahead with their battle plan. The plan was to cut across the Seir Mountains, enter and attack the Eshcol Valley giants.

Unfortunately, the Jews appeared to have overlooked one minor detail. They completely forgot about the belligerent and powerful people that dwelt upon the Seir Mountains itself. These were the Edomites and their Kingdom, Edom, was in fact upon the Seir Mountains.

Thus dwelt Esau in mount Seir: Esau is Edom. [Genesis 36:8]

The mountain-dwelling Edomites were indeed strategically situated. They were in a position of strength to block the entry of the Jews. This they happily performed. They swarmed the Jewish army like bees and chased them howling all the way to Hormah. Eventually, that is to say after a prolonged and acrimonious altercation, the Jewish army was seen to take an alternative route. This alternative route is described as 'compassing or circumventing the Seir Mountains' by way of a route that passed alongside the Red Sea. The journey is described as a torturously long and soul-searing one.

> *And they journeyed from mount Hor by the way of the Red sea, to compass the land of Edom: and the soul of the people was much discouraged because of the way. [Numbers 21:4]*

One pertinent point to note here is that the Edomites repulsed the Jews when they initially tried to cross over, using the direct route along the mountains. However, they did not attack them when they eventually passed by under their very nose through the valley, after having gained entry via the Red Sea route. Thus, what we may take home here is that the Edomites were strictly a 'mountain-dwelling' people and that they were situated upon the mountain on the approach route to Canaan.

Do the secular ancient world sources concur with the Bible's geographical picture? Do they have a kingdom of mountain-dwelling Ethiopians situated 'on the direct route to Ethiopia' in their arena?

Secular Source Concurrence

The Ethiopians were said to have inhabited the land immediately above Elephantine. Herodotus is specific on this point. That would mean that the mountainous region that extended for about four days journey by boat, where the river meandered treacherously, too was occupied by Ethiopians. In other words, Ethiopia began right after Elephantine. Here is the evidence:

> *Then you will come to a level plain, in which the Nile flows round an island named Tachompso. (Now in the regions above Elephantine there dwell Ethiopians at once succeeding, who also occupy half of the island and Egyptians the other half.) [Herodotus 2.127 (G. C. Macaulay)]*

The Ethiopians, it is said, dwelt in the regions above Elephantine. The 'at once succeeding' mentioned in this paragraph would mean that Ethiopians inhabited the mountainous region immediately above Elephantine. Since this was a considerable stretch that took 'four days by boat,' we may assume that it demarcated the kingdom of the 'mountain dwelling' Ethiopians.

Admittedly, the above is not much to go by and as if to make up for it, Strabo goes ahead and mentions Edom by name and offers a clear perspective of its geographical position. Here take a look:

> *The western extremities of Judæa towards Casius are occupied by Idumæans, and by the lake [Sirbonis]. The Idumæans are Nabatæans. [Strabo 16.2.34]*

The 'Idumaea' mentioned here is none other than the 'Edom' of the Old Testament. **Idum**-aea=**Edom**, of this we may be certain and even modern-day scholars are happy to concur. Casius mentioned here is of course Mount Casius and therefore we may presume that a mountain range too existed in the region upon which we may comfortably position the Edomites. Judaea is mentioned next. In short, it would appear that Edom was sandwiched between Egypt and Canaan. Thus, a direct and short route from Egypt (anchored in the above extract by Mount Casius) to Canaan (represented here by Judaea) would necessarily pass through Edom. The Judaea mentioned here is of course the later-date incarnation of the original Jewish kingdom of Israel & Judah. Judaea in fact re-grew around the original temple at Jerusalem after 586 BC and therefore suitably represented the older kingdoms and therefore Canaan. In short, Strabo's geographical picture wholly reflects the geographical picture that the Bible itself paints.

However, what is definitely curious about Strabo's setting is the fact that he positions both Edom and Judaea rather close to Mount Casius and the Lake Serbonis, both of which are central landmarks of Egypt's delta region. The proximity suggested here (1000 furlongs or about 100 miles) does not at all reflect the current reconstructed scenario, wherein the distance between Canaan and Egypt is roughly 500 miles.

To conclude, as far as Edom is concerned, both the secular ancient world historians and the Bible appear to have had such a people in their respective arenas. We may tentatively conclude therefore that 'mountain dwelling Ethiopians who dwelt alongside the route meandering to Ethiopia' of Herodotus were in fact the 'mountain-dwelling Edomites situated en-route to Canaan' of the Bible.

Ammon

"We can cross the river... but where are we to land?" This then was the General's main concern. The Persian Monarch Cambyses had sat silently listening to the General's report. Saba, the royal seat of Ammon, it appears, was heavily fortified. He expected that of course. However, what intrigued him was the brilliant way they had harnessed the rivers, the Astapus, the Astaboras and the Nile, to create an impregnable fortress. Ramparts, it appears, were cunningly built right up to the edge of the river. This engineering detail, a seemingly minor one to the untrained eye, was what had stumped the General.

Ammon would certainly be a hard nut to crack. Cambyses considered leaving it alone. It would mean leaving a pocket of resistance behind his back, which though not desirable, was at this point, acceptable. But then he recalled the Oracle of Ammon. It was situated on this confounded island kingdom and had the power to rally all Ethiopia against him. It would be foolish to let this war-mongering Oracle stand. After a few more minutes of deliberation, he made up his mind and instructed, "Take fifty thousand soldiers from the main body of the army and attack the island citadel." The General, who knew his warfare and was indeed angling for more troops, was visibly relieved. It was exactly what he wanted to hear. "And do me a favor," continued the great Cambyses, still in a dark and pensive mood. "Yes, my lord?" queried the General with his eyes still carefully averted. "Burn the Oracle of Ammon!"

Ammon, the same oracle to which Alexander the Great made a pilgrimage to enquire of his fate and to find out if he was the son of a God. However, you do not have to be an historian to be familiar with Ammon. The Bible cries itself hoarse denouncing this very Ammon, where the Oracle of Ammon, steadily eroded the God of the Old Testament's hold on the Israelites.

Where then was this Ammon? Biblical scholars, if asked, would readily give you an answer. Err, two actually. Two Ammons, that is to say. And, while you look askance, the scholar with a spade in his hands will beam happily and oblige you with an explanation. "One is near Siwa in modern-day Egypt and very nicely holding up the Egypt reconstruction for the Egyptologist. The other, he would continue in his best scholar's voice heavily embellished with jargons, is in the Middle East, better known as Amman, the capital of Jordan and planted there by us biblical scholars to complete the biblical reconstruction. You see, we needed it here and they needed it there, so... " But before he can establish the cornerstones of his quirky logic, you promptly jump off the nearest ledge. On the way down you wonder how scholars can blithely duplicate a place just to fill holes in their reconstruction.

Surely, our ancient world friends are more conscientious. Let us see if they can help resolve the Ammon enigma. Consider the following extract:

Here you come upon a smooth and level plain, where the Nile flows in two branches, round an island called Tachompso. The country above Elephantine is inhabited by the Ethiopians, who possess one-half of this island, the Egyptians occupying the other. [Herodotus 2.29]

We have already established that Tachompso was a tract of land amidst rivers or a river island, and as such, very highly rated during ancient times. No rogue army could gallop right into the town square at unearthly hours, to disturb your sleep. They would first have to cross any one of the rivers that surrounded the island. And, while they were struggling to do so, the inhabitants of the river island could have a hearty breakfast and decide over tea exactly what countermeasures to take—if that is, the enemy was still at it.

It is hardly surprising therefore to learn from Herodotus that the island was jointly occupied. Half the island belonged to the Ethiopians and the other half belonged to the Egyptians, presumably an immigrant colony. It short, two separate kingdoms co-existed on this cozy 'land amidst the river,' on the Plain of Ethiopia.

Moving on, in another part of his history, Herodotus provides the following information:

The Ammonians, who are a joint colony of Egyptians and Ethiopians, speaking a language between the two; hence also, in my opinion, the latter people took their name of Ammonians, since the Egyptian name for Jupiter is Amun.[Herodotus 2.42]

From this second extract, it appears that Ammon too comprised of a 'joint colony of Ethiopians and Egyptians.' Now, we already have Tachompso described as such and therefore we may tentatively assume that Ammon and Tachompso were in some way connected.

Moving on to another extract from Herodotus, we find Ammon under attack. This extract documents Cambyses' campaign against the Ethiopians, the same that I have dramatized above. Here it is:

At Thebes, which he (Cambyses) passed through on his way, he detached from his main body some fifty thousand men and sent them against the Ammonians

*with orders to carry the people into captivity and burn
the oracle of Jupiter. Meanwhile he himself went on
with the rest of his forces against the Ethiopians.*
[Herodotus 3.25]

It appears that Ammon was heavily fortified. Cambyses had to detach fifty thousand men from the main army to overthrow the Ammonians. An Oracle of Jupiter too existed in Ammon. Since this bit of information is not immediately of use to us, let us file it away for later use.

First we have the joint colony similarity, that suggests that Ammon was in some way connected to the island Tachompso. In addition, now we have Cambyses sending a large contingency of soldiers to capture Ammon, which suggests that Ammon was somehow heavily fortified. This once again suggests the island Tachompso. Remember that the island Tachompso too was secured by rivers on all sides and was very difficult to access. In other words, apart from the joint colony similarity, we now have 'the heavy fortification,' to strengthen our assumption that Ammon and Tachompso were intrinsically connected. Let us see if we can get some reference to the river-fortification of Ammon, to make this a near certainty.

Incredibly, a fortified island that appears to be Ammon is mentioned in Josephus' text. Fortunately, the extract also mentions the campaign that Cambyses ordered against Ammon. He records:

*At length they retired to Saba, which was a royal city of
Ethiopia, which Cambyses afterwards named Mero,
after the name of his own sister. The place was to be
besieged with very great difficulty, since it was both
encompassed by the Nile quite round and the other
rivers, Astapus and Astaboras, made it a very difficult
thing for such as attempted to pass over them; for the
city was situate in a retired place and was inhabited
after the manner of an island, being encompassed with*

Here indeed is mention of a well-fortified island in the heart of Ethiopia. The Ethiopian royal city upon it was called Saba, which was later renamed Meroe. Saba or Meroe was located on an island formed by the twin tributaries Astaboras and Astapus and therefore very difficult to breach. Apart from the river barriers, the city appeared to have had high ramparts all around that made it nearly impossible to defeat. Cambyses apparently had a difficult time capturing it.

Let us now scurry back to our drawing table and add these interesting new scraps of information to our emerging picture. We have Tachompso and Saba-Meroe, both in Ethiopia, documented as difficult to breech, heavily fortified, 'river island kingdoms.' The two rivers, Astaboras and Astapus, the tributaries of the Nile and the Nile itself, appeared to have encompassed Saba-Meroe as well as Tachompso.

Making an intelligent assessment of all the above information, we get: on the Plain of Ethiopia, the river Nile splits into two, forming twin tributaries named Astaboras and Astapus. The river island thus formed was called Tachompso.

Now we know that Tachompso was jointly occupied. One-half was occupied by Ethiopians and the other by Egyptian settlers. That being the case, we may tentatively assume that Ammon was perhaps the name of the Ethiopian kingdom on this island. The Egyptian settlers occupied the other half. Saba-Meroe, was a royal or capital city of one of these kingdoms. My suspicion is that it was the capital city of Ammon. An oracle of Jupiter too was situated on this island. Since we keep hearing of the famous oracle of Ammon, the very same that Alexander the Great stopped by to enquire of his lineage, we may safely place it in the Ammon half of the island.

Wow, Herodotus and his ancient world cronies have certainly opened the floodgates of information. They have executed a perfect double flip, a half turn and finished off with a perfect 10-point landing, with their hi-fidelity documentation. Will the Bible be able to make this jump? Or, will it flounder, fall with its pages aflutter and land with a thud on its spin, to prove the smirking biblical scholars right? Does it have the integrity or the page count to deliver a similar performance? Let us see.

Biblical Concurrence

Let us begin here by establishing the presence of a river island in the core biblical arena to match Herodotus' river island description. As discussed in an earlier chapter, consistent reference to 'a city that is in the midst of the river' in the core biblical arena has puzzled biblical scholars for ages. Here are two verses from the Bible that refer to such a formation.

> *From Aroer, that is upon the bank of the river Arnon and the city that is in the midst of the river and all the plain of Medeba unto Dibon and all the plain by Medeba. [Joshua 13.9]*

> *And their coast was from Aroer, that is on the bank of the river Arnon and the city that is in the midst of the river. [Joshua 13.16]*

What did 'city in the midst of the river' mean? Knowing the Jews, it had to have meant exactly that: a city in the 'midst of a river,' on a river island that is. Land with a natural moat around it, was hot property as far as our warring ancestors were concerned. Familiar as we are with the clockwork consistency with which marauding armies knocked at the doors of Israel and Judah, we can well appreciate this fact. 'The city in the midst the river' mentioned consistently in the Bible is as explained before, an unambiguous reference to a river island that existed in the core biblical arena.

Moving on, consider the following verse from the Bible:

And Joab fought against Rabbah of the children of Ammon and took the royal city. And sent messengers to David and said, I have fought against Rabbah and have taken the city of waters. [2 Samuel 12.26&27]

Rabbah the royal city of Ammon is referred to here as a 'city of waters,' difficult to besiege. Nonetheless, Joab conquered it and patted himself on the back for a job well done. Two facts immediately catch our attention. One, the royal city of biblical Ammon was called 'Rabbah.' And two, for Rabbah to earn the name 'city of waters,' it was very likely fortified with water all around.

Hold on. Is this not exactly how Josephus describes Saba in Ethiopia? Saba, the royal city of Ethiopia, which Cambyses afterwards renamed Meroe, "was to be besieged with very great difficulty, since it was both encompassed by the Nile quite round and the other rivers, Astapus and Astaboras." Saba was fortified by rivers and ramparts, as was Rabbah. Cambyses had just as much difficulty in conquering the island capital of Saba as Joab had in subduing Rabbah. Although one was in Ethiopia and the other in Canaan, both were royal cities. What is more, the names 'Saba' and 'Rabbah' sound strikingly similar. S-**aba**=R-**abbah**. Evidently, at some point in time, someone had mistakenly replaced the script that represented 'S' with an 'R' or vice-versa. This means Saba was after all, the royal city of Ammon of secular scholars. In short, there is overwhelming evidence here to conclude that Saba of Ammon in Ethiopia was Rabbah of Ammon in Canaan. **Ammon=Ammon.**

The Bible is not done yet. Consider the verse given below:

Sihon king of the Amorites, who dwelt in Heshbon and ruled from Aroer, which is upon the bank of the river Arnon and from the middle of the river and from half Gilead, even unto the river Jabbok, which is the border of the children of Ammon. [Joshua 12.2]

'Half' Gilead? What could this mean? Very likely, it is yet another one of those Jewish idiosyncrasies and knowing their penchant for descriptive names, Half Gilead would very likely be a distinct or discernable half of something. Note also that the 'middle of the river' is mentioned in connection with Half Gilead. Even Ammon is mentioned in this extract.

If Half Gilead was half of something, then my money is on the river island that existed in this region. Half Gilead was half that river island. Earlier we had arrived at the conclusion that Ammon was upon the island. And now we here we have Half Gilead making a claim for it. Was perhaps Half Gilead on the other half of the island? Let us see if we can find some more information to go by. Consider the following verse from the Bible:

And unto the Reubenites and unto the Gadites I gave from Gilead even unto the river Arnon half the valley and the border even unto the river Jabbok, which is the border of the children of Ammon. [Deuteronomy 3.16]

Oops, yet, another half equation. This time however, it is half a valley mentioned in connection with Gilead. In seems that Gilead is never mentioned 'whole.' It is always, 'half Gilead' or 'half mount Gilead' or 'half a valley' etc.

Whom else do we have here? Why, here is Ammon again! Now, we already know that Ammon was on an island and have speculated that perhaps Gilead shared the river island with Ammon. Does Ammon too should show up with a half tag? This thinking inspired a dedicated computer search of the Bible for a 'half' reference associated with Ammon. Sure enough, the machine faithfully ferreted out one. Here is the verse:

And their coast was Jazer and all the cities of Gilead and half the land of the children of Ammon, unto Aroer that is before Rabbah. [Joshua 13.25]

"Half the land of the children of Ammon!" Here indeed is Ammon flaunting its very own 'half' tag! That ought to be enough. We can safely conclude that Half Gilead and Half Ammon shared the river island Tachompso. They were the two different colonies on the island Tachompso.

Half Gilead no doubt belonged to the Egyptian settlers who occupied the island as mentioned by secular ancient world scholars. It was a Jewish city, and the Jews, as far as the people of this region were concerned, were Egyptians, for they had indeed emerged from Egypt!

Half-Gilead needs to be congratulated. It has carried this stigma of a 'half' tag faithfully, braving all manners of Bible editors for thousands of years. Perhaps it did so one and one reason alone. To bear witness, here and now!

Tahtimhodshi

The Bible seems to be doing a fabulous job in keeping up with the likes of Herodotus. In the earlier chapter, of which this is a part—the icing on the cake really—the Bible matches point by point, each and every detail offered by Herodotus and his ancient world cronies. Painstakingly it has brought together 'the city in the midst of the river,' Ammon, Rabbah and Half Gilead references to match the secular scholar's description of the island Tachompso on the Plain of Ethiopia. It is rare indeed to find this level of similarity between two ancient world sources.

But there is one tiny bit of the puzzle that is still missing though. I have not been able to find a direct reference to the name 'Tachompso' in the Bible. Herodotus has proffered it; surely, the Bible can offer a match. But alas, the Bible stubbornly refused to offer up a concurrence for Herodotus' Tachompso. Here is that aberrant name in context.

Here you come upon a smooth and level plain, where the Nile flows in two branches, round an island called Tachompso. [Herodotus 2.29]

What is to be done with Tachompso, un-tethered and chomping up my painstakingly compiled proofs? Numerous computer searches of the Bible were done, yet no trace or teeth marks of Tachompso were to be found. In desperation, a manual, page-by-page search was undertaken. It yielded a single find:

Fed up with my persistence and perhaps not wanting to be
outdone by a crank from Halicarnassus, the Bible cranked its
archaic machinery and finally tossed out a name to match.
With Gilead in tag, it left no room for doubt. Discounting
minor variations, 'Tahtimhodshi' of the Bible is strikingly
similar to 'Tachompso' of Herodotus! **Tah-ti-mhod-shi=Ta-ch-
omp-so**. True, Herodotus' 'Ta' does not have the explosive
fullness of the Hebraic 'Tah,' his 'ti' is a misfired 'ch,' his
'mhod' is an off-key 'omp' and his 'shi' a silly 'so'—all in much
the same way as 'shibboleth' becomes 'sibboleth' on a foreign
tongue—ordinarily, reason enough in Gilead at least, to lop
off his head!

Hurrah to Herodotus and the Bible, the two much
maligned ancient world sources! The first, thought to have
had the sensibilities of a giddy tourist and often called a liar
and the second, accused of raving about a glorious history of a
people when even a brick of their fabled kingdom could not
be found! Yet, here they are, tap dancing in breath-taking
synchronicity! The above hi-fidelity similarity—the dearest of
my finds—demonstrates without a doubt that the two ancient
world sources are true and in step. Increasingly, it appears as
if it is the modern-day scholars who are the ones with two left
feet!

COROLLARY

Here is an interesting corollary. Gilead traded in spices and
myrrh. Apart from Gilead's association with spices and myrrh,
I have already established in the earlier chapters that that the
royal city of Ammon, of which Gilead was a part, was called

Rabbah or Saba. Keeping these bits of information in mind, consider the verse below:

> *And she gave the king an hundred and twenty talents of gold and of spices very great store and precious stones: there came no more such abundance of spices as these which the queen of Sheba gave to king Solomon. [1 Kings 10.10]*

Allowing that 'Saba' was the true name instead of the 'Sheba' mentioned and bundling the spices association with it, we get an interesting inference. The Queen of Sheba gave King Solomon an abundance of spices. Is it not possible that it was the Queen of 'Saba' of Ammon, who lived around the block and indeed had all the spices in the world to give, who had nipped across to bewitch the wise Solomon?

TAHTIMHODSHI VANDALIZED

While doing a bit of information gathering on Kadesh, I was shocked to stumble upon my Tahtimhodshi under extreme circumstances. I had thought that Tahtimhodshi was so remote a reference that even biblical scholars would have trouble placing it. However, clearly, that was not the case.

After resorting to what can only be described as 'some obscure processing that would shame an alchemist,' modern historians have deduced the term 'chittim qadheshah' from 'Tahtimhodshi' of the Bible and thereafter forced the name 'Kadesh' out of it; possibly to anchor Kadesh-on-the-Orontes located in modern-day Syria.

The process involves the use of the 'LXX' and is elaborated below.

The Septuagint, commonly designated 'LXX,' is the oldest Greek version of the Bible. It is not a particularly good version since it was translated from the Hebrew Bible by Hellenistic Jews (70 to be precise, hence the name), who were not very familiar with Hebrew, during the period 275-100 BC. It was also established that the LXX was translated from a Hebrew version that is thought to be older and slightly different from the one in use today. In short, the LXX is the oldest 'though badly translated' version of the Bible we have on hand.

Now, 'oldest' and 'badly translated' makes a deadly combination. While the 'oldest' tag lends it more authority, the 'badly translated' tag opens up the portal to facilitate boundless fanciful interpretations.

This is how the con works. If the regular translation is not to your convenience, then it is time to take out the LXX. Since it is acknowledged to be the oldest, it probably contains a little more information. Little nips and tucks that the regular Hebrew version had undergone after 275 BC can all be spotted and if necessary reverted. So is the justification.

Now just suppose you need a textual reference, say for a second Kadesh (located on the Orontes) in the Bible. It not there of course, but that is not a problem that cannot be fixed. Remember the LXX was poorly translated. It might well be there but probably got obscured in translation. Now, even if it is not there, who is to stop one from taking an obscure reference such as 'Tahtimhodshi' and massaging a Kadesh out of it? And that is how Tahtimhodshi became 'chittim qadheshah' and eventually Kadesh.

Clearly, the scholars who engineered this fanciful word jugglery did not expect anyone to find a correlation between the obscure Tahtimhodshi and Herodotus' Tachompso. Indeed, compared to my direct, guileless and eminently believable interpretation of Tahtimhodshi, the biblical scholar's 'chittim qadheshah' effort does come across as an alarmingly artificial one, that reveals the callous and casual nature of scholarship that exists in this field of study.

As far as I am concerned, Tahtimhodshi of the Bible was Tachompso of Herodotus. Nevertheless, let us say you prefer to go by the biblical scholar's current interpretation. In which case, you should ask yourself, why another Kadesh? Do we not have one already near Sinai? Where is the need to resurrect another? So, why did this urgent need to fabricate yet another Kadesh arise? And why here, in Syria, on the banks of the Orontes? Is it possible that irrefutable evidence for the real Kadesh was found in this region? Was the real Kadesh perhaps in Syria?

As later date note, let me add one last paragraph. As regards to the question of 'why another Kadesh,' I finally found a rather strange answer. Without getting into too many details, it is as such: Two distinguished scholars founded the two different Kadeshes. One was politely asked to relinquish his claim, but refused. In short, the biblical landscape carries the burden of two Kadeshes to satisfy the whim of one unyielding scholar.

CHAPTER 21

MIDIAN

The Bible is indeed a brilliant piece of literature complete with background noises and other 'visual' details, that manage to impart a streaming-video like quality to its narrative. The scenarios rapidly change from royal courtrooms to wall-top brothels in mid-sentence, giddily panning from the resplendently royal, to the starkly nomadic, in the blink of an eye.

Even Moses for that matter, experienced acute cultural shock, when he was suddenly catapulted from the royal settings of Egypt, to the rustic nomadic setting amongst his future Midianite in-laws. Such was his displacement and desolation that he named his son, born in these environs, 'Gershom' for he said, "I have been a stranger in a strange land."[Exodus 2.22]

It is through such picturesque descriptions that one can discern that the Midianites were nomadic by nature. The settings in which we find them are consistently nomadic. Uninhabited wilderness is often the backdrop and jostling livestock the inevitable foreground. The scenario is patently rustic and vastly different from the royal or the wall-city tenement aura that we see in Egypt or Israel.

The Midianite's nomadic way of life is evident from other parts of the text as well. We are told that Midianite men were recruited to serve as guides, to lead the Exodus through the wilderness, demonstrating their nomadic knowledge of the land. Finally, to round off this argument, here is an unmistakable snapshot of Midian. For, here are camels at their snarling best and in such profusion, that one can almost smell them!

> *The multitude of camels shall cover thee, the dromedaries of Midian and Ephah; all they from Sheba shall come: they shall bring gold and incense; and they shall show forth the praises of the LORD. [Isaiah 60.6]*

"The multitude of camels shall cover thee, the dromedaries of Midian..." This is a conclusive indicator that the Midianites were indeed unyielding nomads in nature, not unlike the Bedouins of the Middle East. Thus when Herodotus refers to an Ethiopian people who were nomadic in nature, we know exactly whom to smell or suspect. It is suggested that the Midianites existed on the core biblical arena as nomadic settlements.

But does Herodotus concur? Does he have nomadic settlements in his Ethiopia?

Secular Source Concurrence

Moving on to the next group of Ethiopians documented by Herodotus on the Plain of Ethiopia, we have a settlement of 'nomadic' Ethiopians who lived around the great lake.

> *Above the island there is a great lake, the shores of which are inhabited by Ethiopian nomads; after passing it, you come again to the stream of the Nile, which runs into the lake. [Herodotus 2.29]*

Here the term 'nomadic' catches our attention. Surely, were not these nomadic Ethiopians the Midianites of the Bible?

To attest the above, Ptolemy, the geographer from antiquity, offers a stunning piece of evidence. In his book 'Geography,' Book IV, chapter 7, titled, 'Location of Aethiopia below Egypt' he writes:

To the west, from this part of the Nile river, those occupy the land after the Greater Cataract, who pasture the Triacontaschoenus region between the Aethiopian mountains and the Nile river, a after these toward the south are the Euonymitae; then Aethiopia Media and the Sebridae; these races also inhabit the island of Meroe. [Ptolemy, Geography 4.7]

Here then is unambiguous proof that one of the Ethiopian settlements was Midian of the Bible. Indeed, Ptolemy calls this settlement of Ethiopians 'Aethiopia Media.' Other familiar landmarks and key words, such as Meroe and indeed the Sebridae (very likely is a corrupted version of Strabo's Sembritae; **Se-bri-dae=Sem-bri-tae**), a direct reference to the Deserters or Jews, are also available in the extract. We may therefore tentatively conclude that Aethiopia Media of Strabo was indeed the Midian of the Bible.

AROER

"The other Ethiopians, whose capital was Meroe," says
Herodotus, referring to yet another kingdom on the Plain of
Ethiopia. In lieu of proper names, notice how our friend
Herodotus is having trouble with his generic label 'Ethiopians.'
He has far too many groups of Ethiopians on hand and is seen
here resorting to associative names, to identify the
bewildering array of barbarians. Fortunately, by his doing so,
we get one piece of information that is useful. He identifies
one set of Ethiopians as 'other' Ethiopians whose capital city
was Meroe. Let us see what the Bible has to offer on Meroe.

Biblical Concurrence

The Bible offers us 'Aroer' instead. Note the striking similarity
in names. Me-**roe**=A-**roe**-r. Besides, like Meroe, Aroer too was
situated next to a confluence of rivers.

Now, we already have Josephus informing us that Saba,
the royal city of Ammon, was renamed 'Meroe' by Cambyses.
Based on this information, we have placed Meroe in Ammon
on the island Tachompso. However, here was Meroe snuggled
up with the 'other' Ethiopians.

Admittedly, there is some confusion here. But then again,
confusion existed over Aroer even during biblical times! Aroer
changed hands so often that rulers of the time were unclear
as to whom it originally belonged and were therefore
continually squabbling over it. The Bible itself is seen referring

to yet another book from antiquity called the 'Book of Jasher' to resolve this issue!

To conclude, 'Meroe' is certainly a reference to 'Aroer' of the Bible. The 'other Ethiopians' whose capital was Meroe, is perhaps a reference to the Moabites of the Bible.

BAAL

Amongst the landmarks of Ethiopia Herodotus includes an Oracle of Jupiter. The Oracle of Jupiter in Ethiopia was apparently a popular one and said to have "directed the warlike expeditions of the Ethiopians." Earlier, from numerous other clues, we learnt that the Oracle of Ethiopia was in fact located in Ammon. Here are two more extracts from 'The History of Herodotus' of Herodotus that testify to this fact:

> *The dove which flew to Libya bade the Libyans to establish there the oracle of Ammon. This likewise is an oracle of Jupiter. [Herodotus 2.55]*

> *At Thebes, which he passed through on his way, he detached from his main body some fifty thousand men and sent them against the Ammonians with orders to carry the people into captivity and burn the oracle of Jupiter. Meanwhile he himself went on with the rest of his forces against the Ethiopians. [Herodotus 3.25]*

The first extract indicates that there was an Oracle of Jupiter in Ammon. The second is a reference to Cambyses' Ethiopian campaign, and confirms that an Oracle of Jupiter was indeed located in Ammon.

Let us see if the Bible has anything to say about an Oracle of Jupiter in the core biblical arena.

Biblical Concurrence

The Bible has an abundance of information on a 'Baal or Baalim' instead. Indeed Baal makes his presence felt rather vigorously in the Bible. Baal apparently even managed to wean away the Israelites from the God of the Old Testament. This sad development is highlighted in the Bible in a number of places. Here is a verse that testifies to Baal's increasing popularity.

> *Then said Elijah unto the people, I, even I only, remain a prophet of the LORD; but Baal's prophets are four hundred and fifty men. [1 Kings 18.22]*

Four hundred and fifty prophets of Baal overran Israel during the time of King Ahab. Prophet Elijah alone bravely canvassed for the mercurial God of the Old Testament. These numbers gives the correct perspective on what was happening at the altars of Canaan.

Speaking of numbers, the Bible actually refers more often to Baal that to the God of the Old Testament. A computer search of the Bible reveals that there are fifty-five references to Baal and Baalim, whereas there are only four to Jehovah or Yahweh. Seeing the Bible's keen focus on Baal, some scholars suggest that Baal, which appears to mean 'lord,' and was perhaps a reference to Jehovah. Not true. These are but desperate remedies. Baal was actually another God who was fast gaining popularity in Canaan including in Israel.

It appears therefore that Canaan cavorted and cart wheeled around Baal, just as all Ethiopia revolved around Jupiter. And who exactly was Baal? Oh, Baal is none other than Jupiter! Jupiter is merely the Greek name for Baal! All Canaan worshipped Baal-Jupiter, as indeed did the Ethiopians. We may therefore add this to our growing tally of similarities between Ethiopia and Canaan.

ANCIENT ISRAEL

Finally, we come to the settlement of the Deserters on the Plain of Ethiopia. We have already tentatively identified this settlement as the Kingdom of Israel, based on the legend or history that emanates from this settlement. Now, with the neighborhood coming alive with alacrity, this tentative identification becomes a near certainty. Let us examine Herodotus' information from a political perspective and see what additional information can be gleaned.

From Herodotus' extract, it appears that the Deserters colonized a region further down the river, at a considerable distance from Meroe.

> *On leaving this city, (Meroe) and again mounting the stream, in the same space of time, which it took you to reach the capital from Elephantine, you come to the Deserters, who bear the name of Asmach. [Herodotus 2.30]*

On the Plain of Ethiopia, beyond the island formation, beyond the great lake, beyond Meroe the capital city of the 'other' Ethiopians identified here as the kingdom of Moab and a considerable distance further, lay the settlement of the Deserters.

The same is confirmed by Strabo in his book 'Geography:'

> *Above the confluence of the Astaboras and the Nile, he says, at a distance of seven hundred stadia, lies Meroe, a city bearing the same name as the island; and there is another island above Meroe which is held by the*

Aegyptian fugitives who revolted in the time of Psammitichus and are called "Sembritae," meaning "foreigners." [Strabo, Geography 17.1.2]

Here is Strabo proffering exactly the same information. As mentioned earlier, "Sembritae, meaning foreigners" is an unambiguous reference to the Deserters of Herodotus and therefore to the Kingdom of Israel.

Actually, Herodotus hints at two different settlements that can be identified as that of the Jews. One is that of Half Gilead upon the island Tachompso referred to as 'former Egyptians.' And, the second is that of the Deserters, was located deep inside Canaan-Ethiopia, possibly in the mountains.

Let us see if the Bible has anything in particular to add to this subject.

Biblical Concurrence

The Bible informs us that the Jews were able to carve out two separate parcels of land in Canaan. The first one was on an island Half-Gilead and the second, a much larger settlement, was established in the mountains that appeared to have adjoined the Canaan Plain.

The smaller island terrain was rich and suitable for cattle rearing. The Reubenites, Gadites who owned cattle, put in a plea for it and on the promise that they would continue to fight until all the tribes were comfortably berthed, were given this land. Upon survey, it was discovered that the land consisted of halves. Half a hill, half a valley, half an island and so on and so forth. Thus, it was happily rechristened 'Half Gilead.' Halves being the state of things, the half tribe of Manasseh too asked to move to it with the Reubenites and Gadites. The second tract of land was larger and therefore gradually became the true seat of the kingdom. This parcel of land was equitably divided and given to the rest of the tribes of Israel and here they lived for about 444 years (1030 BC to 586 BC).

By about 586 BC, after that is, the Kingdoms of Israel and Judah were dismantled, the Jews perhaps existed only in scattered Diaspora colonies. By about 450 BC, when Herodotus recorded this region, all that remained of their glorious kingdom was a faded impression of their most memorable deed—the Exodus from Egypt. However, it registered with all the outsiders as an inglorious act of desertion and thus they stole their way into the pages of secular world history as the 'Deserters.'

Chapter 25

Canaan-Ethiopia

Ethiopia of the ancient world Greek Scholars and Canaan of the Bible has registered astonishing historical, topographical and geographical similarities. We may therefore safely assume that Canaan and Ethiopia were not two different kingdoms, but merely two different perspectives of the same kingdom. Canaan was the biblical name and perspective of the said kingdom and Ethiopia represented the Greek or Egyptian version. There is absolutely no ambiguity here. Indeed, the fact that we are able to see a near one-to-one similarity between the two perspectives proves this point without a doubt.

So, how exactly would I go about reconstructing my 'Canaan-Ethiopia'?

I would at first set the Nile down in my reconstructed scenario. There is no disputing the fact that the Nile was the lifeline of Canaan-Ethiopia and that it was situated much further up-river than Egypt.

How much further up-stream? Well, Herodotus says that the Nile twists and turns here like the Meander and therefore it would take you about four days to reach the Plain of Canaan-Ethiopia. Herodotus also records that 'the land rises.' Therefore, be prepared to be towed up-river by a pair of draught animals, for not only are we going up-stream, we are moderately going up-hill as well.

After a period of four days or so, a large, oblong, shield-shaped island would be reached. It is not a 'sand bar in the midst of the river' type of island, but is very likely a tract of land circumscribed by rivers. In fact, the island Tachompso-Tahtimhodshi was formed by the two or three rivers. The island tract is said to have been quite large and had rolling hills, valleys and forest tracts. I would keep my eyes open for such a tract of land.

The next geographical feature of Canaan-Ethiopia was an extensive, well-watered plain. Of course, Herodotus presents the plain first and then the island. However, taking my cue from Strabo, I have reversed the sequence, for I cannot see how an island with rolling hills and valleys could co-exist in the same space as a plain.

On the plain, there was a large, sea-like lake. This then is the working topographical picture.

The reconstructed scenario described above has been concurrently gleaned from two or more textual sources. Furthermore, it does present a cohesive picture. That being the case, I would be very surprised if I am unable to find my Canaan-Ethiopia exactly as described.

But where exactly was Canaan-Ethiopia? How would one reach it? Where would one begin? As to the first question, I have no answer yet, but the second two questions, I will readily answer.

Continue upstream beyond Egypt upon the Nile. Make sure that you meander upon the river for many days. After four whole days of meandering, you ought to find yourself in Canaan-Ethiopia.

CHAPTER 26

KNOCK, KNOCK, KNOCK!

Modern-day scholars have inadvertently reconstructed a separate Ethiopia and a separate Canaan. While, Ethiopia was reconstructed south of Egypt as per the evidence available in Herodotus' history and other ancient world texts, Canaan was reconstructed in the East Mediterranean belt, based on the broad evidence available in this region.

Would this duplication have affected the biblical reconstruction? Yes, certainly. Without a doubt, the core biblical reconstruction would have been profoundly affected by this major archaeological reconstruction error. However, the exact extent of the damage cannot be determined at this stage. This is because the Canaan-Ethiopia duplication is itself more of an effect rather than the root cause. The root cause seems to lie elsewhere in the Levant reconstruction.

How did this duplication take place? Why did scholars not see the traces of a duplication as I have so effortlessly seen? Why did they not pull at the loose ends and unravel this mystery as I have done? Why did they prefer instead to create a patently illogical scenario of a separate Ethiopia and a separate Canaan? What indeed stopped this genre of scholars, whose imagination otherwise knows no bounds, who are capable of coming up with the manifestly manipulative 'Ebers Sothic Calendar' argument, or the 'LXX fix' from resolving this issue of duplication that is plainly evident? What stopped them cold?

The simple answer could be that perhaps they did not see the similarities, at least to the extent that we see now. A more complex one could be that, perhaps they did see, but were constrained from resolving it immediately for a very compelling reason and therefore prudently left it on ice.

What could the compelling reason be?

The answer is as such. If one were to logically follow this lead, it will unerringly lead to the doorstep of reconstructed Egypt. Indeed, it is this grand reconstruction that comes under pressure if one prods or ponders the Canaan-Ethiopia duplication. Reconstructed Egypt is indeed the pivot from where both Canaan and Ethiopia have been speculatively extrapolated. Any attempt to resolve this duplication would almost certainly require irreverent tampering with this sacred pivot.

One can see therefore exactly why the Canaan-Ethiopia anomaly would have been left so prudently on ice. For, ancient Egypt, the grand and glittering citadel of the Egyptologists, the veritable mother ship of all archaeology, is definitely the wrong address to be knocking at, looking for core reconstruction discrepancies. Built up by thousands of scholars who have over the years ferreted out a wealth of details from its ruins, down to obscure palace intrigues and who-slept-with-who trivialities; where scholars can supposedly read the hieroglyphics off the walls; where even the history makers, referring to the embalmed kings, are available for the doubting Thomases to poke and prod... all of them cannot be mistaken in matters as fundamental as this. When respectable publications unceasingly pay obeisance to this reconstruction, yellow-bordered glossies on its every stone, every broken nose and the heady brew of countless coffee table publications, dissertations, expositions in their thousands, nay millions... all of these cannot be so terribly wrong.

Even so, even so, not all the gold in Egypt can save this anomaly-on-ice from thawing now. For, the Canaan-Ethiopia duplication, which is solidly supported by the entire phalanx of ancient world scholars—Herodotus, Strabo, Artapanus, Josephus, Ptolemy, Bible and other mute witnesses—brings one powerful idea home to roost. The days of quirky logic followed by roasted duck are officially over. The Canaan-Ethiopia duplication, which is at the heart of the biblical anomaly, is traceable to the doorstep of the Egypt reconstruction. This grand and glittering reconstruction that underpins the entire Levant's reconstruction is somehow responsible for the Bible's loss. This much is certain. It is time now therefore to strip the gold off Egypt, in search of biblical bronze!

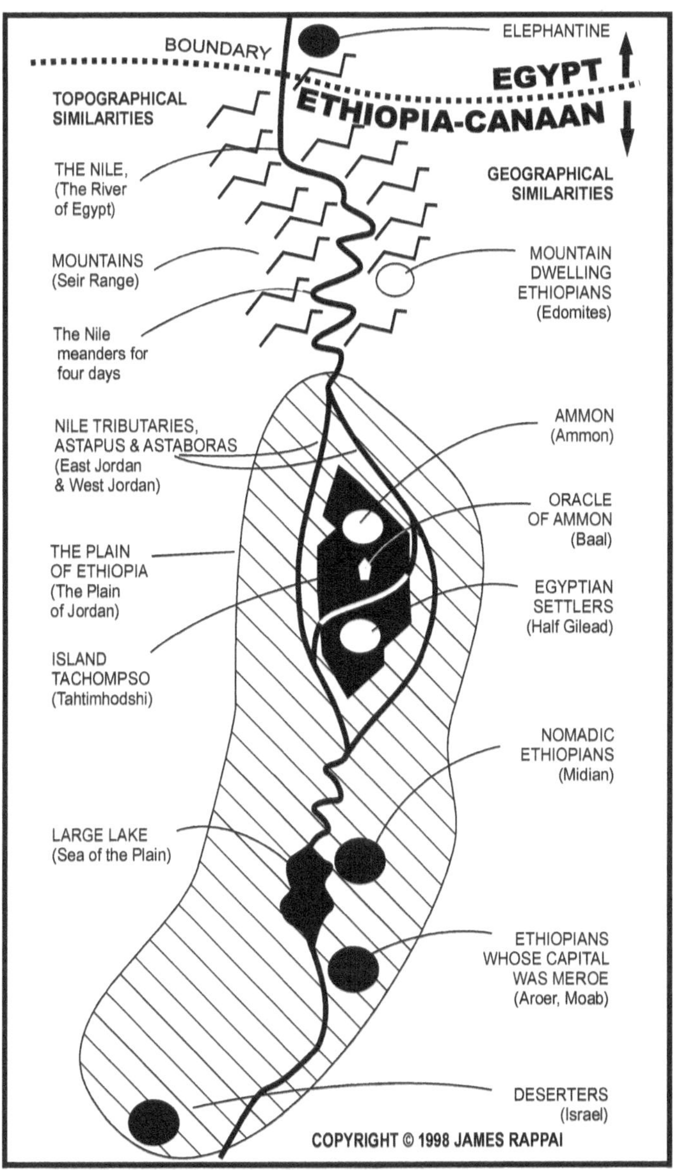

Diagram 1: **Canaan-Ethiopia.** The picture that emerged using the corroborative route. It was located by the banks of the Nile up river, south of Egypt, after about four days of mountains.

BENEATH THE GOLD: THE EGYPT ENIGMA

CHAPTER 27

EGYPT: NIGGLING DISCREPANCIES

The Great Pyramid of Giza, with its awesome size and singularity, continues to amaze anyone who stands in its ancient shadows. Commercial airline pilots flying thousands of miles above Cairo, obligingly inform their passengers of the pyramid's clearly visible apex view—a salute of sorts, by a nine hundred thousand pound flying feat of modern cutting-edge technology, to an ancient colossus of equal inconceivability.

The pyramids are without a doubt an enduring and eerie enigma. Indeed, the theory that they were built possibly by aliens, using inconceivable technology and served an yet unknown function, has yet to be convincingly put to rest. It is therefore arguable that the pyramids may have been partly responsible for identifying the ruins in Africa as that of ancient Egypt. Egypt was after all, the veritable hub of the ancient world. Fine art and architecture are indeed the hallmarks of a mature civilization, and the pyramids leave absolutely no room for doubt in this regard.

However, on close examination, these very pyramids, in all their colossal majesty, help realize a different reality. True, they speak volumes about architectural refinement. Yet, from an economic, social or political perspective, the 'sophisticated civilization argument' fails to make sense. For, to build these mountains, for whatever reason, one would have had to engage almost the entire work force and resources of the kingdom. This would have been a severe drain on the country's economy. The indisputable fact is that the pyramids did not, could not, have happened innocuously on the side. The entire nation's focus would have been on them, as they engaged in the various tasks of executing these gargantuan construction projects. The reality was that, as modern archaeologists are beginning to find out, this was a nation totally stripped of all civic rights, poverty stricken, illiterate and entirely exploited. Generation after generation were engaged slavishly in the continuous construction of pyramids, one after another, without respite, to appease perhaps a cruel and perverse royalty. In other words, the pyramids and other massive and elaborately decorated superstructures that we so admire, though wonderful, speak of obsession, rather than progress. They darkly hint of depravity, abuse, isolation and abnormality.

To complicate matters, Herodotus records that the 'real' Egyptians were in fact poor builders. Meaning, from the architectural point of view, Egypt incredibly had very little to show. The truth is, real Egypt, according to this historian who purportedly walked its ancient roads, was in fact a commercial hub, much like the modern cities ones sees today. All it really had were bursting warehouses, buzzing ports, bustling bazaars and broiling brothels. It reverberated not with the sound of chisel on stone, but with the din of commerce and the tinkle of money feverishly changing hands.

Real Egypt, the one described by Herodotus, Strabo, Manetho or any other ancient world historians, was anything but abnormal. It was spared the quirkiness of aberrant rulers, of autocratic monarchs. It engaged in perfecting the art of living well, much in the same fashion as modern-day progressive nations do. The historical accounts of Egypt speak of a sophisticated populace, comfortably settled and enjoying numerous civic amenities. A sense of democracy prevailed in its corridors of power and the general populace nurtured a sense of liberty. Even foreigners were welcome, allotted choice lands to settle in and peaceful co-exist. Poverty and illiteracy were perhaps conspicuous by their absence.

Ancient Egypt rang with laughter and not with the groans of an oppressed people, slavishly engaged in one construction project after another, to appease a perverse royalty.

Could such an advanced and sophisticated civilization have put up with this incredible pyramid-construction mania? Does this Egypt, whose kings and governments protected the interests of the common people, encouraged trade and traders with land grants and other concessions, absolutely spoiled their soldiers with high income and land grants; reflect exploitation or oppression? Does it reek of despotism, or God obsession as evident in the land of the pyramids? Can the oppressive, spine-crushed people who subsisted in the shadow of the pyramids, ever be mistaken for the Egyptians, who perhaps took pride in the 'Egyptian way of life?' To all the above questions, the answer is a resounding no.

Here is an interesting peek in to their medical profession. In Egypt, a host of doctors, specialists really, for each and every part of the body, plied their trade. Our GPs of yesteryears would have been laughed right out of the BCs were they to come armed with their antacids, aspirins, and cortisones. Our heart surgeons though, with their open-heart theatrics, pacemakers and pigskin valves would have been welcomed with open arms, and our cloning specialists... why, they could expect to be deified and booked all the way into the ADs!

The Egyptians wore a linen tunic fringed about the legs called a 'calasiris.' Over this, they wore a white woolen skirt. Also, the Egyptian male, from early childhood, had his head shaved. Regarding their shaving their head bit, our man from Halicarnassus even spun a theory complete with a 'scientific experiment' to establish this fact. By throwing stones on the sun-bleached skulls scattered on a battlefield, where the Egyptians and Persians had fought, he found that some broke easily, while others did not. Herodotus concluded the Egyptians who regularly shaved their heads were the case-hardened skulls, while the weaker ones belonged to the Persians, thanks to their turbans and long hair. Now admittedly, Herodotus does have his unhinged moments, nevertheless, thanks to his bizarre experiment, we know that all Egyptian males, from priests to the pilferers, king to the commoners, regularly shaved their heads.[1]

But do we see shaven heads in the frescoes or wall carvings in the Egypt-in-Africa scenario? No, never. On the contrary, the people are always depicted with hair. They definitely did not shave their head as Herodotus documents.

So where did Herodotus' shaven-headed Egyptians go? Was Herodotus making this up, as modern-day scholars are inclined to believe?

To the above questions all I can say is, Herodotus' shaven headed Egyptians existed and there is even archaeological proof for it. Artifacts carved in stone, marble and basalt have been excavated, that strikingly resemble the historian's Egyptians. An array of shaven headed men with beards, exactly as Herodotus describes, bearing mute testimony to the remarkable accuracy of his documentations, are to be found in almost any book of history. The only thing is, they are not considered Egyptians, for they were not found in Egypt, but in Mari and numerous other archaeological sites in modern-day Syria. One is struck with wonder by the keen similarity of these shaven-headed figurines, complete with full beards and fluffy sheepskin skirts over their calasiris (pleated white cotton skirts), with that of the historian's Egyptians. Butchers, bakers, barbers, priests, pilferers and pharaohs... all fashioned in roughly the same style. Go on, take a look at the accompanying picture. Surely, these are Herodotus'

Diagram 2: **The Real Egyptians?** Spitting images of Herodotus' bearded, shaven headed Egyptians, complete with calasiris and woolen skirts. These genuine, 2500 BC artifacts were found in modern-day Syria.

Egyptians... but whatever are they doing in Syria?

Distance Discrepancies

The arrow hit Alexander on his right shoulder as he let his guard slip for a fraction of a second. Fortunately, it only managed to put an impressive dent on his bronze armor. Alexander however did not notice, let alone feel it. His full attention was on Darius, Monarch of all Persia, who he saw withdrawing, preparing to flee from the battlefield of Issus.

Quickly mounting a horse at the head of a Companion cavalry, Alexander gave chase at full gallop, with his mind galloping at a faster pace, furiously analyzing the situation. It did not add up, it did not add up at all. The Persian army was much larger and the battle was nowhere near its end. It all seemed too premature and seems somewhat unnatural and contrived. What was Darius trying to accomplish by withdrawing now? A headless army was bound to get demoralized and quickly defeated. Everyone knew that. Moreover, Darius was fleeing alone, leaving even his family behind to uncertain fate, possibly even slaughter. The Persians had this curious habit of bringing their families along to the battlefield, as if it were a picnic. Why did they do that? It was all too middle-eastern for his straightforward soldier mind. Then it struck him. Perhaps it was a trap—a sly middle-eastern one at that—to draw the unsuspecting enemy flushed with a sense of victory, in a hot pursuit, deep into enemy country. If it was, it surely was working, for every fiber in his body willed him to give chase. With great difficulty, he reigned in and let that Persian fox run, disappear into the darkness. [1]

Instead, Alexander proceeded to capture Egypt.

Why did Darius prematurely run away from a battle that was far from over and one that he could just as easily have won? For that matter, why did Alexander let Darius go? Why did he go instead to Egypt, which was after all, 600 miles away, far removed from the middle-eastern arena, actually on another continent? None of it makes sense.

Are we perhaps missing something here?

If Egypt was right around the corner, say, in the Syria region... yes, then of course, it would all make perfect sense. Only then would it have seemed an attractive alternative to Alexander. Only then would Alexander's abandoning his chase after Darius add up. After all, Egypt was the then Persian capital and Alexander had come on ships with just a small army. Finding an immediate base in the middle-eastern arena would fit in well as his primary agenda.

Having Egypt right around the corner, in the near eastern arena would also explain Darius' anxiety to lead Alexander away from Egypt. Egypt was his new capital and even he could well see that all would be lost, if Alexander were to capture Egypt.

Brilliant though this explanation is, we cannot have it. There is a minor problem. Someone has gone and stuck Egypt a good 600 miles away from this arena—on a different continent actually. In short, our options are - either Alexander did not attend a single class in strategy under the tutelage of the able Aristotle and the great Darius was a coward, or, some idiot has misplaced ancient Egypt on the map.

The matter does not quite end here. Although it is indisputable that Alexander did go to Egypt, curiously there is no detailed record of this long and arduous journey. His return from Egypt too is lacking in detail and modern-day historians are not quite sure which route he took back. Did he cut across the Saudi-Arabian desert, or did he trace his route along the Mediterranean coast?

Distance discrepancies such as the one described above, which appear to suggest that Egypt has been wrongly positioned on the map, will fill a sizable, if sonorous book. Reconstructed history of this region is teeming with such instances. The Persians, the Scythians and Assyrians, and a host of other marauding armies are said to have attacked Egypt, but when one considers the prodigious distances that these armies would have had to march to reach Egypt located in Africa, one is left in some doubt. These armies, on an average, would have had to cover an approximate two-way distance from the point of origin to Egypt-in-Africa of around 2000 miles! This does not make business sense. Furthermore, the said journey involved crossing the barren and unforgiving Sinai desert. That all these armies did go to Egypt cannot be denied. What is in dispute is the incredible distance involved, all of which clearly points to a reconstruction discrepancy. Indeed, all of the above–mentioned encounters would become viable if we give the archaeologist's sensibilities a pass and re-engineer but a single change. Reposition Egypt, move it into the middle-eastern arena where all and sundry can easily reach it and cross swords with it at will.

So, whose sensibilities do we go by here? With that of a master strategist like Alexander, who in a blitzkrieg military campaign won all Asia or his equally astute enemy, Darius, the Persian Monarch—or with that of our man with his pocket full of shard?

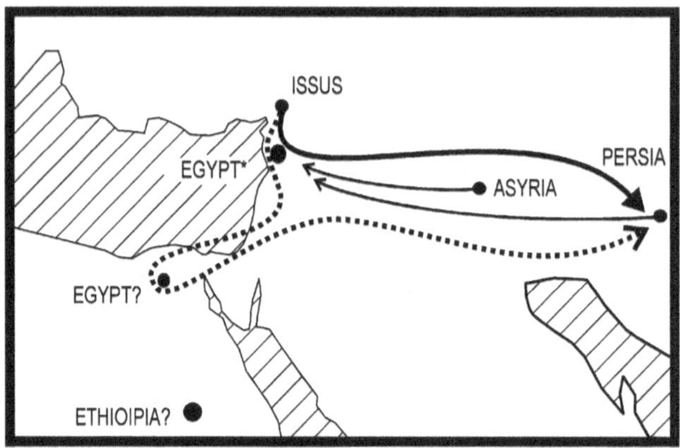

Diagram 3: **Alexander's logic.** From Issus **to** Egypt **to** Persia. This is how Alexander decisively moved his army to capture all Asia. His would not have succeeded however had he taken the loopy, 2800 odd miles (dotted line) grueling journey through desert terrain suggested by the modern-day scholars. Egypt in the Near Eastern arena will resolve this discrepancy. Similarly, marauders would have to travel prodigious distances to reach Egypt and Ethiopia located in the Africa continent. This does not make good business sense and puts the spotlight on Egypt's faulty position.

CHAPTER 29

AN UNKNOWN LEVIATHAN

In 1928, in coastal Syria, a farmer snagged an ancient buried flagstone with his plough and discovered a subterranean chamber, in which he could dimly see fine vases and other artifacts. This accidental discovery at Ras Shamra and subsequent discoveries in and around the Turkey-Syria region, proved the existence of an advanced civilization in the Levant arena. The plough had done its job all right. Levant reconstruction, the product of many years of careful jugglery, was furrowed, and utterly turned over.[2]

All the evidence discovered here, established the presence of a juggernaut commercial hub in this region that served the entire Near Eastern arena. However, all the known superpowers of this region were already satisfactorily identified and properly berthed. Egypt, Babylonia and Assyria were all in the bag! A fourth superpower was simply not on the cards. Who in heaven's name was this?

To find out, let us look at some of these findings in some detail.

UGARIT

In 1929, the Academie des Iscriptions et Beles-Lettres in Paris sent Claude Schaeffer on an archaeological expedition to Ras Shamra. Findings of great archaeological significance were obtained in the first few years itself. Items such as pottery and ceramics, deities, jewelry and other everyday objects were unearthed. Evidence of extensive foreign trade established the fact that this was the main hub of commerce in the Middle-Eastern arena. Ras Shamra appeared also to have been the major terminal for land travel to and from Egypt, Greece, Syria and Mesopotamia. Documents discovered at this site mention a wide bazaar of trading goods that came from great distances. Foodstuffs such as olives, barley, dates, wheat, honey, wine and spices converged at this bazaar from distant destinations. A thriving livestock fair that dealt in horses, donkeys, sheep, cattle, geese and other birds flourished at this hub, attracting traders from distant lands. Metals such as lead, iron, copper, tin, bronze, were traded here. Timber formed an important trade commodity at this bustling marketplace.[3]

A well-oiled industry that existed alongside to serve this commercial hub too is evident. Rows and rows of industrial units, wood and metal workshops, much like in modern times, with carpenters and smiths bent in earnest, churning out a bewildering array of goods such as chests, wooden furniture, baskets, weapons, vessels, tools, glass and cosmetics to feed this insatiable market. Curio objects made of hippo teeth, elephant tusks and scales too were carved and competed to find wholesale buyers.

Such being the demand for white goods and trinkets, could heavy industry be far behind? Evidently not. Heavy industries, like shipbuilding too, had sent down deep roots. Wooden ships for the nation's traders, as well as export orders from far-flung maritime cities were undertaken. Needless to add, a robust slave market that feverishly supplied the workforce is said to have kept pace with this run-away development.

Ras Shamra had a very cosmopolitan flavor. Foreign nationals including diplomats from various kingdoms resided here. This apparently led to a flourishing real estate industry.

With the outsiders being so well taken care of, what then is there to speak of the treatment meted out to the good citizens of this empire? Merchants of this nation received grants of land in return for their undertaking of trading voyages, on the behalf of the farsighted rulers of this clearly progressive nation. Similarly, soldiers too were given land grants in return for service in the army. Clearly, this was a nation well and truly on the path of progress, as we define it today.

The royal archives consisting of a large number of clay tablets bearing a cuneiform script of an unknown origin too were found. The unknown script used, proved to be the earliest evidence of a comprehensive alphabetic system used for writing. Deciphering of this text brought even more excitement, this time for the biblical scholars. These texts were written in one of four languages identifiable as Sumerian, Akkadian, Hurritic and one exclusive to Ras Shamra. These tablets were found in the royal palace and in the house of the High Priest and leading citizens. What came as a surprise was that they shared a common literary and linguistic lineage with the Old Testament!

Even Ras Shamra's pantheon seems hauntingly familiar. In fact, the often-heard denouncement of the Canaanite gods of El, Baal, Asherah in the Bible makes infinitely more sense when one realizes that these were the ruling deities of the region. These indeed were the gods worshipped at Ras Shamra!

Incidentally, the Bible too refers to 'El' and gives him a place of honor to such an extent that modern scholars decided that El was perhaps a generic name for Yahweh. This confusion has now been put to rest, thanks to the Ras Shamra discoveries. El was the competition. Scholars are now even willing to concede that the Psalms in the Bible, ascribed and dedicated to Yahweh, the God of Israel, were originally ascribed and sung in praise of El, the omnipresent presiding deity of the Ras Shamra-Canaan region.[4]

Finally, after years of deliberation, the Ras Shamra ruins were identified as Ugarit. We are informed that the name Ugarit came from the Ras Shamra texts itself and learn that it took nearly two years for someone to ferret out. What is strange about this name is the fact that no other ancient world texts mention such a name. In other words, Ugarit distinguishes itself as a name by being patently obscure.

EBLA

In 1964, an Italian expedition under the direction of Paolo Matthiae, discovered yet another rich ruin at the 50-feet high Tell Mardìkh mound in Northern Syria on the road to Aleppo. Clearly, a contemporary of Ras Shamra close by, it too yielded its share of royal palaces, monumental city gates, ramparts, temples and private houses. In 1974, the royal archives—a cache of tens of thousands of tablets written in the now familiar cuneiform script was found. Of special interest to Bible scholars, are the number of Old Testament cities referred to in the Tell Mardìkh text. Even the name 'Urusalima' (Jerusalem) occurs in the text, and is considered the earliest known reference to the city. There is even a direct reference to the 'five cities of the Plain' as in the Bible, referring to Sodom, Gomorrah, Admah, Zeboiim and Zoar, on the well-watered plain of the Jordan! Even records of a creation remarkably similar and apparently predating the Genesis account, too have been found.

Tell Mardìkh was eventually identified as Ebla. However, as before, the name Ebla has little or no significance from an ancient world perspective.

Mari

In August 1933, at a remote place roughly 75 miles southeast of Deir Ezzor in Syria, a group of Bedouins who were looking for stones, discovered a statue weighing nearly six hundred odd pounds. This chance discovery let to yet another great city-state being brought to light. Tell Hariri was known earlier, but this discovery led to intensified digging.

Tell Hariri appeared to have had strong ties with Mesopotamia and the Mediterranean and was considered an important trading point. Of great interest are the numerous statuettes with clasped hands that clearly evoke prayer, which were found at this site. The statuettes appear to have been made according to the same criteria and are made out of stone, although a few are made out of metal or alabaster, their height varying from a few inches to a couple of feet. They are all represented wearing a kind of sheep or goat's hair skirt, which men usually wore like a skirt and the women as a tunic that covered the whole body, leaving at times one shoulder bare. The eyes are made from shell and lapis lazuli set in bitumen, their hair is long and the top of their heads shaved. What is startling about this discovery is that these figurines exactly match the description given of the Egyptians by the 450 BC Greek historian Herodotus. Tell Hariri has been tagged 'Mari.'[5]

Currently there are more than three dozen or so Tells or mounds being actively excavated in the Turkey-Syria region. Some of the others are: Abu hureyra, Tell ain el-kerkh, Tell arbid, Tell ashara, Tell aushariye, Tell bazi, Tell beydar, Tell brak, Tell chuera, Djade el-mughara, Dura-europas, Emar, Tell es-sweyhat, Tell halula, Hammam al-turkman, Tell hamoukar, Jerablus tahtani, Jerf el-ahmar, Khisham, Tell leilan, Tell mashnaqa, Tell mishrife, Tell mozan, Tell munbaqa, Tell beydar, Palmyra, Tell qarqur, Tell sabi abyad, Tell shiukh fawqani, Tell tuneinir and Umm el-mara.[6]

WHAT LIES BENEATH

Why are there so many contemporary city-states in the Turkey-Syria region? Is it possible that these numerous, near identical city-states were perhaps interrelated cities and perhaps formed one big kingdom rather than independent city-states?

Scholars, it would appear, are afraid of making this very assumption. Indeed, they are careful never to mention these city-states in the same breath, lest such a slip give rise to the 'one super-power kingdom' theory. Clearly, they do not desire this at all.

It is not difficult to see their reasoning. After their initial shock and inadvertent admittance of not knowing a thing about these ruins during the initial days, archaeologists decided that it was best to underplay these discoveries. Later, that is say, when it was discovered that it was merely the tail they had inadvertently caught and that the beast extended exponentially underground, that there were not one or two but innumerable such sites, they decided it best to identify and tag these as a rash of independent city-states. No eyebrows would be raised if a host of tiny independent city-states, all neatly tagged with obscure names, were tucked into the Levant scenario. Imagine, on the other hand, if they were required to berth a single gargantuan kingdom into the Levant arena, which is already under great strain with the biblical anomaly!

Could the one kingdom scenario be true? Is there evidence to suppose that a major kingdom, instead of small independent ones, actually straddled the Levant arena in the Syria region?

It is an interesting ideology, especially when you consider that the innumerable 'Tells' of this region share many things in common. Each one of them reflects near identical level of development, language use, culture, religion, trade and industry. What is more, there is even irrefutable evidence to support that nearly all of them dramatically declined at about the same period. All of this suggests the one giant kingdom scenario.

To conclude, a bustling commercial hub, an Egypt-sized kingdom, straddled the Syria region. Of this, there is no doubt. The only question is which was this juggernaut kingdom?

CHAPTER 30

ANCIENT HISTORIAN'S EGYPT

Amongst the first thing that strikes anyone who reads Herodotus or Strabo on ancient Egypt is, that all of them provide the exact same unambiguous set of geographical pointers with which to identify and place ancient Egypt. Meaning, there is absolutely no ambiguity or mismatch concerning the information they provide on Egypt.

The fact is, Egypt was a popular subject, a sweet heart really, with Greek scholars. Any and everyone who could passably string words together and afford the ship fare, was out there furiously scribbling away, documenting this vivacious princess for posterity. Thus, if ambiguity exists concerning its exact location, then you may be sure it is patently artificial and created by our not so forthcoming friend, the modern-day scholar.

Let us briefly examine exactly how the ancient world scholars picture or paint Egypt.

Egypt is often described as 'the tract of country, which the Nile overspreads and irrigates.' Another popular remark is, 'Egyptians were the people who lived below Elephantine and drank the waters of this river.' Strabo graphically describes the country as a 'girdle-band' or a strip of land (extending, say roughly five miles on either side of the river) that essentially follows the river's course. In short, Egypt occupied the lower half (the upper half being occupied by Ethiopia) of the river valley created by the Nile.

The above general description is followed by a systematic and detailed description of Egypt's key regions, which, in Herodotus' case, is imaginatively worked out as a voyager upriver upon the Nile. Using this as a template, the key regions of Egypt were:

- **The Egyptian Sea and the islands**: This was the sea that washed the Egyptian shore and had islands in it. It is described as a shallow sea and calculated as a day's sail from the open sea to the Delta region.
- **The Coastal Region of Egypt**: This was the coastal region that extended along the base of the Delta.
- **The Delta or Lower Egypt**: This was a hemmed in triangular piece of low-lying land. In antiquity, this region was underwater. Later, that is, after the land was raised, thanks largely to the Nile's abundant gift of sediments, it went on to become a heavily populated region. It is described as a vast, spread out region that contained numerous swamps.
- **Red Sea**: A very large lake or inland sea called the Red Sea appears to have been a key landmark feature.
- **Upper Egypt**: This was the portion that snugly fitted in a long cloistered valley between two parallel mountain ranges. Egypt's territories ended here with Elephantine. After Elephantine, the land rose and after a distance of four days journey following the Nile's course, one reached the tract called Ethiopia.
- **The River Nile**: The River Nile was the lifeline of Egypt. One could traverse all along the length of Egypt upon this river all the way upstream, from the coast to Elephantine. The Nile emerged from Ethiopia, entered Upper Egypt, passed through this narrow valley and finally reached the apex of the Delta region. Here it branched out into two principal tributaries (that defined the Delta region) and

numerous others natural and artificial canals, and eventually exited into the sea.

This then is the Egypt that ancient world scholars consistently document.

Keeping this broad framework in mind, let us begin our search for specific clues by which we can successfully place Egypt in its true ancient world settings.

CHAPTER 31

THE EGYPT CLIMATA

"If I were not Alexander, I should wish to be Diogenes." So said Alexander the Great of the philosopher Diogenes, the Cynic of Sinope. Well, these great men have long gone, yet the ancient city of Sinope, continues on and has even cynically retained its name, perhaps as a tribute to its lone illustrious son. Abbreviated to 'Sinop' having lost merely an 'e' to all those long and turbulent years, it is still right where it always was: on a slight promontory jutting out into the Black Sea, though now presumably in modern fineries, flashing neon signs and breathing noxious fumes, laced no doubt with that odd bit of radioactive fallout. Yet unknown to itself, Sinop anchors more that its insignificant self.

Consider the following extract:

Egypt lies almost exactly opposite the mountainous portion of Cilicia, whence a lightly-equipped traveler may reach Sinope on the Euxine in five days by the direct route. Sinope lies opposite the place where the Ister falls into the sea. [Herodotus 2.34]

Now, Herodotus mentions four easily identifiable landmarks to anchor ancient Egypt on a yet to be identified coastline. The landmarks that include the above-mentioned Sinop are: the Euxine, the Ister and the mountainous portion of Cilicia.

Now Sinop lies on a promontory that juts into the Black Sea (or Euxine). Any map will confirm this. What is more, its position wholly agrees with the statement, that it lies "opposite the place where the Ister enters the sea." The River Ister, now renamed the Danube, enters the Black Sea from the Romanian coast at a point that is roughly opposite to the location of Sinop. Both are easily identifiable, regardless of their change in names. There is no mystery here; this triangulation of the recognizable landmarks is accurate.

Now, the mountainous portion of Cilicia is an unambiguous reference to the Taurus Mountains (Toros daglari), that fringes the Gulf of Iskendrun on its northwestern side. From here, apparently, a lightly equipped traveler could reach Sinope by the direct route in five days. This is conceivable and does accurately represent the distance between the Taurus Mountains and Sinop. The name Cilicia is no longer in use, yet any number of ancient world maps will identify the region by this name. Modern maps, at any rate, will identify the 'Cilician Gates' in this region, which should serve as an accurate pointer.

Opposite the Cilician Mountains lies the coastline of modern Syria, including a small portion of Turkey. According to conventional history, this coastline was occupied in ancient times by an assortment of Syrian tribes of little significance. As mentioned earlier, none of the above descriptions by Herodotus contains any mystery whatsoever. If anything, you idly wonder how little the world has changed even after so many years and give full marks to Herodotus for accurately establishing the position of a number of recognizable landmarks, in some manner of triangulation, with a view it seems, to anchor the Egyptian coastline.

What comes next rudely snaps you out of your reverie. Herodotus observers too jump up and decide that the man needs careful watching after all. As for the Egyptologists peering over his shoulders, why, they are foaming in the mouth with righteous anger! For, according to Herodotus, opposite the Cilician Mountains on the Turkish-Syrian coastline, lay not Syrian tribes of little significance, but ancient

Egypt! That is right. Egypt the commercial hub of the ancient world was located on the Turkish-Syrian coastline roughly where Samandagi is currently situated.

However preposterous this information may seem, let us give Herodotus some leeway and try to make sense of his innocent but incredible claim. He has, after all, given us the Canaan-Ethiopia similarity.

Now, Herodotus had a keen scientific mind. Keeping this in mind, I re-examined the anchor points given for Egypt and made a startling discovery. All the anchor points given, fall in a straight-line! The mouth of the Ister, Sinope, the mountainous portion of Cilicia and the Syrian coastline opposite the mountains, all appear to form the straight-line coordinate of Egypt!

After further reading, I realized that these straight-line coordinates proffered by Herodotus are possibly the precursor of the 'climata' that Strabo, Ptolemy and others used at a much later date. In other words, Ister, Sinope, the mountainous portion of Cilicia is the straight-line Climata of Egypt, which I have taken the liberty to call the 'Egypt Climata.'

Climata, in turn, after further refinement, went on to become the latitudes and longitudes of today. Thus, what we have here is a first! This indeed is the very first instance wherein the ideology of using a number of points, all falling in a straight-line, anchor a kingdom (in this case, Egypt) on a map.

There is absolutely no ambiguity here. If Egypt was on this coast, one definitely has to concede that the statement made by Herodotus, 'Egypt lies exactly opposite the mountainous portion of Cilicia,' is accurate, and highly original!

Take a closer look at this coastline. You will soon note that we have been directed to look long and hard in an area acknowledged even by modern experts to be the very cradle of ancient civilizations! Herodotus could not have chosen a better site even if he were speculating!

It is here on this coastal belt that archaeologists have found the presence of a juggernaut commercial empire 'where none was thought to exist.' The Ras Shamra ruins and numerous others in this region speak of an advanced civilization that has been described by archaeologists as 'larger and infinitely more advanced than Mesopotamia.' This region also holds the distinction of having evolved the first modern script, which according to Herodotus, was yet another fine Egyptian achievement.

Admittedly, truly spectacular architectural accomplishments are somewhat lacking here. But then again, that too is in keeping, for according to Herodotus, the Egyptians were in fact poor builders. Ports, sweatshops, warehouses, evolved script and snatches of Bible stories are all it embarrassingly tosses up. Yet, these indeed—and not pyramids—are the crown jewels of a mature nation.

Herodotus was of course merely documenting. Meaning, there was no need for him to speculate, ferret out information, and reconstruct a scenario and so on, for Egypt was still very much around. Yet, with unbelievable foresight, he hammers in a good many tacks to anchor ancient Egypt on this coastline. A good thing too. For, Egypt is now truly lost. Indeed, in a bizarre twist of fate, another has taken its place. True Egypt, the superpower of the ancient world, stands forlorn and forgotten—no doubt paying the karma price for its former, unbridled glory.

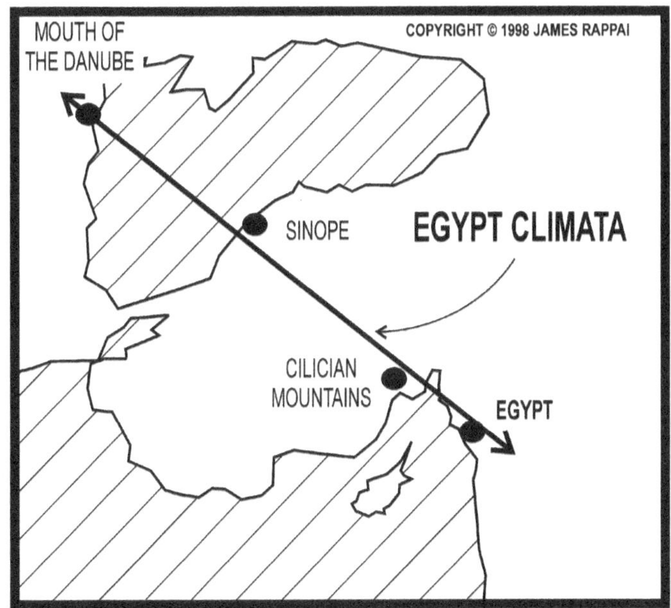

*Diagram 4: **Egypt's Straight-line Co-ordinate or the 'Egypt Climata.'** Herodotus often set a straight-line co-ordinate of a place by identifying a series of places that were in line with it. Using this ideology, he fixed the position of Egypt by using: the mouth of the Ester, Sinope, and the mountainous portion of Cilicia, as its straight-line anchor-points. As can be seen, this firmly places Egypt in Syria.*

CHAPTER 32

MOUNT CASIUS

A gulf profound as that Serbonian Bog Betwixt Damiata and Mount Casius old, Where Armies whole have sunk. [Milton, Paradise Lost 2. 595]

Incredibly, pinning down the Egyptian coastline on the very stretch of East Mediterranean seaboard currently occupied by Syria and a portion of Turkey, is yet another immovable landmark that is readily identifiable. Herodotus writes, "The length of the country along shore, according to the bounds that we assign to Egypt, namely from the Plinthinetic gulf to Lake Serbonis, which extends along the base of Mount Casius, is sixty schoene."[1]

Herodotus has always been very fastidious with his triangulations. He wanted readily identifiable landmarks at the two extreme ends of Egypt's extended coastline to demarcate it for posterity. Therefore, he chose the Plinthinetic Gulf at one end and the Lake Serbonis at the base of Mount Casius at the other, to do the job of anchoring this eventful coastline.

Now, gulfs are notoriously difficult to identify. At least I have trouble with them. Fortunately, my luck with the mountain in this scenario is much better. Indeed, someone had already identified a Mount Casius for me on the Syrian coast very near Samandagi. All I has to do was look at a map.

It is not there anymore though. For some reason, modern-day scholars are now shying away from mentioning or locating the Syrian Mount Casius on a map.[2]

Even so, Mount Casius' original position on the coast of Syria would be known to all students of history. Furthermore, any ancient world map or text would readily identify it for you. For instance, Thomas Milner from the distant past, in his book 'Geography of the World' written in 1868, mentions Mount Casius, along with other recognizable landmarks, such as the ancient city of Antioch and the river Orontes. He writes, "Antakia, on the left bank of the Orontes, about twenty miles from the sea is the poor modern representative of the vast and splendid Antioch of former times." Thomas Milner goes on to add, "This city, for several centuries, the favorite residence of the Syro-Macedonian Kings and afterwards of Roman governors, was built partly on the plains through which the river winds its way and partly on the rugged ascent towards Mt. Casius, the slopes of which were once covered with vineyards." [Thomas Milner, Geography of the World] [3]

Antakya in modern Turkey, located on the East-Mediterranean coast, can of course be easily located on the map. It was formerly known as Antioch and figures prominently in the history of Christianity. Incidentally, the very name 'Christian' originated here and Antioch had become a prominent centre of the Eastern Church. Earlier to that, the Jews were partial to this city owing to the 'jus civitatum' or right to citizenship offered by Seleucus. We may therefore be reasonably sure that Mount Casius was near Antakya.

But where exactly? Now, Herodotus also informs us that Mount Casius, apart from having a lake at its base, jutted out into the sea. He writes:

...after Jenysus the Syrians again come in and extend to Lake Serbonis, near the place where Mount Casius juts out into the sea. At Lake Serbonis, where the tale goes that Typhon hid himself, Egypt begins. [Herodotus 3.5]

As for the Typhon reference, it may interest readers to know that the River Orontes that passes through this region was formerly called the Typhon.[4] And, as mentioned before, Mount Casius jutted out into the sea.

The Syrian Casius of old, the one that was known to Thomas Milner, Sir Leonard Woolley and their contemporaries, was I believe on the sea shore, and not entirely to my satisfaction. I believe it to be correct in the broad sense, but am not so sure if the mount jutted out into the Mediterranean Sea. I do not know how it came to be identified, but my guess is, its placement was largely determined by early-date modern-day scholars and that it is entirely based on Antioch's history.

So, where would I place my Casius? Into which sea did the Mount Casius intrude? This being the specific criteria, I scanned the Antakya region and was able to find a mountain that was an astonishing fit. However, I am unable to find the local name by which to identify it! The coordinates are: 36.0354 E, 36.0914N and it appears that the ruin called 'St. Simon's Monastery' is located upon it.

But where is the sea? Well, my Mount Casius stands in a low-lying and wide passageway of sorts that lies approximately between Samandagi (at the coast) and Antakya in modern-day Turkey. Formerly, this corridor was occupied by a long sea intrusion called the 'Tongue of the Egyptian Sea' (read chapter, 'Tongue of the Egyptian Sea' for more on this subject). Thus, Mount Casius' rude stance right in the midst of this passageway cannot but be considered an intrusion upon this now extinct sea.

Actually, this particular detail of the mountain 'jutting out into the sea,' I feel, had to have been something as distinctive as this to have found mention in books of history. Meaning, there you are sailing calmly down the sea and suddenly this lone mount looms large, standing insolently right in the pathway like a titanic iceberg. This perhaps is how one should picture Mount Casius.

The above reconstruction is wonderfully supported by Lake Serbonis situated at the base of Mount Casius. I say this because a lake situated in a passage wherein the sea intrudes, is certain to be overwhelmed by it. And, this indeed is the ever-changing picture documented of the Lake Serbonis by ancient world scholars. We see it documented as a lake; we see it being overwhelmed by the sea; we see it struggling to retain its integrity and its waters when the sea pulls out and finally, we see it as a bog, broken and defeated, licked by the Tongue of the Egyptian Sea.

Comment

A shocking bit of skullduggery in connection with the Mount Casius has been resorted to by archaeologists, this time the very strident group who call themselves Egyptologists, and it needs to be exposed here. Did you know that they actually have gone and identified a low hillock as the Mount Casius in their Egypt-in-Africa reconstruction? This would explain their deliberate silence regarding the Syrian Casius. Although the Syrian Casius served invaluably as a sheet anchor in the Ancient Near Eastern arena for the earlier generation of scholars such as Thomas Milner and Leonard Woolley, modern-day scholars seem to be making a conscious effort to erase it from memory. Clearly, one can sense a house-cleaning happening here.

At any rate, I assumed that they had at least a low hillock to label as their Mount Casius at the new site. A cursory Google Earth search though, did not reveal one in the said region.

Every once in a while, an easily recognizable tract of land disconcertingly appears in textual sources in entirely different settings. Earlier, I had highlighted the reoccurring of a known topographical scenario in two different eras or settings that were seen in Josephus' text. The island Saba-Rabbah with the confluence of rivers appears twice, documented once in an Ethiopian setting and the second time in a Canaanite setting.

Similarly, Strabo too documents a particular landmark in two different settings. This time it is the Mount Casius. Here that a look:

> *And it is on this account that the Antiocheians worship him as a hero and celebrate a festival in his honour on Mt. Casius in the neighbourhood of Seleuceia. [Strabo 7.15.2.5]*

> *Thence to Mt. Casius near Pelusium the distance is a little more than one thousand stadia; and, three hundred stadia farther, one comes to Pelusium itself. [Strabo 7.16.2.28]*

In the first extract, we may note that the Mt. Casius mentioned is in the 'neighbourhood of Seleuceia' and Antioch in Syria. In the second, it is near Pelusium in Egypt. The reason for this duplication may be explained as such: to write the history of ancient Egypt, Strabo had to rely wholly on previously documented text by early historians, such as the 450 BC Herodotus and others and therefore laid the geographical foundation of Ancient Egypt as was given there. Later, he went on to document Seleucus' Syria, little realizing that its territories were formerly that of Ancient Egypt.

But how did that happen, you might ask. The fact is, ancient Egypt, had ceased to exist as before. The Persians and Greeks, into who hands it passed on, portioned it into various satrapies and these became part of two different later-date empires. Seleucus' Syria, which extended from Babylonia, got the Delta region of ancient Egypt. Ptolemy's Egypt retained a portion of ancient Egypt, primarily along the East Mediterranean Coast (including parts currently occupied by modern-day Lebanon, the Bekaa Valley, southern Syria, etc) and included portions of Ancient Canaan-Ethiopia's territory (Israel, Philistine, Sidon, etc).

Needless to add, the picture got further obscured and complicated when modern-day scholars removed Egypt and Canaan-Ethiopia from this arena and placed it on the African continent. Translators on their part, busy little bees, invariably massaged the text to reflect the modern-day reconstruction and completed the processes of creating mass confusion. It is thus that we now have two Mount Casiuses. One in Syria and the other in Egypt. In truth there was but one. Formerly, it was in Ancient Egypt and later, when that portion of its territories was hived off to Seleucus' Syria, it appeared there as well.

Of course, now that this gargantuan mystery has being split wide open, the anomaly regarding Mount Casius merely serves to confirm my new reconstruction.

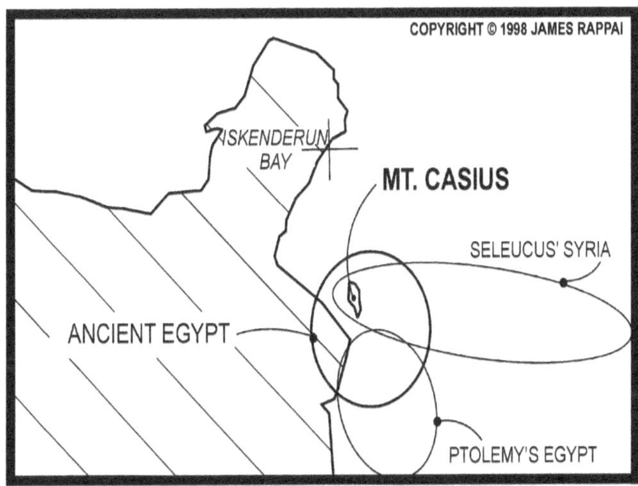

CHAPTER 33

ANTAKYA

I would like to cover an interesting ruin that is situated in this region near Mount Casius. It is Antakya, and this archaeological find is presented here as a sneak preview of what is in store in this region.

When Syria was conquered by Rome in 64 BC, Antioch became the eastern capital of the Roman Empire. The Romans, it is assumed, contributed to the architectural splendors of the city. Yet, in all probability, Antioch or Antakya was formerly an Egyptian city and much of the ruins we see in this region, are probably of Egyptian origin. Indeed, this whole argument is hinged upon one such a ruin.

While conducting my research on Mount Casius, it was revealed that in the Egyptian scenario, the closest city to Mount Casius was Bubastis. Both the city and Mount Casius are mentioned in connection with a canal, which appeared to have begun its passage from near here.

> *The water is derived from the Nile, which the canal leaves a little above the city of Bubastis, near Patumus, the Arabian town, being continued thence until it joins the Red Sea.... From the northern sea to that which is called the southern or Erythraean, the shortest and quickest passage, which is from Mount Casius, the boundary between Egypt and Syria, to the Gulf of Arabia, is a distance of exactly one thousand furlongs. [Herodotus 2.158]*[1]

That Bubastis was the closest city to Mount Casius in the Egyptian scenario seems a safe assumption to make based on the above extracts. Fortunately, this is quickly confirmed by

Herodotus who reveals the same in another portion of his text. Here he states, "The Bubastis of the Egyptians is the same as the Artemis (Diana) of the Greeks."[2] Meaning, Bubastis is Diana. He then goes on to offer an elaborate description of the temple.

> *Other temples may be grander and may have cost more to build, but there is none so pleasant to the eye as this of Bubastis.... Two artificial channels from the Nile, one on either side of the temple, encompass the building... there is a grove of beautiful tall trees growing round the shrine. The entrance to it is by a road paved with stone for a distance of about three furlongs, which passes straight through the market-place with an easterly direction and is about four hundred feet in width. Trees of an extraordinary height grow on each side the road, which conducts from the temple of Bubastis to that of Mercury. [Herodotus 2.138]*

Now, upon reading Herodotus' description of the temple of Bubastis, one gets the queerest sense of déjà vu. For, by an extraordinary coincidence, Herodotus' description of the temple of Bubastis, written in 450 BC, matches almost word for word, the description of the ruins of the temple of Diana in Antakya, written by Thomas Milner in 1850 or thereabouts and with that of George Rawlinson written in 1860 or so. The 2400 odd years that separate these authors, becomes apparent when one realizes that while Herodotus appears to be describing the temple in all its glory, Thomas Milner and George Rawlinson had only its ruins to go by. Of course, as far as Milner or Rawlinson was concerned, they were describing the ruins of the temple of a Roman Diana and not that of an Egyptian Bubastis. Here are both the extracts:

> *The temple of Daphne stood in the neighbourhood (of Antakia), embosomed in thick groves of laurels and cypresses, through which numerous streams were led*

*forming a cool summer retreat for the inhabitants of
the city. [Thomas Milner, Geography of the World]*[3]

Interestingly, George Rawlinson, in his book, 'The History of
Phoenicia' adds:

*On its north-eastern prolongation, which is washed by
the Orontes, lay the enchanting pleasure-ground of
Daphné, bubbling with fountains and bright with
flowering shrubs, where from a remote antiquity the
Syrians held frequent festival to their favourite deity—
the 'Dea Syra'—the great nature goddess. [George
Rawlinson, The History of Phoenicia, Ch 1]*

From Thomas Milner, the author of 'Geography of the World,'
and George Rawlinson's 'The history of Phoenicia,' we find
that the ruins of a temple of Daphne or Diana stood in the
neighborhood of Antakya. Clearly, the Antakya documented
above was the pleasure ground of goddess Diana. The river
mentioned here is of course the Orontes, which is indeed the
Nile according to my hypothesis. The same is matched almost
word for word by Herodotus documentation of the temple of
Bubastis in close to Mount Casius and therefore Antakya.

The points of similarities are: both are temples of Diana,
both had streams from the Nile (the River Nile-Orontes in our
scenario) flowing by, both had beautiful tall trees growing
around the shrine and both authors comment it to have been
a 'pleasing to the eye' sort of a place. Even Canon Rawlinson
with his 'enchanting pleasure-ground of Daphné, bubbling
with fountains and bright with flowering shrubs' happily
concurs!

Perhaps it is no more than a 'celestial conjunction of
prose,' if there is such a thing, or perhaps the Lady Diana did
indeed cast a spell on these dour historians. At any rate, we
have the Mount Casius landmark to go by. Both Bubastis and
Antakya were anchored in place and time by this mount. Thus,

we can say with some degree of confidence, that Antakya was formerly the Egyptian city of Bubastis.

Good citizens of Antakya-Bubastis, here is a bit more history of your beloved city. Of the several festivals that the Egyptians celebrate, the chief, which is better attended than any other, is held at the city of Bubastis, in honor of Diana. Boat loads of men and women come with castanets, pipes and drums, sing, clap and generally make merry. When passing towns upon the banks, they approach the shore and, while some continue to play and sing, others call aloud to the females of the place and load them with abuse. Some even stand up and uncover themselves. After proceeding in this way all along the river-course, they reach Bubastis, where they celebrate the feast with abundant sacrifices. Seven hundred thousand or more attend this festival. More wine is apparently consumed at this particular festival than all the year around![4]

CHAPTER 34

TONGUE OF THE EGYPTIAN SEA

The coastline of Egypt presented a complicated landscape. It had harbors with narrow openings that demanded great skill to negotiate. There were marshes, saltpans, lakes, islands, including a mountain to be skirted or skipped. Decommissioned harbors and all manners of vessels including terracotta boats that needed to be dodged or deflected so much so that most regurgitating historians and rear admirals would readily agree that backing a ship into Egypt was a major pain in the rear!

The impression gained on reading ancient world textual sources is indeed that the last leg of the sea route leading into Egypt was an especially torturous one. The coastline near Samandagi however presents no such picture. If anything, it is featureless and appears to have no decent anchorages even.

Fortunately, the Bible reveals a detail of the sea at this point that is rather illuminative. It speaks of an intrusive bay that appeared to have reached deep inland. The Bible colorfully refers to it as the 'Tongue of the Egyptian Sea.' Here, take a look:

> *And the LORD shall utterly destroy the tongue of the Egyptian sea; and with his mighty wind shall he shake his hand over the river and shall smite it in the seven streams and make men go over dryshod. [Isaiah 11.15]*

The Tongue of the Egyptian Sea appeared to be a narrow 'tongue shaped' bay that the sea (the Mediterranean Sea) shot inland possibly up to the Delta region. Indeed, the seven streams mentioned here in connection with this tongue of the sea, is an unambiguous reference to the Delta of Egypt, where the Nile flowed through seven streams.

Be that as it may, the fact remains that there is no such tongue in this region at present. What is to be done? Many days of frantic search, followed. I scanned ancient world texts for signs of an extinct sea intrusion. Gradually, a picture began to emerge.

There was once such a water body in this region. The clue that cracked opened this mystery was Mount Casius. Apparently, flood waters so inundated this region that Mount Casius, which was located in its pathway, often resembled an island. As is often the case with unraveling mysteries, other pertinent facts that have been sitting right under my very nose all along, began to obediently fall into place.

The fact that a sea intrusion thrust its tongue into this region is well documented. Strabo who delivers the Mount Casius clue also explains that it was due to the breaching and outflow at the Pillar of Heracles (which lowered the Mediterranean) that the Tongue of the Egyptian Sea eventually ceased to exist. Here, is the textual evidence:

...and that in ancient times Egypt was covered by the sea as far as the bogs about Pelusium, Mt. Casius and Lake Sirbonis; at all events, even to-day, when the salt-lands in Egypt are dug up, the excavations are found to contain sand and fossil-shells, as though the country had been submerged beneath the sea and the whole region round Mt. Casius and the so-called Gerrha had once been covered with shoal water so that it connected with the Gulf of the Red Sea; and when the sea retired, these regions were left bare, except that the Lake Sirbonis remained; then the lake also broke through to the sea and thus became a bog. [Strabo, Geography 1.3.4]

Again, the Egyptian Pharos was once an island of the sea, but now it has become, in a sense, a peninsula;

The above scenario is confirmed in the above text as well. Even Herodotus documents the Tongue of the Egyptian Sea. The only difference is that his 450BC documentation actually shows the tongue as a shallow sea intrusion! Here, look:

In the first place, on approaching it by sea, when you are still a day's sail from the land, if you let down a sounding-line you will bring up mud and find yourself in eleven fathom's water, which shows that the soil washed down by the stream extends to that distance. [Herodotus 2.5]

In the above extract, it is said, that for a day's sail you are roughly in eleven fathoms of water. Now, this can be interpreted either as 'the silt built-up in the sea proper' or 'the sea encroached into the land.' However, when you consider the fact that this shallow stretch extended for a whole day's sail, then obviously the sea encroachment into the land scenario seems more likely. In short, this is indeed an unambiguous reference to the Tongue of the Egyptian Sea.

It had taken me nearly six months to discern this diabolic tongue. Indeed, it had nearly licked me in this battle of wits and had brought to me down on my knees in tears. Even then, I was a little skeptical of this reconstruction. All that changed when I chanced upon an explicit mention of the Tongue of the Egyptian Sea in an obscure, ancient world source. Here it is:

And his portion extends along the great sea, and it extends in a straight line till it reaches the west of the tongue which looks towards the south: for this sea is named the tongue of the Egyptian Sea. [The Book of Jubilees 8.12][1]

There was indeed a sea called the 'Tongue of the Egyptian Sea' according to the ancient Jewish textual source known as 'The Book of Jubilees,' or 'Leptogenesis' (lesser Genesis). There is no ambiguity here at all! Indeed, the text emphatically states that the sea was actually known by this curious name.

However, textual records are one thing. Does the terrain here in this region support such a sea? A quick fly past over this region with Google Earth revealed an exciting landscape. A low-lying corridor of sorts, almost like a glacier pathway, roughly between Samandagi and Antakya, emerged forth. A quick peek into archaeological reports concerned with this region confirmed the find. This corridor was the largest fertile tract in all Turkey and served as the breadbasket of the country. The land was marshy and there is ample evidence of shallow lakes.[2]

That this very fertile region was once the bed of a shallow sea in the distant past is thus not difficult to imagine. If this indeed was the Egyptian Sea, then, the islands of the sea such as Pharos-Alexandria, Tyre, etc., could easily have been in this very sea.

A quick scanning of the ruins in this region assures me that there are very good specimens to choose from for my islands. Tell Ta'yinat and Tell Atchana would do very nicely for my Tyre and Sidon. Would you believe that there is a Solomon's Temple like ruins upon one of them? Was this perhaps the original Sidonian temple that served as the model for Solomon's temple in Jerusalem?

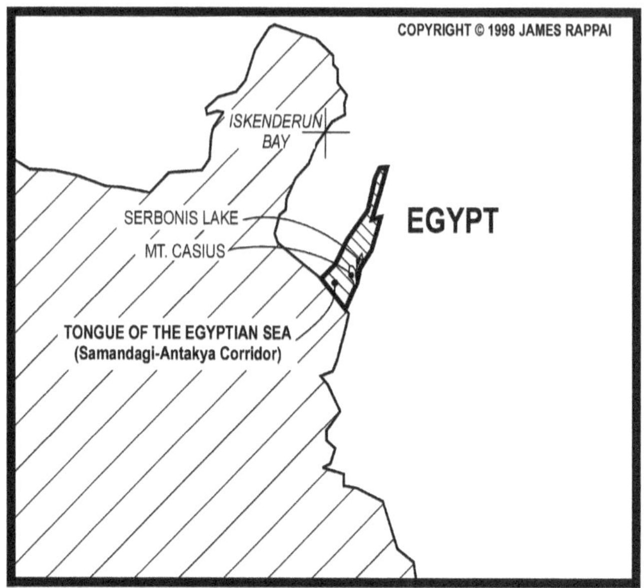

*Diagram 6: **Tongue of the Egyptian Sea.** The Samandagi-Antakya Corridor is a low-lying depression that exists in this region as indicated above. This corridor was once occupied by a sea intrusion, which extended all the way to the Delta district of Egypt. It was called, appropriately enough, the 'Tongue of the Egyptian Sea.'*

CHAPTER 35

THE DELTA REGION

"Delta? They cannot be serious!" Herodotus exclaimed. "It seems such a misnomer!" The region in question was certainly not the delta of the river. Misleading as it was, he could well see the logic of their explanation. He sighed. The Ionians somewhat dazzled him. Their flashy ideas and flamboyant theories, of which they had several concerning the Delta itself, intimidated him, made him look a blundering amateur. Disturbed though he was, he let it pass. He was determined however to attack their foolish theory that 'nothing was really Egypt except the Delta.' The rest of Egypt, meaning, the either sides of the River Nile, according to them, technically belonged to Arabia and Libya. Herodotus snorted in disgust. "There is limit to hair-splitting!" he said to no one in particular.

The impression gained from reading ancient world texts regarding the Delta region of Egypt, is somewhat different from the current thinking on the subject. The Delta region was not exactly a classic river delta, the kind that is formed at the mouth of a river. In reality, it refers to a tract of low-lying land that was distinctly triangular in shape and hemmed in by mountains or highlands on all sides. True, it was a well-watered tract, close to the sea, choked with silt and the Nile flowed through this region in many branches, all of which conspired to give the illusion that it was a regular river delta. Yet, it was not one.

Classic river deltas are formed at the mouth of a river by the fact that the sea is reluctant to accept the bountiful gift of alluvium the river insists upon offering it. This creates a backpressure. The silt is thus pushed right back and accumulates in the form of a wedge or delta at the mouth of the river, which ends up choking the river and splitting it into numerous tributaries. The wedge like shape results from the fact that the river pushes it from one side and the sea blocks it from the other.

The point to note here is, in a classic delta formation, the land is not reclaimed, but is instead lost, being choked and overwhelmed by silt. Good land is actually destroyed by the accumulation of silt. Perhaps the only gain in a classic river delta scenario is when the accumulation of silt pushes itself into the sea to form an embattled promontory.

The documented dynamics or evolution of the Delta region of Egypt was diametrically different from that of a classic river delta described above. What is mentioned in ancient world texts is that the Delta region of Egypt was formerly underwater. Thus, when the river emptied itself into it, being low-lying, it acted exactly as a natural trap for silt. In short, unlike as in a classic river delta scenario, here in the Delta region, the river's bountiful gift of alluvium was not rejected, or pushed back, but instead gladly and abundantly received. Land was raised and reclaimed by silt and not overwhelmed and destroyed by it. Indeed, it rose considerably and alarmingly in height and soon this formerly inundated region became inhabitable. This as we all know, is almost half the story of Egypt. That Egypt was the gift of the Nile, is the favorite story written by every ancient world historian, all of them no doubt taking their cue from the scientific-minded Herodotus, who alone genuinely marveled or understood such things.

Of course, the whole confusion arose because the Ionians, discerning its triangular shape, began referring to this region

as the Delta. Over time, the appellation struck. To Herodotus
the term 'Delta' for this region struck as unsuitable and he
makes a point in mentioning it. One can sense his
dissatisfaction with the term. Perhaps it suggests a wrong
usage. However, he holds his tongue and does not comment
on it.

To the untutored eye, the Delta region of Egypt differed
very little from a regular river delta. Being sediment rich and
located at the juncture of a river and the sea, it looked and
sounded very like the real thing. The difference was so subtle,
that even when they did discern the difference (like
Herodotus above), all they could really do was to make a note
of it. Herodotus thought it a misnomer and obliquely blamed
the Ionians who bewildered him. Strabo too, it would appear,
sensed a discrepancy and therefore insisted on calling it the
'Delta region,' in the vain hope that perhaps future historians
may nail the discrepancy. He also plainly states that the region
"was called a Delta on account of its similarity in shape (with a
'delta' which is a Greek alphabet)." Strabo even goes on to
identify it as a river island.

Of course, there is always the chance that the entire
confusion crept in during the translation stage. Whatever the
cause, what needs to be noted here is the fact that, however
else ancient world scholars referred to the Delta region, no
one ever described this region as the delta of the River Nile.

VISUAL CONFIRMATION

Modern scholars will no doubt railroad the above delicate
arguments. This is because they have identified a regular river
delta and a massive one at that, in their reconstruction. Very
likely, this voluptuous, 'mother of all Deltas,' played a part in
their wrongly identifying Egypt. Indeed, this delta, a classic

river delta if ever there was one, is so huge that it is probably visible from the moon!

A picture, they say, speaks a thousand words and the Nile delta in Africa was certainly doing that for these scholars. This staggering pictorial evidence, that unequivocally supported the modern-scholar's reconstruction, made me pause in my racy re-reconstruction tracks. Could they be right after all? This powerful visual that so heartily confirms their reconstruction ideologies, vaguely distressed me and forced me to look for a pictorial evidence of my very own.

I needed a picture desperately. One that unequivocally and brilliantly supported my theory; one that spoke a thousand, nay a million words.

So there I was, frantically scanning through maps, satellite images and Google Earth images of the Turkey-Syria region, hoping that there was a well-defined delta out there to fire my reader's imaginations.

Unbelievably I found it!

When suddenly I saw the distinct triangular shape of this region for the first time, I was unprepared, shocked. Indeed, like a paleontologist who slips into a dreamy reverie and imagines that the six-inch tooth that he had been lovingly brushing for the last half-hour is attached to a living, breathing Tyrannosaurs Rex, a creature that he only distantly believed in, and gets a fright, I too was startled. Up until now, I too was merrily going on textual steam, bulldozing the considered opinions of thousands of scholars in second gear, without a second thought. I knew that I was right of course, even so, when suddenly I chanced upon pictorial evidence that so strikingly supported my hypothesis, it rattled me, took my breath away!

I got my picture—and considering that it is a perfect fit in my re-reconstructed scenario of Egypt, this picture of the real Nile Delta, does speak a million!

Take out your world maps or hop into your Google Earth cockpit and swoop down on the Amik ovasi, in the Hatay District of Turkey. It is not at all difficult to find, for it is a distinctly triangular-shaped region. The cities of Antakya, Reyhanli and Aktepe roughly represent the three corners of this 'delta' shaped depression. Note its distinct triangular shape outlined by the contour color, by the parameter roadmap of the region, as well as the international border between Turkey and Syria.

The Amik ovasi is bounded on three sides by hills and mountains. The depression is in fact a part of the Great Rift Valley formation. The Orontes River, which is the Nile in my reconstruction scenario, flows through this delta shaped depression in many branches, before exiting into the 'Tongue of the Egyptian Sea.' As mentioned earlier, Samandagi-Antakya corridor was once home to a shallow sea called the 'Tongue of the Egyptian Sea' that intruded inland from the Mediterranean.

The Amik ovasi, which is roughly about 25 miles on all three sides, is studded with numerous ruin mounds or Tells. Some are low but others rise 50 or 100 feet high. From almost anywhere on the Amik plain, a dozen or more mounds are visible. Even so, it has merely attracted cursory attention of erstwhile archaeologists. The more curious ones, I recently read, practiced a new fangled form of archaeology called 'Landscape Archaeology' that involved 'drive past with head stuck out doggie style,' in an attempt to get a 'feel' of the region's archaeological heritage.[1] As they hurtled by in their four-wheel drives getting a 'feel' and in the process, crushing invaluable potshards and what not, having not the faintest idea where they actually were, I silently screamed. Stop! The Amik ovasi was the Delta region of ancient Egypt; it was the very heart of the ancient world!

Citizens of Syria, of Turkey, celebrate like of old, for I give you back your glorious past! There is no question that you were the real, grand and glorious Egyptians. The only question is, when will you pay the piper his dues.

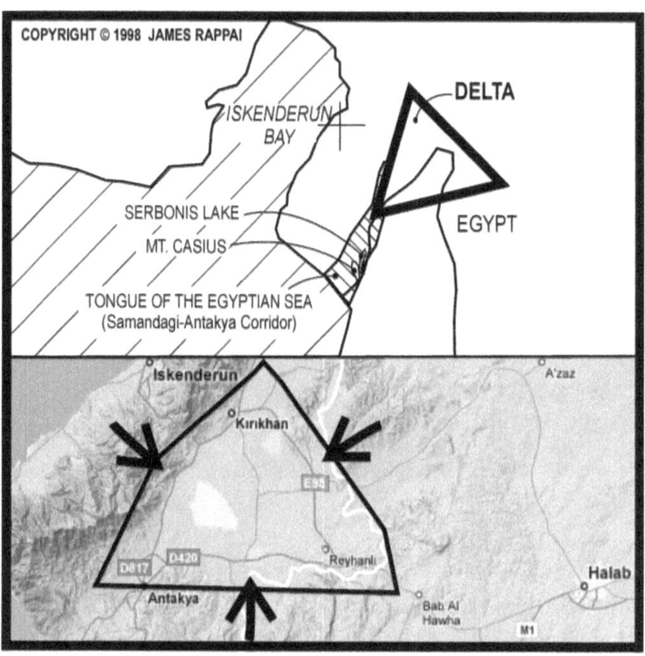

*Diagram 7: **The Real Delta District of Egypt.** Amik Ovasi or Amuq Valley, a triangular depression in southern Turkey (near Antakya), was the real delta district of Egypt. Note its distinct triangular or 'delta' shape as defined by the road map and by the international boundary between Turkey and Syria. The Turkish cities of Antakya, Kirikhan and Reyhanli roughly define the delta's distinctive shape.*

UPPER EGYPT

From the Delta region also Lower Egypt, we enter the region called Upper Egypt. This is in essence, was a long narrow valley that abutted the Delta region. While the lower region was expansive, this part of Egypt was tightly hemmed in by two parallel mountain ranges. Let us examine the description given below:

> *As one proceeds beyond Heliopolis up the country, Egypt becomes narrow, the Arabian range of hills, which has a direction from north to south, shutting it in upon the one side and the Libyan range upon the other.... Above Heliopolis, then, there is no great breadth of territory for such a country as Egypt, but during four day's sail Egypt is narrow; the valley between the two ranges is a level plain and seemed to me to be, at the narrowest point, not more than two hundred furlongs across from the Arabian to the Libyan hills. Above this point Egypt again widens. [Herodotus 2.8]*

Two mountain ranges are described as running parallel to each other in a north-south direction, creating a long valley for a distance of four day's voyage, presumably up the Nile. After a while though, the region apparently opens out once again. This long and narrow valley between two parallel ranges was the region called Upper Egypt.

There is no mystery here. Upper Egypt was essentially a tract between two mountain ranges. While the rest of Egypt was in the plains, a portion, between Heliopolis and Elephantine, was in a narrow valley between twin mountain ranges. More on this subject is available in the chapter titled, 'The Twin Gulf Pointers.'

According to my reconstruction, this region is the narrow valley created by the Jabal an Nusayriyah Mountains and Mount Jebel El Wastani.

Incidentally, the distinct terrain described above is not there in the reconstructed model of ancient Egypt. The parallel mountain ranges that form a cloistered valley, through which the Nile flows, have no place in the modern-day reconstruction. The Arabian Range and the Libyan Range between which Upper Egypt nestled, is wholly absent. In fact, there are no mountains of any kind in their arena. This is a serious anomaly.

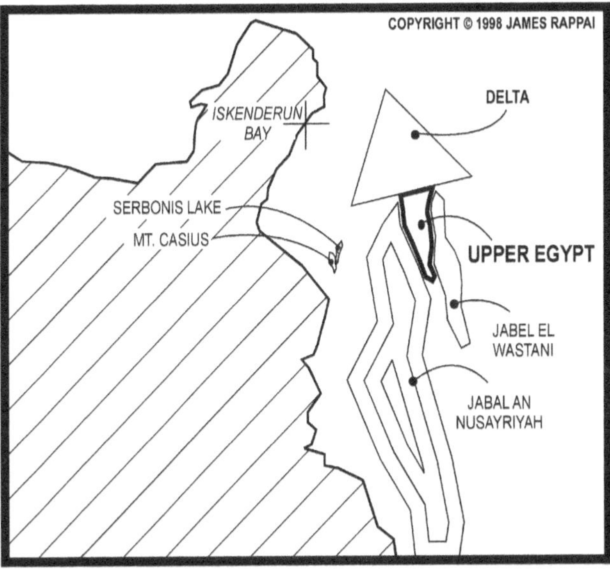

*Diagram 8 **Upper Egypt**. A narrow valley that abutted the delta region and through which the Nile flowed was called Upper Egypt. I have tentatively identified Upper Egypt as the valley formed by the Jabal an Nusayriyah and the Jebel El Wastani as indicated above.*

CHAPTER 37

THE REED SEA

Egyptian textual history records dramatic changes in its topographical features over the ages. Land, it appears, was in constant state of flux, becoming exposed or inundated with clockwork precision. Greek scholars, ranging from Homer to Strabo and representing nearly a thousand years of scholarship, have, on their part, offered all manners of explanation. Sometimes it was because of the outflow at the Pillars that consequently exposed land or it was the river bringing down far too much silt and if honest to goodness scientific principles were not immediately discernable, then it was quietly chalked down to the Etesian winds of yesteryears.

Consider the following extract:

Again, the Egyptian Pharos was once an island of the sea, but now it has become, in a sense, a peninsula; and the same is true of Tyre and Clazomenae. And when I residing in Alexandria, in Egypt, the sea about Pelusium and Mt.Casius rose and flooded the country and made an island of the mountain, so that the road by Mt. Casius into Phoenicia became navigable. [Strabo, Geography 1.3.17]

Egyptian Pharos, was once an island, but now has become a peninsula. The sea about Pelusium and Mount Casius rose and flooded the land, making an island of the mountain. In the first instance, the sea level receded and in the second, no doubt an occurrence separated from the first by considerable time, the sea level rose.

Likewise, from Herodotus we gain the general idea, that the entire Delta region area was marshland and formerly underwater. It was much later, thanks to the Nile's virulent erosive tendencies and possibly by the interventions of enterprising kings, that the region was eventually converted to fertile and usable tracts of prime real estate, into which all of Egypt hastily moved in. Added to the above woes or probably intrinsically related to it, the Nile annually flooded the region and much of Egypt was anyway underwater, for roughly half the year. In short, all throughout its history, Egypt witnessed a fluctuating landscape wherein water competed with dry land in such a manner that most prudent Egyptians invariably had a handy boat parked right next to the buggy in the shed.

Here is an extract from Herodotus that highlights Egypt's plight when the Nile flooded the country:

> *When the Nile overflows, the country is converted into a sea and nothing appears but the cities, which look like the islands in the Egean. At this season boats no longer keep the course of the river, but sail right across the plain. On the voyage from Naucratis to Memphis at this season, you pass close to the pyramids, whereas the usual course is by the apex of the Delta and the city of Cercasorus. You can sail also from the maritime town of Canobus across the flat to Naucratis, passing by the cities of Anthylla and Archandropolis.*
> *[Herodotus 2.97]*

Clearly, here was a country in deep waters and in dire need for civil engineers by the boatloads. Fortunately, the Egyptians were an optimistic and gregarious lot, who only saw this development as an opportunity to take out their boats and have fun. The Nile flooded the land so completely that the whole of Egypt was submerged and just the cities peeked above the water line, making the whole landscape look like the Aegean Sea with its atypical scatter of islands.

Having set this 'blink and your backyard turns to backwaters' scenario for Egypt, I would now like to explore a central landmark or geographical feature of this region. It was a water body and it was called the Red Sea. Consider the following extracts:

> *Eratosthenes adds to what he has said about Ammon and Egypt his opinion that Mt. Casius was once washed by the sea and also that all the region where the so-called Gerrha now is, was in every part covered with shoal-water since it was connected with the gulf of the Red Sea and that it became uncovered when the seas came together. [Strabo, Geography 1.3.13]*

The 'sea that once washed' Mt. Casius and also 'covered with shoal-water' all the region of the so-called Gerrha mentioned in the above extract, is a reference to the 'Tongue of the Egyptian Sea.' The Tongue ceased to exist and the corridor 'became uncovered' when the seas at the Pillars 'came together.' Yes, the seas that 'came together' mentioned here, is a reference to the outpouring at the Pillars. It refers to a cataclysmic seismic event that caused the waters of the Mediterranean Sea to 'pour out' at the juncture of Pillars of Hercules and thereby fall. Due to this outpouring at the Pillars, the land about Mount Casius and the Gerrha or saltpans in the entire Samandagi-Antakya corridor in Egypt, was exposed. In short, after this seismic-triggered outpouring, the Mediterranean Sea level fell, and 'Tongue of the Egyptian Sea' ceased to exist.

Now, consider the following extract:

> *But Hipparchus, interpreting the phrase "to be connected with" to be the same thing as "to be confluent with," that is, that our Mediterranean Sea "became confluent with" the Red Sea because of its being filled up with water, finds fault by asking why in the world it is that, at the time when our Mediterranean Sea, because of the outflow of its*

*waters at the Pillars, underwent its change in that
direction, it did not also cause the Red Sea, which had
become confluent with it, to make the same change
and why in the world the Red Sea continued at the
same level into being lowered with the Mediterranean?
[Strabo, Geography 1.3.13]*

The above extract goes on to say that the Red Sea, although
confluent with the Mediterranean, undergoes no change, by
this seismically triggered outpouring at the Pillars. Presumably
therefore, Hipparchus assumption that 'being connected' was
equal to 'being confluent' is faulty. In other words, the
Tongue of the Egyptian Sea was not confluent to the Red Sea.
Based on this we may assume that the Red Sea was quite
close but not confluent with the Tongue of the Egyptian Sea.

Clarity on this subject of connectivity and proximity
between the two seas in question, comes by with the yet
another extract. Apparently, an isthmus separated the Tongue
of the Egyptian Sea from the Red Sea. Study the following
extract:

*Hence it is nothing to marvel at even if, at some time,
the isthmus should be parted asunder or else undergo a
settling process—the isthmus that separates the
Egyptian Sea from the Red Sea—and thus disclose a
strait and make the outer sea confluent with the inner,
just as happened in the case of the strait at the Pillars
of Heracles. [Strabo, Geography 1.3.17]*

An isthmus merely a thousand furlongs wide separated the
Egyptian Sea or tongue of the Egyptian Sea from the Red Sea.
World wise scholars speculated that a seismic triggered
settling could very easily have parted the isthmus and make
the inner Red Sea confluent with outer Tongue of the
Egyptian Sea. Much as they hoped for this to happen, it did
not. In was one of those doomsday scenarios that did not pan
out. Another doomsday scenario closely related this was the
one about the level of the Red sea being higher and if

someone were to cut a canal between the two seas, then Egypt will surely be inundated by the waters of the Red Sea.

Talks about parting the isthmus, cutting a canal across it to connect the outer sea or the Egyptian Tongue to the inner Red Sea, so as to facilitate commerce with Arabia and India (via Arabia), were indeed bandied about for long. In fact, various attempts were made by kings through the ages to complete the project. This topic is materially covered in the next chapter.

Moving on, here are a few extracts that suggests that the Red Sea was hard to navigate a shallow sea with 'tree growing in it.' Study the following two extracts:

> It is said that Philadelphus was the first person, by means of an army, to cut this road, which is without water and to build stations, as though for the travels of merchants on camels and that he did this because the Red Sea was hard to navigate, particularly for those who set sail from its innermost recess. [Strabo, Geography 17.1.45]

> Along the whole of the coast of the Red Sea, down in the deep, grow trees like the laurel and the olive, which at the ebb tides are wholly visible above the water but at the full tides are sometimes wholly covered; and while this is the case, the land that lies above the sea has no trees and therefore the peculiarity is all the greater. [Strabo, Geography 16.3.6]

The first extract informs us that the Red Sea was hard to navigate, possibly because of shallow waters. The second extract informs us that trees like the laurel and the olive grew along its shores and they were wholly submerged during full tide.

Compiling all the above information, it become clear that the Red Sea in question was 1000 furlongs from the Tongue of the Egyptian Sea, and that it was shallow difficult to navigate body of water that had trees growing along its banks in such a manner that they get inundated during full tide. In short, the Red Sea mentioned here was in reality a large inland lake that looked like a sea, very much like how the Lake Moeris is described by Herodotus.

Unfortunately, such an inland sea does not exist anywhere close to Antakya. So, where would I fit the Red Sea in my reconstruction?

The answer to the above question is 'in the Al Ghab depression.' In fact, exactly such a shallow sea did indeed exist not very far back in the past in this region. Sadly, however, a 100-million dollar reclamation project has effectively wiped out this famous geographical landmark feature from the face of the earth. The Syrian government built dams, irrigation canals and what not and drained the Al Ghab to recover some 85,000 acres of farmland. The indigenous marsh people, who dwelt in this marshy sea and its vicinity, have being resettled on this reclaimed land. New villages have been laid out in ingenious clusters, complete with roads, power and telephone lines. The fishermen's cottages that were thatched with reeds from this sea and were visible until very recently, too have gone. The only trace or evidence of the Red Sea is the watermark that is still visible halfway up the mountainsides.[1]

Modern-day scholars assume that the Red Sea and the Arabian Gulf referred to here, were the modern-day Arabian Sea and that the Persian Gulf respectively. This is erroneous. The Red Sea was a shallow inland sea and the Arabian Gulf associated with it, was a long narrow gulf of this inland sea.

Actually, the Bible puts the Red Sea in the proper perspective and at once establishes the true nature of this sea in clear and unambiguous terms, by calling this sea the 'Sea of Reed.' Being in essence a swampy sea, this sea was perhaps overgrown with papyrus or byblus reeds and it is conceivable that it looked like a vast undulating sea of reeds. Being in the habit of renaming everything under the sun with descriptive names, the Jews had longed since named it the 'Yum suph' or the Sea of Reeds.

Even from amongst the Greek scholar there is Damastes (whom Eratosthenes quotes and who in turn is quoted by Strabo) who suggests the same thing. According to Damastes, the Arabian Gulf (a gulf of the Red Sea) was actually a lake. Here is the reference:

> *Eratosthenes himself tells us one of the absurd stories of Damastes, who assumes that the Arabian Gulf is a lake. [Strabo, Geography 1.3.1]*

As can be seen, even Strabo has difficulty in accepting this concept. This confirms a fact that I have suspected all along. The Red Sea and its Arabian Gulf had ceased to exist long before Strabo's time. Possibly these too were partially drained by the tectonic event that is said to have caused the outpour at the Pillars and drained the Tongue of the Egyptian Sea. The 100-million dollar reclamation project merely removed what was left of it.

To conclude, in my reconstruction, the Red Sea reassumes or reverts to its original biblical term for this sea. Indeed, I see no earthly reason to doubt the Bible's accurate, keenly sensitive and descriptive name, the 'Yum suph' or 'Reed Sea' for this body of water. For the Red Sea was exactly that: A vast undulating Sea of Reeds. The term 'Red Sea' or even

'Erythraean Sea' was never used in the Bible. It was always Reed Sea. Later however, it was changed to read 'Red Sea' in accordance to the vacillating dictates of the biblical archaeologists, a fact that is now readily admitted to by this beleaguered fraternity in these trying days.

Comment

The Reed Sea was a central landmark of Egypt. The burgeoning Jewish population in Egypt knew it well of course, having on many an occasion sat by its shores and wished that they too had a little sea like this one all to themselves, with maybe just a little bit of land to go with it.

While deep in such idle talks, perhaps it was noted by the Jewish men of yore, let us say, by a threesome, bosom buddies who unduly chafed under the ever increasing Egyptian yoke, that the Reed Sea was shallow enough to be waded through, but would readily bog down chariots, if that is, chariots were to follow, say in pursuit. One amongst them, his wit sharpened by a recent lashing, added that the lake was very long but hardy a tenth or so wide. If a man were to wade across, he could put a prodigious distance between him and his pursuers. The chariots, been unable to follow, would have to go all around. Another subversive mind contributed that escaping into the marshy sea was not a novel idea at all. On the contrary, it was the traditional escape route for Egyptian fugitives. Any and everybody who wanted to throw off a pursuer promptly splashed into the Yum suph and took shelter in any one of the numerous islands in the sea. It would therefore be a mistake to make a beeline for the lake. Best to mislead the pursuers at first, say, by going in the opposite direction and later on try and make a dash through the Yum suph, was his considered opinion.

After much deliberation, denunciation, delegating and dilly-dallying, the three compatriots were observed making a hesitant PowerPoint presentation (read drawings in the sand) to a man named Moses whom they knew to be at his wit's end wondering how he could possibly outwit the pursuing Pharaoh's chariots, were he to lead the Jews out of Egypt. Much to their horror and delight, Moses did exactly that. He planned an elaborate subterfuge that confused the enemy, confounded its infantry in the wilderness and then made a dash through the Yum suph to successfully evade the Pharaoh's chariots!

The above-mentioned three compatriots... well, at least their PowerPoint presentation, is entirely fictitious of course! But, without a doubt, the low-lying region known as the 'Al Ghab' that extends almost along the entire length of Jabal an Nusayriyah Mountains in Syria and formerly a vast reed-choked sea, was the Sea of Reeds that Moses so famously cleaved!

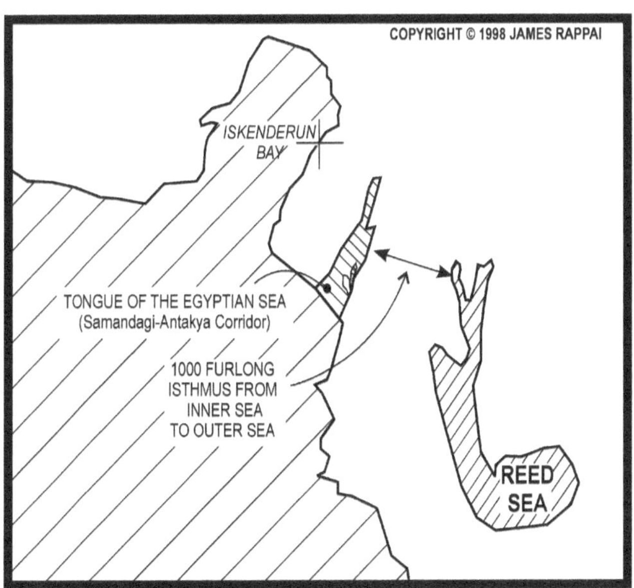

Diagram 9a: **Reed Sea:** *A shallow, vast marshy sea that previously existed in the Al Ghab region was the Sea of Reeds. The Arabian Gulf was in reality a gulf of the Reed Sea. A narrow, 1000 furlongs wide neck portion or isthmus separated this inland sea from the outer Mediterranean or then called Tongue of the Egypt Sea.*

CHAPTER 38

THE NECOS-DARIUS CANAL

An isthmus separated the Tongue of Egyptian Sea from the Reed Sea. Study the following extract:

> *Hence it is nothing to marvel at even if, at some time, the isthmus should be parted asunder or else undergo a settling process—the isthmus that separates the Egyptian Sea from the Red Sea—and thus disclose a strait and make the outer sea confluent with the inner, just as happened in the case of the strait at the Pillars of Heracles. [Strabo, Geography 1.3.17]*

The isthmus that separated the Egyptian Sea, or more accurately the Tongue portion of the Egyptian Sea, from the Reed Sea was merely a thousand furlongs wide. Talks about cutting a canal across it, to connect the outer sea or the Egyptian Tongue to the inner Reed Sea, so as to facilitate commerce with Arabia and India (via Arabia), were bandied about for long. In fact, various attempts were made by kings through the ages to complete the project.

> *Psammetichus left a son called Necos, who succeeded him upon the throne. This prince was the first to attempt the construction of the canal to the Red Sea— a work completed afterwards by Darius the Persian— the length of which is four days' journey and the width such as to admit of two triremes being rowed along it abreast. The water is derived from the Nile, which the canal leaves a little above the city of Bubastis, near Patumus, the Arabian town, being continued thence until it joins the Red Sea. At first it is carried along the Arabian side of the Egyptian plain, as far as the chain of hills opposite Memphis, whereby the plain is bounded and in which lie the great stone quarries; here it skirts the base of the hills running in a direction from*

*west to east, after which it turns and enters a narrow
pass, trending southwards from this point until it enters
the Arabian Gulf. From the northern sea to that which
is called the southern or Erythraean, the shortest and
quickest passage, which is from Mount Casius, the
boundary between Egypt and Syria, to the Gulf of
Arabia, is a distance of exactly one thousand furlongs.
[Herodotus 2.158]*

Pharaoh Necos, it is said, was the first to attempt to connect the Egyptian Sea with the Reed Sea by means of a canal. The distance was roughly a thousand furlongs and it would have greatly facilitated commerce with the Arabians.

Necos was however dissuaded from completing it. Apparently, the level of the Reed Sea was higher than the Egyptian Tongue and the engineers feared that opening a canal would inundate Egypt. Another fear was that the canal would facilitate aggressors... that it would compromise the kingdom's safety... and so the development project was abandoned halfway. Much later, the Persian Monarch Darius, ruler of Persia and Egypt, completed the project.

As can be seen, the Necos-Darius canal fits snugly into my reconstruction scenario. The two seas, the thousand furlong wide isthmus which the canal was required to cut through, are all available here. The Arabian and Syrian neighbors mentioned in this context, who also perhaps used the canal, too are here at the periphery, at the required distances.

Egyptologists too, have reconstructed this canal in their reconstruction scenario. Having erroneously identified Egypt in Africa, and anxious to have this canal in their settings, these enterprising scholars have literally dug a canal connecting the Nile-in-Africa to the Red Sea by means of a canal that connects these two parallel water bodies. Although they may get full marks for innovation and engineering excellence, this canal is patently false.

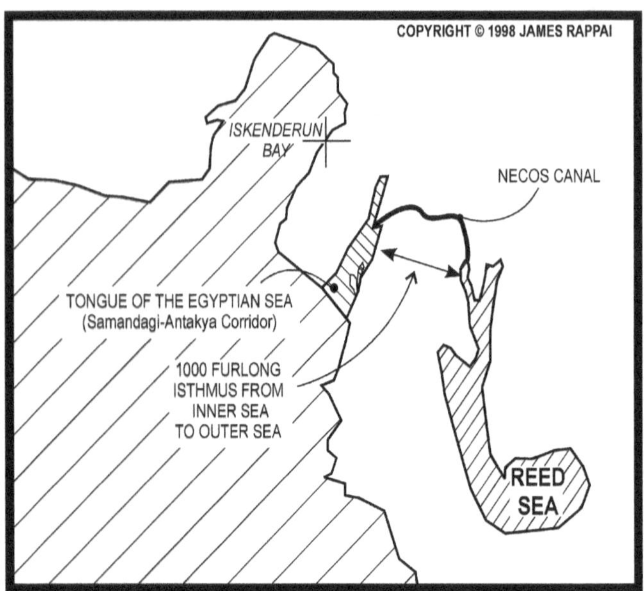

Diagram 9b: **Necos canal:** A canal was cut through the 1000 furlong isthmus that separated inland Red Sea from the outer Tongue of the Egypt Sea. Pharaoh Necos King of Egypt had initiated it, but gave up, fearing the oracle's words, that he was merely facilitating his enemies by creating an easy of passage for them. Another fear was that the waters of the Red Sea were thought to be higher and cutting a canal would cause its waters to rush into Egypt and flood it. The Persian Monarch completed the canal, regardless of these doomsday scenarios, but had blocked it when Alexander was right around the corner. The canal, the 1000 furlong isthmus, the two seas, all of it, you will find forming a perfect fit in my reconstruction model

CHAPTER 39

CIRCUMNAVIGATION

Scholars of old believed that one could set sail from the Red Sea, circumnavigate the land, and eventually sail in into the Mediterranean and the Pillars. However, after a few attempts at making this crossing, it was felt that perhaps the seas were not connected after all and that a landmass or an isthmus separated the two seas. Here is the extract:

> *But Ethiopia may be divided in still another way, quite apart from this. For all those who have made coasting-voyages on the ocean along the shores of Libya, whether they started from the Red Sea or from the Pillars of Heracles, always turned back, after they had advanced a certain distance, because they were hindered by many perplexing circumstances and consequently they left in the minds of most people the conviction that the intervening space was blocked by an isthmus; and yet the whole Atlantic Ocean is one unbroken body of water and this is particularly true of the Southern Atlantic. [Strabo, Geography 1.2.26]*

Ancient world scholars during Homer's time had this idea that the Oceanus was an unbroken body of water that rimmed the land and that all the seas were gulfs of this ocean. According to this model, the Red Sea and the Mediterranean, being 'gulf seas' were connected to the main Oceanus and therefore it should have been possible to go from the Red Sea to the Mediterranean Sea (and the Pillars) and vice versa. In short, one could come down from either of these gulfs make a u-turn in the Oceanus and happily sail up the other gulf.

Perhaps not all were convinced by this ideology. This is why some of them did undertake to sail from the Red Sea to the Mediterranean via the Oceanus. That an isthmus blocked the passage came as a shock, and sent scholars back to their drawing boards, to worry that rudimentary map of the world (that looked like a shrunken rotten orange) they had so painstakingly drawn.

To be sure, the existence and finding of this particular isthmus must have upset quite a few apple carts. Not only did it effectively overturn all their preconceived geography of this region, but very likely it also broke the back of the then held sacred ideology that the Oceanus was an unbroken body of water that circumscribed the world. Furthermore, with the dismantling of the Oceanus ideology, the flat world ideology too must have taken a severe beating.

These then were the wonderful days when man was just beginning to garner the courage to sail across a 10-mile stretch of deep sea and see what manner of people were their neighbors. The reason for the failure of the above expedition was lack of knowledge. The Red Sea was an inland sea and not connected to the Oceanus. Even the Oceanus concept was a faulty one. In fact, the whole model of the world needed to be brought in for a major bout of overhauling.

If we were to reconstruct this region based on the then held beliefs, then Ethiopia would be no further than where Tartus in modern-day Syria is situated. Not much further, south of this latitude, one would reach the shores of the Oceanus, the outermost and continuous body of water that circumscribed the world and rimmed this particular region at this point. This is why Homer believed that the Ethiopians lived at the edge of the world, on the shores of the Oceanus and that they were 'sundered in twain' by the Nile (as they lived on either sides of the river) and what not.

However, before you laugh at Homer, be aware that the ideology of the Oceanus as described above is, in essence, true. What is more, this concept from antiquity has been adopted by modern-day oceanographers and now masquerades under the contemporary name of 'World Ocean.' It appears that reclassifying the contiguous body of water that covers and encircles most of the Earth's surface as one gargantuan ocean, rather than smaller seas and oceans,

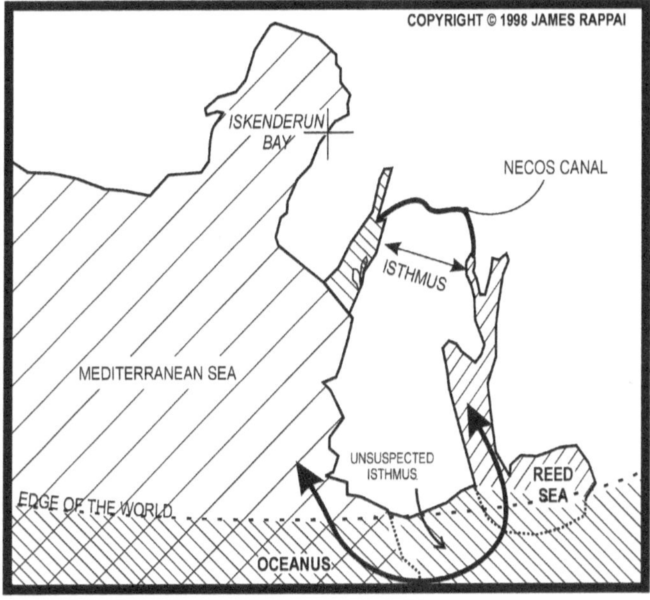

*Diagram 10: **Sailing from the Reed Sea to the Egyptian (Mediterranean) Sea:** (Above) Based on the then assumed geography of this region, the Reed Sea and the Mediterranean were thought to have been gulf seas of the circumventing Oceanus. Therefore, it was assumed that one could traverse from one sea to the other after making a u-turn in the Oceanus. Numerous failed voyages later revealed this model to be deficient. An isthmus (as indicated) blocked passage.*

apparently makes more oceanographic sense.

CHAPTER 40

THE TWIN GULF POINTER

In Arabia, not far from Egypt, there is a long and narrow gulf running inland from the sea called the Erythraean, of which I will here set down the dimensions. Starting from its innermost recess and using a row-boat, you take forty days to reach the open main, while you may cross the gulf at its widest part in the space of half a day. In this sea there is an ebb and flow of the tide every day. My opinion is that Egypt was formerly very much such a gulf as this—one gulf penetrated from the sea that washes Egypt on the north and extended itself towards Ethiopia; another entered from the southern ocean and stretched towards Syria; the two gulfs ran into the land so as almost to meet each other and left between them only a very narrow tract of country. [Herodotus 2.11]

In this paragraph, Herodotus proves himself to have been more than a gifted historian. He doggedly pursues a pet theory and establishes himself as a geologist of superlative distinction as well. That Egypt was gifted by the river was old news now. Even the Egyptians were aware of it and beginning to give our obsessed little historian a wide berth. He therefore speculates wildly, desperately. Fortunately for us, his theories that may have won him no more than a few tolerant smiles or bewildered looks from the besieged Greek academia, serve invaluably to establish the true whereabouts of Egypt.

Incidentally, what Herodotus is referring to here is the fact that the Egypt valley was situated in a unique geological formation that gave it a 'trough' like look. Adjacent to it in another similar 'trough' was the Arabian Gulf of the Reed Sea. It is a simple thing really, but Herodotus appears to have sniffed out something else here as well. Let us see what it is this time.

Herodotus notes that formerly the Egypt trough was a water-filled gulf, like its southern counterpart. However, thanks to the River Nile's marked tendency to deposit silt, it was filled and became an eminently habitable valley. He then speculates. If the Nile were to flow into the Arabian Gulf instead, then that gulf would have been filled up, say, in a span of twenty thousand years.

Any ideas what is going on in his head? No? Well, that is because this particular theory is a tad unbaked; our man was not quite able to crack it. Let us therefore, examine this convolute theory with a little bit of help from modern technology and see if we can set it free.

Resorting to satellite photography, we realize with a start, exactly what our heroic historian was struggling to conceptualize. The eye in the sky sees a massive rift, beginning from Mozambique in Africa and extending all the way to Syria in the Near East. In its Near Eastern sector, it is home to various water bodies, beginning with the Gulf of Aqaba, the Dead Sea, the Jordan Valley, the Sea of Galilee, the marshes of the Hula Valley, the Bekaa Valley and finally ending with the Al Ghab depression in modern-day Syria. Segments of this rift are home to various water bodies. The rest of the rift presents itself as incredibly fertile valleys, converted as such, by silt deposited there for eons. The sides of these rift valleys have a classic 'slipped or sheared off' profile, which too must have caught the historian's attention. Incidentally, this is the longest rift valley in the world and is known as the Great Rift Valley.

It is this massive rift valley that snagged on poor Herodotus' line! What had originally caught the historian's attention were the sedimentary deposits in the Egyptian valley and possibly the valley's unique 'sheared off' sides. He was astute enough to catch all these details, but the full picture still eluded him.

Incidentally, this is typically how we make a brilliant discovery. Little details are dangled in front of our eyes, until finally, after many a failed attempt, it finally registers on us. This is laboriously followed up with the next clue. Again, dangle, dangle, and so on until we begin to 'discern the pieces falling together' and finally make the discovery. In short, while we may consider ourselves great scholars, brilliant discoverers, or inventors, the humiliating truth is that 'cosmic intelligence' sits on our shoulders and literally spoon feeds us every morsel. What is more, everything is done for us in a carefully orchestrated manner, intended to make us believe that we are indeed the doers. In truth, we are puppets, incapable of doing anything independently. The infinitesimal particle soul is incapable of manipulating matter. If and when we manage to see through this deception, then we can consider ourselves to have become self-realized.

Getting back to Herodotus and his latest preoccupation, we see him mentally transpose the virulent Nile into the other valley, play around with the timeframe and generally think aloud, trying to make sense of it all. Indeed, one can see his mind take those baby steps... see him laboriously trying to make sense of it all... and note that he is actually no more than a few clicks away from cracking it—and discover in the process, the Great Rift Valley. But no, he is too thick headed and falls short.

Although Herodotus failed to haul in the Great Rift Valley ideology, he did leave us with some vital clues regarding the exact location of ancient Egypt. The key observation here is of course the fact that the Nile could easily have diverted its waters to the Arabian Gulf of the Reed Sea, instead of flowing through the Egypt valley. This would mean that the two gulfs in question were adjacent to each other in such a manner, that the Nile could have chosen to flow into either of the said gulfs.

I closely examined my reconstructed arena for the above topographical feature and eventually managed to find it. The north of the Al Ghab Basin is bifurcated into two by the Jabel El Wastani mount. The mount effectively separates the basin into two troughs. The western trough was Upper Egypt and the eastern trough (the Balou trough) was occupied by a long narrow gulf of my Reed Sea that was called the 'Arabian Gulf.'

Incidentally, the twin gulf scenario cannot be established in the currently accepted reconstructed scenario of Egypt. Modern-day scholar's Upper Egypt does not lie in a trough created by parallel mountains and neither can their Red Sea be filled up with sediments by their Nile in 20,000 years. All these are grave discrepancies that would ordinarily be enough reason to reject the current reconstruction model.

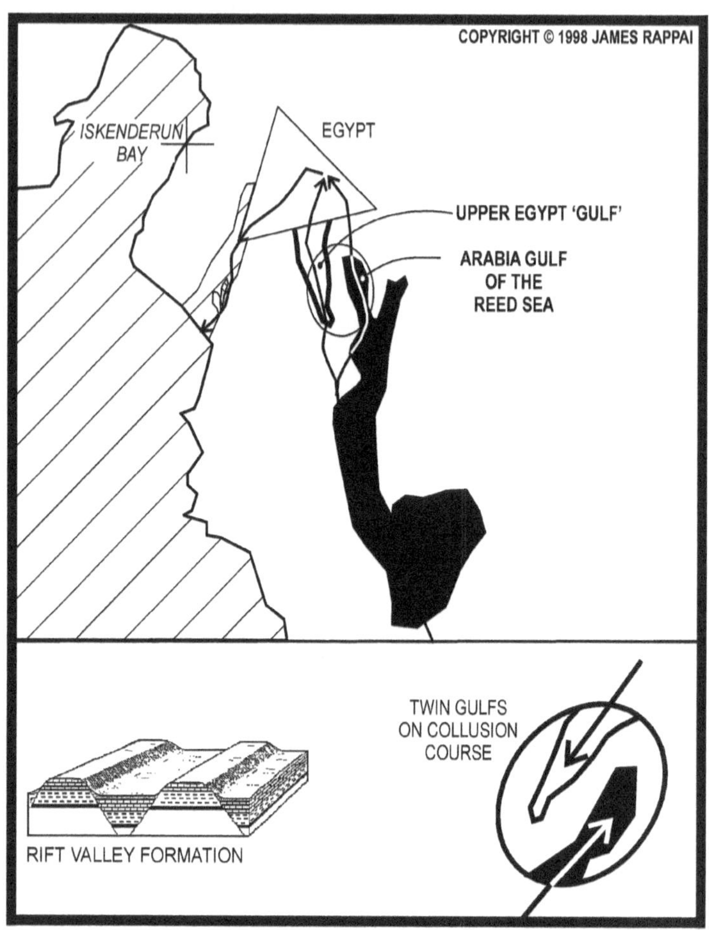

Diagram 11: **Herodotus' 'twin gulf on collusion course' observation explained.** *The key observations are: one, the Egypt valley and the Arabian Gulf (of the Reed Sea) presented similar but curious 'troughs shaped' valleys (possibly with sheared-off sides) with heavy silt deposits. Two, the Nile, instead of flowing through Egypt, could just as easily have diverted its waters into the Arabian Gulf (and eventually choked it with silt). The first we may reinterpret as Herodotus struggling to conceptualize the 'rift' valley formation. The second suggests that the troughs in question were adjacent to each other and that the Nile could theoretically flow into either trough.*

CHAPTER 41

THE NILE-ORONTES

We have now identified the shoreline of Ancient Egypt, the distinctive Delta region and the narrow region called Upper Egypt, all unambiguously and irrefutably located in the region currently occupied by Syria, including a portion of southern Turkey.

Our next task is to determine if the river present in our scenario fits the profile of the Nile. The river in question is the Orontes or Asi, which flows into Syria from the Bekaa Valley in Lebanon and exits into the Mediterranean Sea close to where Mount Casius is located.

With its banks lined with tamarisk, the Orontes may not exactly simulate images of the mighty River Nile. This I suspect may be partially due to the fact that scholars who came after Herodotus, such as Strabo and others, say roughly after 100 BC, consciously or unconsciously used the 450 BC historian's documentation of Egypt as a template. They did so because, one, it was available as a document to peruse and two, the Egypt documented in its pages had changed or no longer existed.

Whatever the reason, what I would like to point out is the fact that while busy regurgitating handed-down wisdom, they perhaps failed to take in the fact, that Herodotus' fascination and extensive documentation of the River Nile, was largely a scientific journey of discovery. All that did register upon them was the fact that there was much written about the river and therefore they too should follow course.

However, in the hands of these later-date scholars (who perhaps did not have a single scientific bone between them), Herodotus' scientific expositions on the Nile's idiosyncratic colors made no sense. They were therefore perfunctorily reinterpreted into commoner hue, that better suited a river—such as accentuated girth and depth—and before long the Nile surpassed even the mighty Amazon in its strides. Indeed, what afflicted the Nile was the same malady that invariably smites all our yesteryear heroes. In real life, they were perhaps ordinary looking men but allow a few hundred years to go and invariably they are transformed into men of great stature, strength and achievement.

The truth is, the Nile was a funny bird and not particularly a fabulous one. It flooded at odd times, served an a border between two continents in a manner that created much controversy (somebody forgot to make room for Egypt!), gave forth no breezes from its surface and so on and so forth, so much so that Herodotus though it "opposite in nature to all other streams."

> *I was particularly anxious to learn from them why the Nile, at the commencement of the summer solstice, begins to rise and continues to increase for a hundred days—and why, as soon as that number is past, it forthwith retires and contracts its stream, continuing low during the whole of the winter until the summer solstice comes round again. On none of these points could I obtain any explanation from the inhabitants, though I made every inquiry, wishing to know what was commonly reported—they could neither tell me what special virtue the Nile has which makes it so opposite in its nature to all other streams, nor why, unlike every other river, it gives forth no breezes from its surface. [Herodotus 2.19]*

The Nile was very likely curious to some extent, but I suspect that its mild eccentricities got racked up a notch or two by

Herodotus himself, who was obliged to churn out interesting material for his book. Indeed, he had hit upon the theme that 'Egyptians did just about everything the opposite way compared to the rest of the world.' The women attended the markets and trade, while the men sit at home at the loom, they worked the warp up the woof, their women carry burdens upon their shoulders, while the men themselves carried it upon their heads, eat their food on the streets but defecated inside their homes, knead dough with their feet and clay with their hands, kept animals indoors so on and so forth, all of which the rest of the sane world did the other way round. Very likely, the good historian was trying to jam this topsy-turvy hat on the Nile's head as well.

Yet another reason why the Nile assumed Amazonian dimensions may be due to the fact that the river in the reconstructed scenario of Egypt in the African continent, is in fact an Amazonian river and this may have slanted the description of the Nile in the translation stage. Canon Rawlinson's robust and rubicund demeanor that strongly suggests 'not averse to nudging the heathens along' might well be responsible in consciously tweaking Herodotus' 'funny' to 'fabulous,' thereby giving us an 'mighty Amazon' instead of a 'niggling and quibbling Nile' that Herodotus strains to portray!

In truth, the Nile was a 'rebel' river of sorts and not surprisingly, this indeed is the appellation given to the Orontes as well. In fact, the local name of the river is 'Asi,' which means rebel! What is more, each and every eccentricity that Herodotus documents with regards to the Nile, is immediately observable in the Orontes.

Archaeological finds on the banks of the Orontes too may help discern the truth. These include a few biblical names such as Kadesh (on the Orontes) and the Hama Pass that may offer some insights into the matter.

Incidentally, 'Kadesh on the Orontes' here represents a double entry, as bewildering as the double entry practiced by accountants and signals that something is seriously wrong with the reconstruction. At any rate, this second Kadesh, the one fashionably called 'Kadesh on the Orontes,' is reasonably close to where I would place my Kadesh, the real and only one that is, in my reconstructed scenario of the biblical arena.

Inspired by this unexpected largesse from the Levantine scholars, if I were to extrapolate instinctively, freely, I would without hesitation, equate the Tamarisk Mannifera that lined the banks of the Orontes, as the genus that bountifully supplied manna to the Jews on their sojourn. The extensive marshy lake formed by the Orontes in the Al Ghab depression would be the 'the Yum suph,' the same marshy sea that was parted by Moses. 'Kadesh on the Orontes' will anchor the real Kadesh and the Homs Gap near this region in Syria would be 'the entrance to Hamah' of the biblical text. All of these are a natural, hand-in-glove fit that require no stretching of the imagination or elaborate fixes. But enough of instinctive extrapolation, lest my detractors call me a capricious fool. As before, I shall plod on collating and presenting evidence of a more substantial nature to help resolve the Nile-Orontes equation.

THE SNOW MELT THEORY

Someone, not Herodotus (though he graciously recorded it), mentioned that the river Nile flooded in the summer months due to the melting of snow. Herodotus however does not support it. He not only rejected the snowmelt theory, but goes on to present a hypothesis of his own that leaves much to be desired. Let us see what tripped our intrepid historian here.

> *Now, as the Nile flows out of Libya, through Ethiopia, into Egypt, how is it possible that it can be formed of melted snow, running, as it does, from the hottest regions of the world into cooler countries? Many are the proofs whereby any one capable of reasoning on the subject may be convinced that it is most unlikely this should be the case. The first and strongest argument is furnished by the winds, which always blow hot from these regions. The second is that rain and frost are unknown there. Now whenever snow falls, it must of necessity rain within five days, so that, if there were snow, there must be rain also in those parts. Thirdly, it is certain that the natives of the country are black with the heat, that the kites and the swallows remain there the whole year and that the cranes, when they fly from the rigours of a Scythian winter, flock thither to pass the cold season. If then, in the country whence the Nile has its source, or in that through which it flows, there fell ever so little snow, it is absolutely impossible that any of these circumstances could take place. [Herodotus 2.22]*

Above, Herodotus heatedly argues that the Nile flowed from the depths of Ethiopia, which was one of the hottest regions of the world. Hot winds constantly blew into Egypt from this region, he avers. Also look at the inhabitants; they are burnt black due to the region's extreme heat. Attacking it from the opposite flank, he states, that if it did snow, it ought to rain as well. But Egypt received almost no rainfall! Expertly netting in a bewildered flock of migratory birds to support his arguments he says: Scythian Cranes and other migratory birds flock to Egypt, to evade the harsh winter. Why would they come to Egypt if it snowed here as well?

After having melted down the snowmelt theory with a blast of fiery arguments, steeped in keen scientific observations, Herodotus offers his own take on the subject. Unfortunately, it has not the brilliance or the cutting-edge scientific reasoning that he employs to overthrow the snowmelt theory. On the contrary, this one has something to do with an alchemy of dark forces, typical of the ancient world and threatening to shatter the image of a 'scientist' we had so painstakingly built for the man.

Why did Herodotus go so wrong? What really caused the Nile to flood so unreasonably, so unseasonably in summer? To unravel this Gordian knot, let us transport this whole scenario into our Egypt-in-Syria reconstruction theatre.

The Nile here is the River Orontes and immediately, one mystery at least, is quickly resolved. The Orontes does in fact draw its waters from the snowy peaks of the Lebanon and Anti-Lebanon Mountains. Unknown to Herodotus, perpetual snow and ice is indeed found atop these mountains. It melts during the summer months and consequently the Nile-Orontes floods the Egyptian plains during the summer. The snowmelt theory offered by an unknown Herodotus source is accurate.

But, why was Herodotus unaware of this fact? The reason is simple. Herodotus had no clear knowledge of the river Nile's source, as he himself admits. In fact, finding the Nile's source was one of his main agendas. He tried, but was unable to make his expedition deep into the heart of Ethiopia, to find the fount of the Nile. His knowledge of the terrain here was acquired by quizzing Ethiopians at his interview stand high up in the mountains of Elephantine. Indeed, he had gathered some very wide-eyed information about this dark region... of cattle that grazed backwards, of beasts with eyes on their chest and what not, all of which threatened to turn his head away from the newfangled science that he was preaching. Dismissing these with an effort (cattle grazing backwards can be very disconcerting) and focusing on more reasonable things, such as the region was hot and the people burnt black and adding to it, his own observation on migratory birds, etc., he thought that he had sufficiently researched grounds to rubbish the snowmelt theory. The place was much too hot for snow and ice.

Unfortunately, for once, he was wrong.

It may interest readers to know that modern-day scholars had readily vetoed the snowmelt theory. Perhaps they did so without thinking, basing their reasoning on their innate experience with snow and ice and its propensity to melt and flood rivers. Had they given it a thought, they would have realized that finding snow for their Nile near the Sahara Desert would be a bit tricky. But commit they did and so hastily trotted off into the desert to find their snow. Finally, after a desperate search, snow was reportedly found in the Abyssinian Mountains. There is much controversy however regarding this find. Was it snow or guano... now that we will never know!

NORIAS

Perhaps the most romantic and visually attractive feature of the Orontes is the Noria, or waterwheel. Water is lifted up from the river by these wheels and carried dripping to the top, where it spills out into aqueducts and runs down to the fields or houses below. The system is inefficient, but cheaper and more reliable than pumps and of course, infinitely more charming. At night, when traffic noise ceases, the town echoes with the creaking music of these wheels.

The most impressive aspect about these wheels is their immense size. They are monstrous contraptions, of which there are many on the Orontes, often in excess of 70 feet in diameter. Besides, they are ancient. Indeed, waterwheels were reportedly seen on the Orontes in 1812, by John Lewis Burckhardt. Here is the extract:

> *There are four bridges over the Orontes in the town. The river supplies the upper town with water by means of buckets fixed to high wheels (Naoura), which empty themselves into stone canals, supported by lofty arches on a level with the upper parts of the town. There are about a dozen of the wheels; the largest of them, called Naoura el Mohammedye, is at least seventy feet in diameter. [John Lewis Burckhardt, Travels in Syria and the Holy Land, page 146][1]*

Burckhardt was incidentally a thoroughly energetic gentlemen, a regular crusader sort, who bulldozed his way through the Near East a number of times, furiously documenting everything in his path.

However, 1812 is perhaps not early enough. The Norias very likely went much further back in time. That would mean we ought to find mention of the Norias in Herodotus' or Strabo's text.

But before I undertake this impossible task, I think that perhaps I should raise the stakes, super-size it, as they say. Let us see now... perhaps I should strive to produce proof of the waterwheels way back in antiquity and that too in the vicinity of the pyramids. There now, this should satisfy even the most skeptical of my readers. Indeed, what could be more convincing than to see a Noria creakingly at work right at the foot of the pyramids?

Here then is a verse by Strabo documented in 64 BC that would do very nicely:

> *There is a ridge extending from the encampment even as far as the Nile, on which the water is conducted up from the river by wheels and screws; and one hundred and fifty prisoners are employed in the work; and from*

A curious contraption apparently was used to transport water of the Nile up a ridge. "...water is conducted up from the river by wheels and screws... from here one can clearly see the pyramids... at Memphis!"

There it is! Waterwheels on the Nile by the pyramids at Memphis! What, not good enough? Perhaps, Herodotus then has something to report about waterwheels way back in 450 BC.

Alas, Herodotus does not mention waterwheels. But wait, let us not write him off as yet. I have a minor side theory here that may well tie him to the norias.

Now, Herodotus certainly was the first to notice that the land in Egypt was rising alarmingly. He had then direly predicted that if this trend continued, then Egypt would soon face a major water crisis. Perhaps the Egyptians did take Herodotus doomsday scenario seriously after all and devised the ponderous Norias to resolve their impending water crisis.

The proclivity to sense a doomsday scenario, to see a trickle and somehow sense an avalanche in waiting, one that would surely send the world hurtling out of control, if a grave and well-informed person such as himself (or the scientists in question) did not immediately intervene has defined our men of science. Herodotus here is no exception. Scientists, the ones who take a quick peek behind the curtains so to speak, invariably surface with a bad case of 'God blues.' It has, I have always believed, something to do with the number of balls that God so effortlessly juggles.

> *Now according to him the Nile is nine hundred or a thousand stadia distant towards the west from the Arabian Gulf and is similar in shape to the letter N written reversed. [Strabo, Geography 17.1.2]*

In the extract quoted above, Strabo offers two distinct pointers by which we can identify the Nile. One, it is about a thousand stadia west of the Arabian Gulf. And, two, the Nile's course through Egypt was similar in shape to the letter 'N' written in reverse.

Now, the first clue that the Nile was nine hundred or a thousand fathoms west of the Arabian Gulf, is an oblique reference to the 1000 fathoms wide isthmus between the Tongue of the Egyptian Sea (the Mediterranean that hugs the Near East coast) and the Reed Sea. The Arabian Gulf mentioned here was a long narrow gulf of the Reed Sea. Here is Herodotus' original version:

> *From the northern sea to that which is called the southern or Erythraean, the shortest and quickest passage, which is from Mount Casius, the boundary between Egypt and Syria, to the Gulf of Arabia, is a distance of exactly one thousand furlongs. [Herodotus 2.158]*

> *In Egypt the tract is at first a narrow neck, the distance from our sea to the Erythraean not exceeding a hundred thousand fathoms, in other words, a thousand furlongs.[Herodotus 4.41]*

Both the above extracts offer the thousand furlongs wide, isthmus ideology that separated the two seas. The sea mentioned as northern or 'our' is the Mediterranean Sea, and by extension the Tongue of the Egyptian Sea. Southern or Erythraean, and the Gulf of Arabia all refers to the Reed Sea. Having discerned that the Nile presumably hugged the western side of the isthmus, Strabo merely repackaged the above information as the distance between the Arabian Gulf and the Nile. It is the nine hundred that he offers here that gives his game away.

The second clue that Strabo offers is unique. The Nile traces a reverse letter 'N' is an entirely new observation. The Nile-Orontes does in fact trace exactly such a zigzag pattern. See attached diagram.

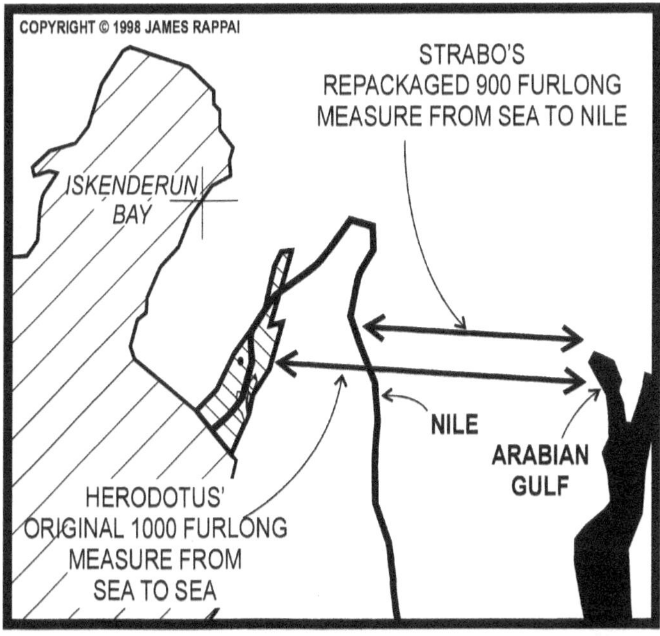

*Diagram 12: **The Nile's 900 furlong.** Strabo documents that the Nile was 900 furlongs (roughly 78 miles) west of the Arabian Gulf of the Reed Sea. This seems to be a back-of-the-envelope calculation based on the pervious observation made by Herodotus, which states that the neck region or the distance between the two seas was 1000 furlongs. Diagram 13: **The Nile's inverted 'N' shape.** (Next page)The Nile had an inverted 'N' shape, documents Strabo. The above-indicated shape of Nile-Orontes was perhaps what he was referring to here.*

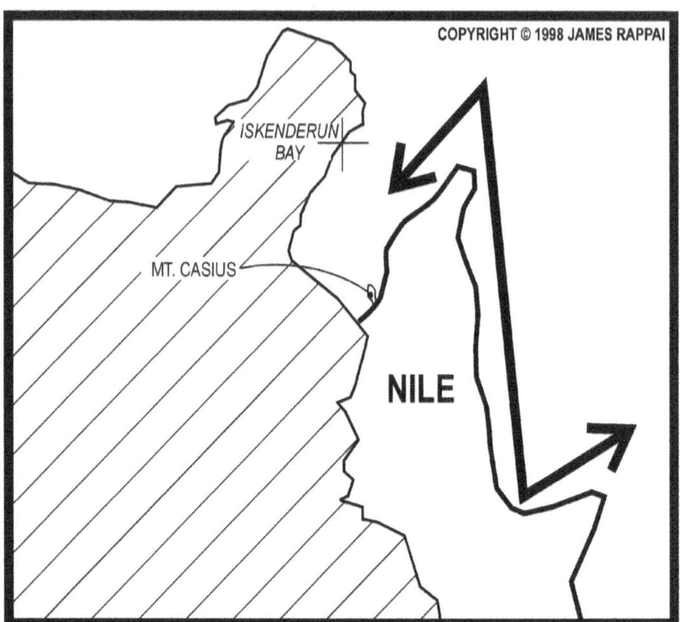

*Diagram 14: **Noria.** (Next page, below) Evidently, these gargantuan waterwheels were an Egyptian invention that were possibly inspired and indeed dimensioned on Herodotus' doomsday scenario calculations!*

LIBYA

In a bid to bring order to the world, ancient world Greek scholars divided the known world into three continents. Europe, Asia and Libya. Separating Europe from Asia was easy as the Black Sea, Sea of Marmara and the Aegean provided a clean break between the landmasses. Separating the Libyan continent from Asia, on the contrary, was plagued with confusion.

Someone floated the idea that the River Nile be chosen to form the line of demarcation between the Asian and Libyan continent. Very likely, the river was chosen as it was a water body, and as such, could physically separate the landmasses in question with a clean break. However, this decision did not go down well with most, for rivers served as lifelines of settlements that invariably straddled the river, spread out on either banks, and ingeniously used it as a fluid, multi-accessed highway. Using a river as a line of divide, would split these settlements right down the middle. Ancient world historians, who recognized this conflict of ideas, invariably raised a stink about this issue.

But why was the Nile chosen in the first place? How could it conceivably have served as representing a clean and unambiguous break between two landmasses that needed to be differentiated? Why for that matter, was it felt that Libya had to be set adrift on a separate continent in the first place?

Let us begin by answering the last question. Libya presented itself as an altogether different race, probably of Sub-Saharan African stock, that struck the Greek scholars who were meditating on these things, as definitely warranting a different continent. The Libyans were also a geographically separated people, they felt. Libya was separated by expanses of water on all sides, except where it was connected to the

Asian landmass. Now, it so happens that the Nile lay exactly at the 'seam' where Libya supposedly connected to Asia and therefore it was chosen to demarcate the two continents. Indeed, the Nile's role here was seen as providential.

Incidentally, the use of the Nile to demarcate the Libyan continent serves invaluably to overthrow the modern-day reconstruction. The reasoning here is as such: The modern-day Nile in the African continent could not have served as a line of demarcation between continents. If that were so, then the sliver of Africa, meaning the portion north and northeast of the Nile that is adjacent to the Red Sea would fall to the Asian continent. This is patently anomalous. Why would anyone let a sliver of a well-defined landmass fall to another continent? I mean, would this not make a mockery of the whole exercise of demarcating continents, wherein the convention always was to separate 'large, continuous, discrete masses of land, ideally separated by expanses of water?'

Also, there is the modern-day Red Sea to consider. Why would anyone disregard this wonderfully demarcating sea (really, nature seem to have especially wrought this slender sea for exactly such a role) and use the modern-day River Nile instead? Clearly, this discrepancy signals a reconstruction anomaly.

Libya's troubles did not end there. Indeed, its woes were compounded with the advent of modern-day scholars. Modern-day scholars inadvertently assumed that the African landmass was in fact Libya. The African landmass does cleanly break-off and satisfy all the preconditions of a continent.

This however is erroneous for they do not consider the fact that geography during these times was woefully incomplete. Very likely, the African landmass was yet to be discovered by the then Greek-centric world of scholars. As Eratosthenes says, "In ancient times no one had the courage to sail on the Euxine Sea, or along Libya, Syria, or Cilicia." [Strabo, Geography 1.3.2] Sailors did not have the courage to sail the Black Sea merely because it was huge expanse of unchartered waters, and not because it was especially treacherous. Eratosthenes also includes here the sea 'along Libya, Syria or Cilicia.' In short, sailors had not yet found the courage to sail down to the African landmass and therefore Libya cannot have been on the African landmass.

If the African landmass was not Libya, than what was? To find out, let us consider what our ancient world secular textual sources reveal, beginning with Herodotus' statement, "For is it not their (Ionians) theory that the Nile separates Asia from Libya?" [Herodotus 2.16] Since the Nile served to demarcate Libya, the landmass that lay west or southwest of the River Nile, we may assume, was Libya. Setting aside the known reconstruction and applying this to my new reconstruction, we will get the following answer. Given that the Orontes is my Nile, the East Mediterranean coastal region, including the Sinai Peninsula would roughly be Libya.

Consider now the following extract:

Libya belongs to one of the above-mentioned tracts, for it adjoins on Egypt. In Egypt the tract is at first a narrow neck, the distance from our sea to the Erythraean not exceeding a hundred thousand fathoms, in other words, a thousand furlongs; but from the point where the neck ends, the tract which bears the name of Libya is of very great breadth. [Herodotus 4.41]

Evidentially, Libya was narrow at the top and wide at the bottom. This roughly indicates a triangular shape. In addition, it had a distinct 'neck' that was formed by two seas squeezing it from either sides. Since it specifically states, 'from the point where the neck ends' we may assume that the neck region was distinguishable as such and that it had a reasonable 'length' of squeezed or isthmus like tract. Beyond this point, Libya was of very great breadth. In short, squeezed at one end, and broad at the other. That was Libya.

Now consider the extract given below:

As for Libya, we know it to be washed on all sides by the sea, except where it is attached to Asia. [Herodotus 4.42]

Here Herodotus reveals that Libya was washed on all sides by the sea, except where it was attached to the Asian continent. Okay, let us add that bit of information to our file on Libya.

We now have enough to information to go by, with which to identify the Libyan continent. It was west of the Nile, was roughly in the shape of a triangle and it was washed on all sides by the seas, except where it was attached to Asia.

Let us now open our maps and look for such a triangular piece of landmass. Right away, a distinctly triangular shaped landmass catches our eye. It is, in essence, the Sinai Peninsula landmass. Now, if we were to add to it the East Mediterranean Seaboard all the way to the modern-day city of Samandagi, ensuring that only the portion west of the Orontes (or west of the Great Rift Valley) was taken, it would indeed give a satisfactory triangular shape to Libya. Here, the base is the Red Sea side, the Mediterranean side would be the perpendicular, and the Great Rift Valley (which includes the river Orontes) the hypotenuse. The narrow neck portion of Libya mentioned by Herodotus can be taken as the region that lies between Samandagi and Beirut. The Al Ghab Basin, lies parallel to this region that was originally the Reed Sea, and distance between the Mediterranean Sea and the Red (Reed) Sea is indeed quite narrow.

The above reconstruction will satisfy the equation that the Nile-Orontes formed the border between Libya and Asia. It is washed on all sides by sea except of course where it is 'attached to Asia' by a long seam, the one that runs along the length of the Rift in this region.

Incidentally, Strabo also gives Libya a triangular shape and specifically a right-angle triangle one. This is very likely a tweaked version of what Herodotus himself states (narrow at one end, broad at the other) concerning Libya.

Libya has the shape of a right-angled triangle, conceived of as drawn on a plane surface, having as base the coast opposite us, from Aegypt and the Nile to Maurusia and the Pillars and as the side perpendicular to this that which is formed by the Nile as far as Aethiopia and by me produced to the ocean and as the

Strabo's Libyan triangle was as such: The East Mediterranean Coast (from Samandagi to the mouth of the Suez Canal) as side one, the Great Rift Valley side as side two, and the Suez Gulf side as side three. The landmass so demarcated, is remarkably in the shape of a triangle and is exactly how I have demarcated Libya.

However, Strabo complicates matters by calling it a right-angle triangle, and indeed places the right angle at the Egypt (Samandagi) corner. This poses a difficulty, for this region is narrow and can form the 30-degree angle at best. Actually, this is the corner that Herodotus himself identifies as the narrow end, for this is the region that falls in the 'neck' region. Thus, Strabo runs contrary to Herodotus.

However, Strabo is not known to run contrary to Herodotus. At least he does not generally appear to and certainly, he does not claim to either. The only plausible answer therefore is that either this discrepancy is the handiwork of the modern-day translator, who possibly rearranged the sides to reflect the modern-day reconstruction Or, Strabo's geography possibly was a bit skewed. An inadvertent altering of the length of any one side will readily skew a right angle triangle, and change it to an acute angle one or so.

Modern-day scholars too take the triangular shape of Libya seriously. This is why in their map of the ancient world, Africa, which is indeed their Libya, is depicted as an austere right-angle triangle. The all important 'neck' region however has been conveniently omitted, and they achieve the desired triangular shape by the injudicious use of the scissors. The bold and powerful shape of the African landmass, you will find, has been alarmingly trimmed down to obtain the right-angle triangle shape. What is more, it is done in a manner that shocks the sensibilities and shatters ones romantic image of the Dark Continent.

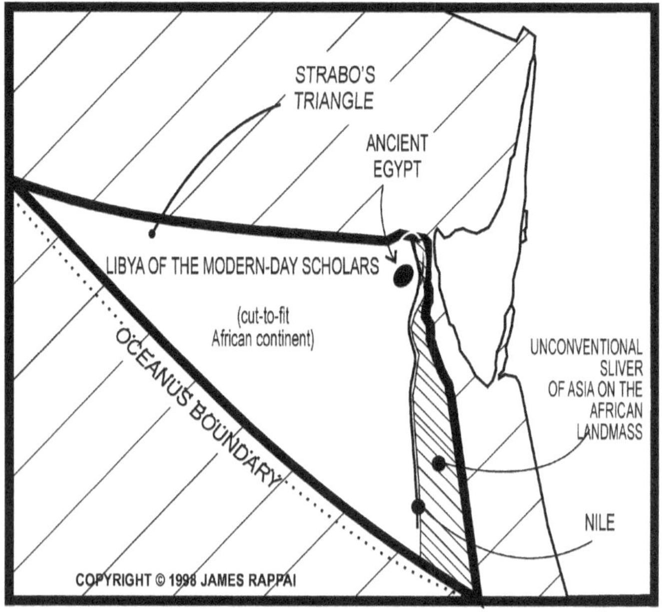

*Diagram 15: **Libya of the modern-day scholars.** (Previous page) Here, the African continental landmass is Libya. The triangular shape of the landmass is derived by assuming the Oceanus boundary. A sliver of the African landmass falls unnaturally to Asia. This is patently anomalous.*

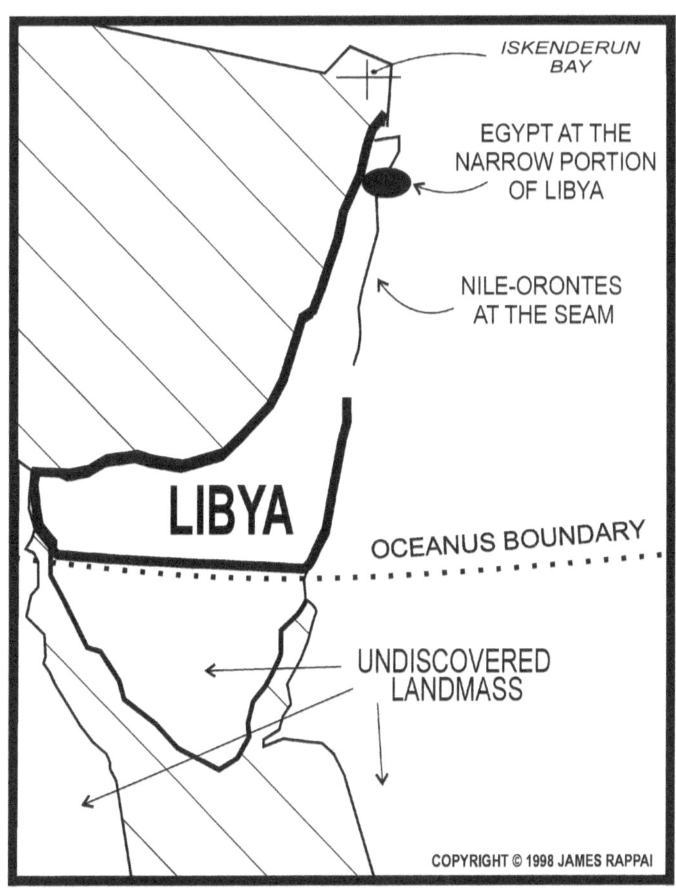

*Diagram 16: **My Libya.** (Above) Libya was narrow at one end and broad at the other says Herodotus. Strabo tweaked this to a right-angle triangle. He added that Libya was surrounded by water except where it joined with Asia and that the Nile runs exactly at this seam. This was why the Nile was chosen to demarcate the two continents. My Libya satisfies all these conditions. The Nile here is of course the Orontes. Also, one must factor in the geographical inadequacies of these times including the belief that the Oceanus truncated this identified landmass to perhaps three-fourth its size.*

CHAPTER 43

THE PHILISTINES

& SIDONIANS

Remember the final bit of advice that the God of the Old Testament gave to the Exodus assemblage when they were just about to exit out of Egypt, like an over-protective parent? The one about not taking the route to Canaan through the land of the Philistines, "lest peradventure the people repent when they see war" and return to Egypt? No? Here it is then:

> *And it came to pass, when Pharaoh had let the people go, that God led them not through the way of the land of the Philistines, although that was near; for God said, Lest peradventure the people repent when they see war and they return to Egypt: [Exodus 13:17]*

The Jews were asked to take the alternative, possibly longer or more difficult route to Canaan from Egypt. From this, we assume that the Philistines were a formidable people and that they inhabited the region through which the direct or possibly easier route to Canaan passed.

Apart from the Philistines, the other settlers often mentioned in the Bible are the Sidonians. Five settlements of the Philistines and two of Sidonians are mentioned. These then were the two prominent coastal neighbors mentioned in the Bible. We may safely assume 'coastal' here because both the Philistines and the Sidonians were intrinsically connected to the sea and therefore the easier route from Egypt to Canaan was possibly along the seacoast.

Who were the Philistines? From the Bible we gather that the Philistines were a people who did not practice circumcision, worshipped other gods and possessed a technologically superior armory. They were indeed the people who introduced 'brazen' full-body armors to this region. Goliath from Gath, who had "a helmet of brass upon his head and was armed with a coat of mail; and the weight of the coat was five thousand shekels of brass," provides us an accurate snapshot of the Philistines. In fact, the Goliath story reveals how full-bodied bronze armors created a sudden imbalance in battlefields of the Ancient Near East. Philistine smithies, it is said, went on to supply this entire region with all manners of weapons, farm implements and what not. From all the above information provided by the Bible, we may conclude that the Philistines were foreign settlers who had freshly landed on the Ancient Near Eastern coast.

The Bible goes on to inform us that there were five kingdoms or settlements of Philistines along the coast adjoining Canaan. They were Gath, Ashdod, Ashkelon, Gaza and Ekron. What is more, due to their proximity to the Jewish kingdoms and the constant skirmishes they had with them, all faithfully, blow by blow, documented in the Bible, most Bible readers are intimately familiar with these foreigners. Indeed, the Philistines managed to become very much a part of the geopolitical scenario of this region and I would most certainly have to accommodate them in my brand-new reconstruction.

But before we do that, let us run them by the ancient world secular Greek historians. Let us see what they have on record, concerning a brazen-armored sea people, in their Egypt-Ethiopia arena.

From Herodotus we learn that the coastal stretch from Egypt to Ethiopia, was in fact inhabited by colonies of Lacedaemonians or Spartans, who arrived from the island kingdom of Thera. They had reluctantly colonized the Libyan coast upon the advice of the Oracle at Delphi. Having tentatively set up an island settlement off mainland Libya, at a place called Platea, they progressively moved on to the mainland, putting up one settlement after another, at Port Menelaus, Aziris, Cyrene and Barca. Of these, Cyrene became the main settlement and attracted many more Spartans to this coast. Cyrene grew exponentially, until finally the native, the Ethiopians and the Egyptians, awakened to this menace and jointly attacked it. Alas, it was already too late. The Spartans were, by then, already well entrenched; they stoutly repulsed the attackers and went on to become a permanent fixture on this coastal belt.

So, were the Cyrenaeans of the ancient world secular historians, the Philistines of the Bible? Was Sparta or Lacedaemon their kingdom of origin? I cannot say for certain, but considering that we are on the lookout for exactly such a people, a brazen-armored seafaring lot who had recently colonized this very coast, and had energetically made elbowroom for themselves, crossing swords with the Jewish kingdoms on a regular basis, yes, it does look promising.

Frankly, there is no ambiguity here at all. However, if you want more, I could give you some name-matches. Ashkelon, Ashdod and Gaza of the Bible, are in fact mentioned by these very names, by the secular ancient world sources as well.

Ashkelon

Herodotus mentions a city of Palestine by the name of 'Ascalon' in his 'Histories' that had caught my attention in the very beginning, even before I had formulated my hypothesis. I had chanced upon it and had assumed that 'Ascalon' was indeed 'Ashkelon' of the Bible. It had to be. The name co-relation and the simple logic that there cannot have been more than one Ashkelon in this part of the world was the thumb rule applied here. Later of course, I became acquainted with archaeologists in general and biblical archaeologists in particular and learnt that in their books, what is obvious is not always right. Fortunately, I did not need to conform.

Could Ascalon of Herodotus be the same Ashkelon of the Bible, one of the five Philistine settlements? Let us find out and begin by examining the extract from Herodotus' history that mentions this name.

> *The Scythians became masters of Asia. After this they marched forward with the design of invading Egypt. When they had reached Palestine, however, Psammetichus the Egyptian king met them with gifts and prayers and prevailed on them to advance no further. On their return, passing through Ascalon, a city of Syria, the greater part of them went their way without doing any damage; but some few who lagged behind pillaged the temple of Celestial Venus. The Scythians who plundered the temple were punished by the goddess with the female sickness, which still attaches to their posterity. Those who suffer from it are called Enarees. [Herodotus 1.107]*

On studying the above extract, two interesting points caught my attention. One was that the temple of celestial Venus existed in Ascalon and the other was the 'female sickness' that affected the men and resulted in a growth that attached to their posteriors. The sufferers or possibly the growths were called 'Enarees.'

With a sense of déjà vu, I heard myself saying, "Surely I have heard of 'Enarees' before?" But where? In the Bible? I quickly reached for my Bible and before long, my suspicions were confirmed. The Bible reveals a strikingly similar story:

> *And it was so, that, after they had carried it about, the hand of the LORD was against the city with a very great destruction: and he smote the men of the city,*

Ah yes, it was 'emerods' not 'enarees' but clearly the same dreaded disease. The Philistine settlements of Ashdod, Gaza, Ashkelon, Gath and Ekron were afflicted by 'emerods' which is described as an 'incurable disease that afflict the private parts of men.' To obtain a cure, the Philistines, it is said, made gold emerods and offered it to the God of the Old Testament. The Celestial Venus mentioned by Herodotus is very likely Ashtoreth the goddess of the Sidonians.

However, the Philistines, it is said, worshipped 'Dagon' and not Ashtoreth. This is a minor discrepancy. It is possible that Herodotus got his gods mixed-up. Or possibly, the Philistines also worshipped the Sidonian Ashtoreth just as they did Yahweh of Israel, all in a desperate bid to get rid of their enarees. At any rate, demigod worshippers, afflicted with enarees or otherwise, unlike the straitlaced monotheists, had no qualms about dashing off a quick prayer to a friendly neighborhood God, and if need be, make room for the deity in question upon their already crowded home-altar!

Female sickness that afflicted men and resulted in a growth, would appear to indicate some form of venereal disease. A quick search however revealed that venereal diseases generally do not cause visible tumors. A soft, non-cancerous growth resulting from the tertiary stage of syphilis called gumma was the best I could get. Gumma is a form of granuloma and is most commonly found in the liver but can also be found in brain, heart, skin, bone, testis and other tissues. Then again, this is the current scenario. Earlier days, even a relatively small complaint would balloon up to unimaginable sizes. I remember seeing a photograph of half-a-dozen glum men with basketball-sized scrotal hernias, wherein the entire intestines, all twenty-one and a half feet of it that is normally housed in the abdominal cavity, had slithered down into the scrotal sac. Surely, syphilis, or any of the other forms of venereal disease, if left untreated, could be counted on to come up with some very alarming and grotesque growths.

Incidentally, 'enarees' appeared to mean female-like men as well. Therefore, I would go with a disease that primarily affects the male genitalia. 'Some form of venereal disease' is therefore my best guess. At any rate, I would be happy to go with just the 'enarees=emerods' similarity and take flight. Ascalon of Herodotus was without doubt the Ashkelon of the Bible. The celestial Venus referred to by Herodotus was Ashtoreth of the Bible, a goddess from this very region.

'Hemorrhoids gone awry' is, by the way, the modern-day scholar's take on the subject. It is, if nothing else, very much in keeping with their disconnected-with-reality way of thinking!

Ashdod & Gaza

Strabo, for that matter, mentions not just Ascalon, but Ashdod and Gaza as well in his texts. Here, take a look:

> *But in the interval one comes to Gadaris, which the Judaeans appropriated to themselves; and then to Azotus and Ascalon. Then, near Ascalon, one comes to the harbour of the Gazaeans. [Strabo 11.2.29, 30]*

Azotus, Ascalon and Gaza are mentioned by Strabo to have been next to Judaea, in the region that adjoined Egypt. Surely, one does not need to be very bright to discern that these were the same Ashdod, Ashkelon and Gaza mentioned in the Bible.

The Sidonians were a people who were intrinsically connected with Egypt's bustling maritime trade and who inhabited a portion of its coast near the Canobic mouth of the Nile. Their main settlements were in Sidon, upon an island situated close to Sidon called Tyre, which eventually became equally, if not more prominent than Sidon. The Sidonians were a very adept sea faring people and it appears that they alone made up the maritime workforce, both commercial and naval, of Egypt. The Bible adds that the Sidonians serviced ancient Israel's maritime activities in a similar manner and therefore it may be safe to assume that the Sidonians provided this service to this entire region.

All the ancient world secular historians offer a consistent picture of the Sidonians, whom they called the 'Phoenicians.' Thus, there is no ambiguity here regarding this people. Almost all the ancient world secular sources fully agree with whatever the Bible has to say regarding the Sidonians. The Tyre and Sidon mentioned by the Bible were obviously the Tyre and Sidon mentioned by Herodotus and other ancient world secular sources. So let us take this bit of information and directly file it away in our 'similarities' folder.

CHAPTER 44

THE PYRAMIDS

Such is their timeless grandeur that they still continue to find a place in the revised twenty-first century's list of Seven Wonders of the World. Indeed, they are the only one from the original list of monuments that are still in existence. I am of course referring to the Pyramids of Giza. Such being the case, one would have thought that the Pyramids of Giza would very easily have topped a 450 BC historian's lists by a stratospheric margin. Not so. Herodotus pegs it at a miserable third. [Herodotus 2.148]

In essence, he says, "the pyramids surpass description, but the Labyrinth surpasses the pyramids... and wonderful as is the Labyrinth, the work called the Lake Moeris, is yet more astonishing." [Herodotus 2.148] In other words, first comes the Lake Moeris, followed closely by the Labyrinth and finally, inexplicably, in third place, lag the pyramids. So curious is the lapse that we cannot help but feel we are missing something here.

Let us examine the wonders on Herodotus' list and see if we can find the underlying cause of this discrepancy.

Lake Moeris was nothing more that a large artificial lake. Now, reservoirs, however big, have only a barely legitimate claim to artificiality in the first place. They are, after all, created with little intervention by man. Generally, all the ingenuity required to build such reservoirs is a basic knowledge of building barriers or dams. Large bodies of water by itself too are not an unfamiliar sight and cannot have impressed a normal person. In short, the ingenuity or engineering quotient in its construction or in the end product itself would hardly have merited mention under normal circumstances.

But then again, Herodotus did see things differently and an ingeniously constructed reservoir is just the kind of thing that would have caught his fancy. Even so, how could an 'ingeniously constructed reservoir' have posed a threat to the Pyramids of Giza in terms of grandeur, ingenuity, engineering or peculiarity is still beyond comprehension.

Similarly, the labyrinth, with its 3000 chambers and all, simply could not have overshadowed something that cast its mesmerizing shadows over a whole modern-day city, as does the Great Pyramid of Giza over Cairo.

Such being the case, the unshakable realization that Herodotus did not ever set his eyes upon the Great Pyramid of Giza, takes firm hold. For if he had, it most certainly would have had his undivided attention and he, without question would have placed it at the top of his list of wonders. What is more, he would have documented this truly wondrous and patently artificial creation in the choicest of prose, in a manner that would leave no doubts in the mind of his readers of the Pyramid's identity and grandeur.

The point I am trying to make is, the Great Pyramid of Giza, was, is and always will be a striking monument that overwhelms the viewer. If this does not come through in the text, or shoots right through the top of any fancy list of wonders complied by anyone at any time, then we may most assuredly conclude that the Pyramids of Giza were not seen. Herodotus for one, most assuredly, never set his eyes upon them. Such being the case and assuming that he did see the 'pyramids,' the only reasonable conclusion that can be made here is, that the pyramids that Herodotus saw were different.

Oh yes, there is this possibility as well to consider apart from, that is, jumping up and calling him a liar. Very likely, what he saw were ziggurats.

Ziggurats

Ziggurats were built in the Ancient Near Eastern arena by the Sumerians, Babylonians and Assyrians. The earliest examples of the ziggurat date from the fourth millennium BC. Ziggurats were essentially temple-towers.

Now, ziggurats were as different from pyramids as cheese is from chalk. While pyramids were monuments, artificial Mt. Horebs of sorts, ziggurats were actually multistoried buildings, office blocks and such like, that invariably had a stepped-pyramid-like construction, thanks to the limitation of the building materials available during these times.

Let me explain. Although the idea of building multi-storied buildings had gained currency, building materials, concrete and steel, that would wonderfully facilitate this flight of fancy, had yet to hit the market. Steel was yet to be discovered and concrete awaited the arrival of the Romans. Given that, the only alternative was to build pseudo-multileveled structures. Now, these were cunningly designed stepped structures wherein each floor actually rested upon a solid inner core of earth. In other words, they merely appeared to be multistoried structures.

In essence, building a ziggurat was much like building a terraced building on a mountainside. The only difference is, here it is a wrap-around building and the mountainside was replaced by an artificial mound of compacted earth and rubble at the center.

Once the inner core mound was ready, the building was started top downwards. That is right. This is especially so if you are using megaliths. You had to build the top tier first all around. After that, you built the middle tier followed by the bottommost. The end result is a stepped structure, consisting usually of three distinct tiers and looking somewhat like a stepped pyramid.

Ruins of ziggurats can still be found aplenty in the Middle East. The temple-tower of Etemenanki in Iraq, popularly associated with the Bible's Tower of Babel in Babylon, is one such. An even larger one is located at Choga Zanbil, in Iran. This has a 335 ft square base and had three tiers. It has a solid core of earth and rubble and large slabs of stone used to erect the ziggurat. The best-preserved ziggurat is the one at Ur, in Iraq that was built entirely of bricks in 2113 BC .[1]

Yet another structure that is similar to the ziggurat of Herodotus is mentioned in the Bible. I am of course referring to the Temple of the Jews, the one that Solomon built. It was of course an improved version, one that incorporated the very latest in architectural innovations of the time and therefore seemingly different. Here three levels of stones were built and the tiers fashioned into chambers of decreasing sizes, built as explained before, one above the other, in a staggered or stepped fashion, upon a solid core of earth.

This structure incorporated the very latest in architectural innovations. The stones, for example, were precut monoliths that were cut and polished at the quarry itself. Another innovation that considerably refined the design was a new roofing material that increased the roof-span. Stones slabs restricted the size of rooms, which in turn increased the number of pillars. Indeed, often we see ancient ruins with innumerable pillars and wonder if there was any usable space at all within the building.

The answer was cedar beams. Cedar beams that afforded long span ceilings had finally reached the market. Kings from as far away as Assyria and Egypt were queuing up for this wonder material at the forests of Lebanon, where it grew in rare abundance and presumably was wiped out in a trice. Solomon too managed to get his hands on a few trees and had them shipped to his kingdom at considerable cost.

Bronze was yet another new material on the market. Bronze body amours were the very latest thing in warfare and whole battalions, often sworn enemies from opposite camps, were seen patiently queuing up for the metal at Philistine smithies. The Bible records Solomon's fascination with the metal and he too managed to procure a quantity of this metal. He used it to create a vast tank, two pillars and two dozen or so of pomegranates—presumably decorative elements—for his building projects.

Needless to say, these architectural innovations caused considerable excitement in the fledgling Jewish kingdom. Hoary scribes too, were swept away by the hullabaloo, as science stealthily crept into the camp. They too set aside their gods and hobbled across to record these simple engineering feats in the best of biblical prose. We of the reinforced concrete age, failing to fathom the excitement over cedar beams and bronze pomegranates, surreptitiously plumb these biblical verses for a religious dimension that it does not hide!

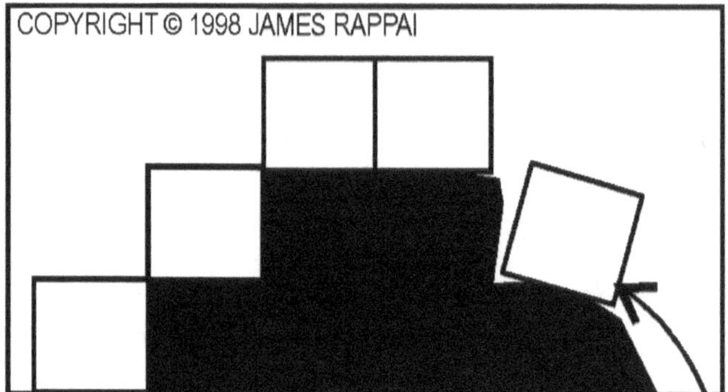

Diagram 17: **Herodotus' Pyramids.** Herodotus' pyramids were distinctly stepped structures and had only three tiers. The upper tier was finished first, then the middle and finally the lower tier. This reversed building suggests the use of megaliths and a core of earth. Add all these up and you get a ziggurat.

RECONSTRUCTION NOTES

Chapter 45

Real Egypt

According to my hypothesis, ancient Egypt was in modern-day Turkey and Syria. Egypt extended along the River Orontes (the Nile in my scenario), occupying say about five miles on either side of the river.

Key regions of ancient Egypt were in the following regions:

- The Tongue of the Egyptian Sea was located in the wide corridor between Samandagi on the coast and Antakya in the interior.
- The islands of the sea, such as Tyre, Pharos-Alexandria-Antioch, were also in the Samandagi-Antakya corridor. These islands ceased to be islands at a later date and this transformation too is recorded in ancient world histories.
- Mt Casius, Lake Serbonis, the Gerrha or saltpan regions were all also located in the Samandagi-Antakya corridor.
- Delta Region or Lower Egypt was in the triangular Amik Ovasi depression (Amug Valley) in Turkey's Hatay district. There are literally hundreds of Tells or ruin-mounds (more than 300 sites have been identified) in this region that will undoubtedly testify this fact.
- Upper Egypt was in a valley between the Jabal an Nusayriyah Mountains and Jabel El Wastani.
- The Reed Sea (Red Sea) was a vast marshy sea and was situated in the Al Ghab basin, which, before it was drained and reclaimed by the Syrian government, did present itself as such until very recently. It no longer exists of course. Watermarks are evident though, halfway up the mountains in this region, and can still be seen. The

Gulf of Arabia was a long narrow gulf of this sea that lay east of the Jabel El Wastani Mountain.

As mentioned before, magnificent ruins lie scattered all across this above-identified region. Many of them and especially the ones loosely classified as 'Phoenician and or Roman' are probably Egyptian. Ruins on the eastern side of the Al Ghab are probably Arabian.

Incidentally, modern-day scholars, as a token gesture, do include the East Mediterranean coastal belt all the way up to modern-day Syria, as extended territories of ancient Egypt. They have done this primarily to include pockets of evidence in this region, such as the battlefields of the Kadesh-on-the-Orontes skirmish in modern-day Syria, and possibly, to satisfy textual evidence, especially biblical, wherein it is stated that the Exodus trail (Sinai regions) and even Canaan was once Egyptian territory.

This then is where and how I would place ancient Egypt in my brand-new reconstruction. It is a theoretical picture and may require fine-tuning with detailed on-the-ground exploration and study, which I will be undertaking shortly.

CHAPTER 46

REAL CANAAN-ETHIOPIA

Locating Egypt is the key to locating Canaan-Ethiopia. We know that Canaan-Ethiopia was Egypt's next-door neighbor and that it was located south of Egypt and upstream upon the Nile-Orontes.

Key regions of Canaan-Ethiopia were as such:

- The Plain of the Canaan-Ethiopia was clearly a portion of the Al Ghab region.
- The island Tachompso, Ammon, the tributaries Astapus and Astaboras, the Sea of the Plain, that were all on the Plain of Canaan-Ethiopia, too were located in the Al Ghab depression. This is why it is said that Ammon, which was upon the island, was at one time on the Reed Sea.
- A sizable portion of the Al Ghab depression was home to various marshy water bodies. The largest of these was the Reed Sea.
- Edom was located in the northern half of the Jabal an Nusayriyah, primarily on its westward slope.
- Ancient Israel was located in the southern half of the Jabal an Nusayriyah again on its westward slope. The Half-Gilead settlement was however, on the island Tachompso located in the Al Ghab depression.

This then is the theoretical picture. The region may well stretch out; the real picture may encompass more territory. A detailed on-the-ground archaeological study alone will iron out the minor kinks in this picture.

If the region indeed stretches out, then it may well extend all the way to Hama in Syria. Then perhaps the Homs Basin was the Plain of Canaan-Ethiopia and the large inland reservoir located in this region, the Qattina Lake, where previously a large lake existed in antiquity, was perhaps the Sea of the Plain. In this scenario, Qatna, which occupies a half-mile square region and is one of the biggest Bronze Age ruin in western Syria and lies between Hama and Homs; would make a perfect Meroe. The two tributaries of the Orontes, one of which is called the Wadi il-Aswad, which are present in this region, may well be Astapus and Astaboras. The fact that Meroe was situated on the edge of a plateau (the limestone-plateau of the Syrian Desert) mentioned by Strabo, is borne out by this setting. The kingdom of Israel will continue to remain in the Jabal an Nusayriyah Mountains in this alternative setting as well.

My job here is done. I have provided the framework and the rest at any rate can only be fleshed out by on the ground research. Let us therefore move on to something a little more interesting. Let us hunt for treasure instead; let us search for Jerusalem!

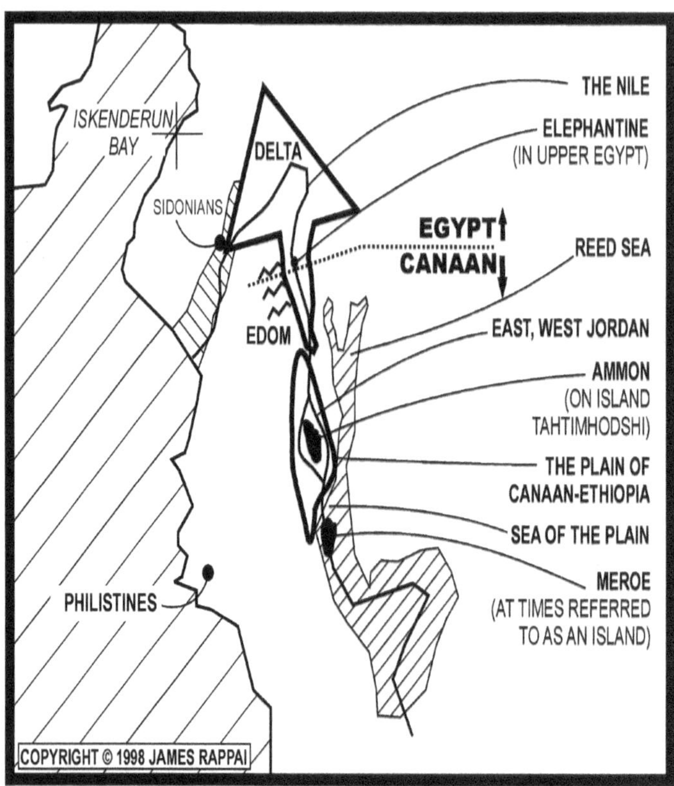

*Diagram 18: **Canaan-Ethiopia**. The concurrently derived geographical map of Canaan-Ethiopia. Diagram 1, which represents Canaan-Ethiopia strictly from a theoretical, concurrently derived perspective, is seen to fit well here on a modern-day topographical map of the Near Eastern arena. In short, while Egypt was primarily in the Amik Ovasi depression, Canaan-Ethiopia was in the Al Ghab depression located to its south. Thus, the appellation 'south country' given to Canaan-*

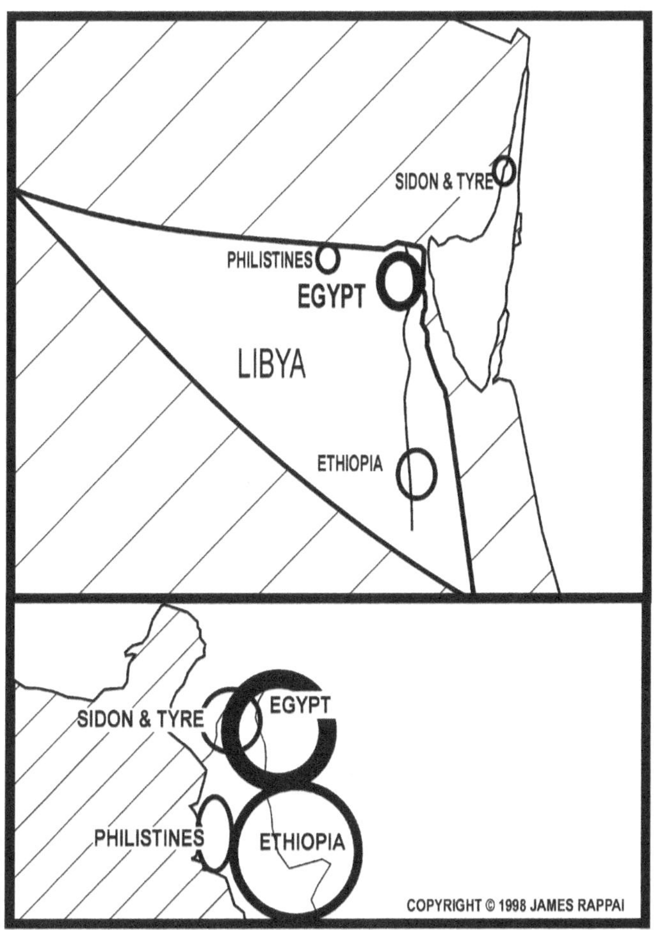

*Diagram 19: **Fundamental Reconstruction Differences.** While the modern-day scholar's model scatters the kingdoms of the Levant across two continents, separated by thousands of miles, thanks to a faulty pivot (Egypt), in my model, we see these kingdoms huddled together on the northern portion of the East Mediterranean Coastal belt, in the Near Eastern*

KEYS TO THE KINGDOM

After the temple of Jerusalem was destroyed in 586 BC and the twin kingdoms Israel and Judah totally dismantled, we see a Jewish settlement take root in this very region and doggedly begin the process of nation building yet again. We see it grow to a full-fledged kingdom and thrive for hundreds of years more. Most of the time though, while Jewish in every sense of the term, it existed as a vassal state, with its territories and high-profile capital city, Jerusalem, changing hands several times between the super-powers of the region.

This then was Judaea. Some might call it new, but in truth, it was the very same embattled Jewish kingdom originally set up by Moses, three thousand or more years ago. And, although politically not in its best years, as far as its main product was concerned, the stars and streetlamps, of Judaea—of Jerusalem—burnt brightly, intently, ready more than ever to perform its primary function of delivering god-men and spiritualism to a deluded world. Indeed, in a not-so-well-lit quarter of this unusual kingdom—in its mangers actually—it gave birth to yet another one of its fine prophets. This one though, hawked a new-fangled version of Judaism, with tenets that were surprisingly mature and as good as any that have been wrought in the by-lanes of Nabadwip, the de facto spiritual capital of the world, located in distant India.

But where exactly was Jerusalem? Certainly, the present day site is not the original site. It is merely a placeholder, a make-believe one—and acknowledged as such by discerning modern-day scholars themselves. The ruins present at the current site, including the Wailing Wall, do not correspond with the evidence available of the temple complex in Josephus' texts. Indeed, quite a few scholars have zeroed in on these discrepancies and are offering ready fixes that in essence, suggest incremental shifts within the same arena. My brand-new reconstruction though, rejects the current site outright.

Regarding Jerusalem, my favorite ancient world scholar Herodotus, has nothing at all to report. But fortunately, Strabo more than makes up for this lacuna. In fact, Strabo has quite a bit to say about Judaea, Jerusalem and even has a sentence or two to spare on Moses. Consider the following extract:

> As for Judaea, its western extremities towards Casius are occupied by the Idumaeans and by the lake. The Idumaeans are Nabataeans, but owing to a sedition they were banished from there, joined the Judaeans and shared in the same customs with them. The greater part of the region near the sea is occupied by Lake Sirbonis and by the country continuous with the lake as far as Jerusalem; for this city is also near the sea; for, as I already said, it is visible from the seaport of Iopê. [Strabo, Geography, 16.2.34]

The 'western extremities of Judaea towards Mount Casius,' appear to indicate either the northern or the southern segment of the western flank. My reconstruction suggests the northern. This would mean that the northwest corner of Judaea was bordered by Mount Casius, Lake Serbonis and the Idumaeans. Now, Idumaeans were the Edomites of the Bible. **Idum**-aea=**Edom**. What is more, when Edom is evoked, the Seir Mountains cannot be far behind.

As regards Mount Casius and Lake Serbonis, we know that they are intrinsically Egyptian landmarks. But here they appear to flank Judaea on its north along with Edom. And surprisingly, these Egyptian landmarks appear rather close to Judaea. Not that I am perturbed. On the contrary, this proximity is desired, for in my reconstruction, Canaan-Ethiopia was in fact located very close to Egypt.

So far so good. Crosschecking with my reconstructed map, and using the Idumaea reference above, it immediately becomes obvious that the Jabal an Nusayriyah Mountains in this region were very likely the Seir Mountains. They had to be, considering that this range was immediately south and perpendicular to the Samandagi-Antakya corridor, where my Mount Casius and Lake Serbonis were situated. Now the Jabal an Nusayriyah range is about 90 miles long. Therefore, let us assume that just a portion, say a 15-mile stretch of the mountain range, was occupied by the Edomites. The remaining portion of the mountain range to the south, including the thickly forested region west to it and up to the coastal stretch, but not wholly including it, was Judaea. Reading off the co-ordinates, we find that according to Strabo, Judaea was between the latitudes N 35.85 degrees to N 35.45 degrees and longitudes E 35.95 degrees to 36.15 degrees.

What immediately strikes one about this positioning is the fact that it sits very well with the boundaries given of Israel in the Bible. During King Solomon's times, Israel was said to have extended from the 'River of Egypt' to the 'Hamath Pass.' Here take a look:

So David gathered all Israel together, from Shihor of Egypt even unto the entering of Hemath, to bring the ark of God from Kirjathjearim. [1 Chronicles 13.5]

Also at the same time Solomon kept the feast seven days and all Israel with him, a very great congregation, from the entering in of Hamath unto the river of Egypt. [2 Chronicles 7.8]

The 'River of Egypt or Shihor' is the Nile (here the Orontes, specifically the segment that flows east to west from Antakya to the Sea at Samandagi). The 'entering of or pass of Hamath' is the Homs Gap, which runs east to west and perpendicularly cuts across the Jabal an Nusayriyah Mountains further south. Both these natural, east-west boundaries, demarcate a segment of the Jabal an Nusayriyah, the same we that we have assigned to ancient Israel, in a manner that would make the statement "from the entering in of Hamath unto the river of Egypt," accurate, the best and most unambiguous way of demarcating the Holy Land. Indeed, the parallelogram defined by these two east-west boundaries (the north-south boundaries being the Al Ghab to the east and the Mediterranean to the west) makes up a well-defined piece of verdant real estate, thickly covered with dense forest, that could well be termed the 'Promised Land' without anyone raising any objection.

Strabo in fact specifically refers to the above-mentioned forests of this region, and informs us that they belonged to the Jews and that it served them well. The Jews were considered robbers and it appears that they could produce up to forty-thousand of their numbers from these forests.[1] Crosschecking with a modern-day topographical map, we realize that we do have dense forests in this region. Indeed, the western side of the Jabal an Nusayriyah that we demarcated earlier, have some of the densest forestlands in all of Syria. Clearly, we are on the right track here.

Strabo then mentions that lope was a harbor on the Mediterranean Sea in this region and was used frequently by the Jews. Carmel too was on this coast and belonged to them. In short, Judaea while largely inland appeared to have owned a small stretch of the coastline and had apparently used it for piracy! The Sidonians and Philistines, one would assume, occupied the rest of the coastline.

Strabo then drops a bomb. He mentions that Jerusalem was in this region. Apparently, it was situated inland and that on a bright day it was visible from the mountains near the Iope harbor on the coast. Here, take a look:

> *Then one comes to Iope, where the seaboard from Aegypt, though at first stretching towards the east, makes a significant bend towards the north. Here it was, according to certain writers of myths, that Andromeda was exposed to the sea-monster; for the place is situated at a rather high elevation—so high, it is said, that Jerusalem, the metropolis of the Judaeans, is visible from it; and indeed the Judaeans have used this place as a seaport when they have gone down as far as the sea; but the seaports of robbers are obviously only robber's dens. To these people belonged, not only Carmel, but also the forest; and indeed this place was so well supplied with men that it could muster forty thousand men from the neighbouring village Iamneia and the settlements all round. Thence to Mt. Casius near Pelusium the distance is a little more than one thousand stadia; and, three hundred stadia farther, one comes to Pelusium itself. [Strabo, Geography, 16.2.28]*

Lest modern-day scholars try to deny the whole thing, Strabo once again confirms that Mount Casius was no more than a 1000 stadia from the Jewish coastal stretch containing Iope and Carmel, and that Pelusium was another 300 stadia more. A stadia is roughly 3 miles. Egypt was therefore no more than hundred miles away. The 'seaboard from Egypt stretching east then making a significant bend towards the north' mentioned in this context, seems to indicate a promontory on the coast. Scanning for such a promontory south of Samandagi on a modern-day map, I see a promontory called 'Ra's al Basit' that seems to fit the bill. 'Stretching out east then making a significant bend towards the north' pretty much describes it. What is more, it has mountains close to it that offer a high vantage point from which to scan the Jabal an Nusayriyah Mountains inland. Ra's al Basit on the coast of modern-day Syria, would certainly do nicely for Iopê.

From Ra's al Basit's high vantage point, Jerusalem situated inland on the western slopes of the Jabal an Nusayriyah was visible on a bright day, it is said. I therefore scanned the Jabal an Nusayriyah near Ra's al Basit that was within a radius of 22 odd miles. This is about as far as you can see from a height of 300 odd feet on a clear day.[2] Jerusalem was in these mountains and I intended to find it today. I had spent far too many hours doing exactly this and frankly, I had long since run out of time.

After many hours of close study of the various ruins in this zone, I stopped at a landmark with which I had recently become quite familiar. It was the Salah ed-Din Citadel. Indeed, for some reason I kept coming to it. Could it have been the Jerusalem citadel?

For some reason I decided to pursue this lead. I resolved to read up more about the Salah ed-Din Citadel but soon realized that there was nothing more to be known than what I already knew. The crusaders, it was generally thought, had built the citadel. I did not particularly care for this conjecture, for the citadel was far too elaborate and expensive for their level of involvement in this region. Moreover, there were many such castles in the region that toted up an investment and involvement that ran the crusaders argument right out of the books of accounts. Also, beneath the castle's later-date construction, there is evidence of an earlier 'Phoenician' structure.

Side-by-side, I stepped up my research on Jerusalem. The uneasy thought that there was a detailed map drawn by Moses floating around somewhere and that I was barking up the wrong tree all along, did occasionally cross my mind. Indeed, I have often conducted surreptitious image searches on the Internet for exactly such a map. Fortunately, such a map never surfaced. However, I did get a whole hoard of later-date maps and diagrams of Jerusalem that were of great use. On examining these, I was able to separate them into three piles. One was essentially a junk pile and consisted of maps, diagrams and photographs based on the current reconstruction, all of them identifiable by the Dome on the Rock that was clearly visible or depicted at its center. The second were a whole series of eighteen or nineteen century reproduction maps. The third were modern-day diagrams of the Mount Moriah complex, that were generated based on textual clues gleaned from Josephus' and other ancient world scholars, including the Bible and the Hebrew Torah, Nevi'im and the Ketuvim and largely produced by 'history mystery' enthusiasts.

On closely examining the second pile, one that consisted of old reproduction maps, I was able to detect two subsets. Here again there were many that tiresomely presented the Dome on the Rock version, which, needless to say, I promptly tossed into the junk pile with disdain. This false Jerusalem has had a pretty good run and I for one had no compunctions about wholly jettisoning it.

What is false is false. The Mount Moriah is sacred because the God of the Old Testament declared it so. Left to our own devise, we may well wonder what the fuss is all about, but God and His entourage, invariably reverted to ancient sacred spots and recommended them to us mortals in no uncertain terms. The reason—if I may give a borrowed one from another corner of the world—is as such. Spiritualism is really a 'rubbed off' phenomenon. Purification can only be attained by direct association with God. However, God is not directly available. What is available instead is His name, His pastimes, including the venues of His pastimes, all of which are non-different from God Himself. You can associate with the name and pastimes (by hearing, remembering) and purify yourself. Additionally, the pastime venues of God can be visited and these too being non-different from God, will burn away sins, exactly as if you were consorting with God in person.

In fact, a sacred venue can be seamlessly included in one's life—as one would choose a holiday spot—to gain immeasurable spiritual benefit. Indeed, you can underpin just about any mundane family activity with the sacred tract and gain immense sacred association. Why, even the entire gamut of homeland nostalgia, which is a powerful emotional bond, can be dovetailed and cashed in for all its worth, to yield rich spiritual dividends. All you have to do is make it (in this case, Jerusalem) your homeland. In short, God's pastime venues are easily the most foolproof, pleasurable and by far the easiest way of purifying oneself and becoming eligible to enter the Kingdom of God.

Admittedly, it all sounds like a mundane chemical reaction where God (His real name, His real pastimes, the real venues of His pastimes) is the reagent. But that is exactly how it is! 'God' is the operative word here, not soulful, not sincere, not sorry or any other sly emotion that we may choose to wring out of our slippery little hearts! Penances, repentances, have little or no intrinsic value by themselves. Only association with 'God' or suffering the reaction for the sinful activity committed as and when it is handed out to you in a future life (which may well be when you are having a good run and under the impression that a better human being than you never walked the face of this earth) can nullify it. You may repent and pray, 'I am sorry for my sins' till you are blue in the face, but you will still find all your sins patiently waiting for you by the blue-berry bush outside the church. This is why finding the real Jerusalem, which is considered a sacred spot, is of paramount importance, for Jerusalem offers direct association with the God of the Old Testament. 'Jerusalem is in one's heart' kind of pulpit pragmatism has indifferent value at best. Needless to add, all this holds true only if the God in question is the Supreme Lord and not a demigod or an Oracle.

Getting back to the two piles of maps on my table, the one that presented the Dome of the Rock version, as I said, I discarded. The second set, I soon realized, appeared to present an altogether different geography of the Holy Land. These clearly were the artistic representations of Jerusalem that existed before Edward Robinson and his team of Bedouin tribesmen gave the world the current make-believe reconstruction. These maps were roughly all the same and depicted Jerusalem as a walled city-state and had many recognizable representations of key elements such as the Via Dolorosa, Maison de Pilate, the Temple, etc.

A citadel depicted at the centre of all these maps caught my attention. On careful examination of one of these maps, it looked like a regular castle. The embattlements and corner towers were all finely depicted. One particular detail of the citadel however, caught my attention. It was the elevated pathway that extended from either side. But more than the pathway itself, what had really caught my attention was a tall needle column that supported one of these pathways. Surely, I had seen this needle column in real life somewhere before.

The citadel in question depicted in these crusader's maps was of course the Fort Antonia that stood adjacent to the temple of Jerusalem. Herod had named it Antonia to please his illustrious patron, Mark Antony, the flamboyant Emperor that Rome nearly had. Mark Antony had captured Jerusalem and the surrounding areas in 37 BC and after installing Herod as the puppet king of Judaea, had gone on to bigger things. Antony's act however fell apart, but Herod's appointment proved to be a winning hand. Indeed, he turned out to be a builder extraordinaire and went on to put Jerusalem right back on the map, with numerous building projects, all named after Roman officials, whom he had assiduously cultivated. This included the 'Tower,' a single ponderous tower of old that stood upon the Mount Moriah, which he repaired, converted into to a full-fledged fort, and renamed Fort Antonia.

This original tower—which appears to have been a single square tower of great proportions—was apparently built in the 2nd century BC by the Maccabeean leader, John Hyrcanus.[3] Herod, repaired the tower, then, presumably as an afterthought, went ahead and built a full-fledged fortress. The newly built fortress encircled and enclosed twice more land of the mount's pinnacle area than earlier, and the thus enclosed area or fortress was used to garrison an entire Legion of Roman soldiers. Herod also carefully dismantled and rebuilt the temple of Solomon that was within this enclosure, on a far grander scale, without disturbing the daily worship, which apparently continued without stop.

The Sanhedrin however, was not terribly impressed by Herod's contributions and even debarred him from entering the temple, as he was an Idumaean Jew. Herod therefore built yet another tower in the east corner of the Fort Antonia, from the top of which he could peer into the temple, offer his prayers and perhaps keep a wary eye on its activities. Here is a portion of the textual source from which I gleaned all the above information.

Accordingly, in the fifteenth year of his reign, Herod rebuilt the temple and encompassed a piece of land about it with a wall, which land was twice as large as that before enclosed. The expenses he laid out upon it were vastly large also and the riches about it were unspeakable. A sign of which you have in the great cloisters that were erected about the temple and the citadel, which was on its north side. The cloisters he built from the foundation, but the citadel he repaired at a vast expense; nor was it other than a royal palace, which he called Antonia, in honor of Antony. [Josephus, War of the Jews, 21.1]

It is appropriate to mention here that some modern-day scholars willfully reinterpret what clearly were regular fortress walls (the kind that we usually see meandering around a mount), as the raised foundation walls of a massive and level platform. They assume that the mount within was leveled, the gaps filled, and the whole thing paved to create a gigantic platform. They identify this massive platform as the same upon which the Dome of the Rock stands, in the currently accepted reconstruction model of Jerusalem.

Unfortunately, there is no mention of such a massive platform in Josephus' text. What is mentioned by Josephus is quoted above and it states unambiguously that Herod encompassed twice more land 'within the parameter walls.' He spent an unspeakable amount to built a "wall," a "cloister" and this great wall, which he "built from foundation upwards" (meaning, it was a new construction and not a repair work), enclosed twice more land of the Mount Moriah. In short, Herod built a regular fortress wall that encircled more of the Mount Moriah's pinnacle surface area than before.

However, biblical scholars have no eyes for reality and are too busy doing what they do best, which is, reverse engineering, misinterpreting Josephus' text, reengineering it to match their defunct reconstruction. A platform was built, they claim, not a wall. What is more, the platform was so great that it straddled the Mount Moriah in such a manner that the mount was overwhelmed, no longer visible and merely a rocky outcrop, the very pinnacle of the mount that is, was all that was visible. Not true.

Look at it this way. The whole idea of building a fortress upon a mount it to enhance its already high level of impregnability. The height of the mountain is indeed of crucial importance. And the exercise of building a fort upon the mount is to doubly ensure its impregnability. This is crucial and cannot be compromised. A superstructure built upon a mount that is seen merely as an exercise to obtain more level land at the top, and necessarily obtained by leveling and lowering of the mount, is a twenty-first century interpretation by fools who do not appreciate the security concerns of the early ages. Why, Titus and the others who did indeed attack this citadel could have stepped off their chariots right on to this ridiculous platform!

With regards to the lone tower that Herod repaired, I have this to add. This tower was apparently referred to as the 'Baris' tower and that John Hyrcanus had supposedly constructed it. However, there is evidence that a tower existed much earlier upon this mount. Indeed, the Bible reports that King David is said to have lived in a 'tower' upon the mount or Jebusite ridge. It also states that the Jewish armies had a very difficult time removing the Jebusites from their ridge. Both these bits of information unambiguously spells 'impregnable tower,' and I for one am willing to accept that this Hyrcanus tower was this impregnable Jebusite edifice. Possibly, like Herod, John Hyrcanus too had merely repaired and reused it at a later date.

The Antonia Citadel was without a doubt, an important landmark of Jerusalem and it had casts its ominous square shadow on many pages of the New Testament as well. St. John was kept imprisoned in its dungeons and later beheaded. Perhaps the praetorium to where Jesus Christ was taken for judgment was in the Antonia citadel.[4] At a later date, when St. Paul was in danger of being mauled by a mob, Roman soldiers promptly pulled him up into the Antonia.

Now, some scholars believe that the Fort Antonia was demolished during the 70 AD destruction of Jerusalem by the Romans. The reason for this belief is fact that there is no archaeological evidence of a fortress at the current reconstructed site of Jerusalem. Josephus however, will have none of it. Consider the following extract:

> *So Titus retired into the tower of Antonia and resolved to storm the temple the next day, early in the morning, with his whole army and to encamp round about the holy house. [Josephus, War of the Jews, 6.4.5]*

The above extract offers vital clues that clearly demonstrate that the Fort Antonia that stood alongside the temple on the mount was not destroyed in the 70 AD war. It states above that Titus retired into the tower of Antonia and resolved to storm the temple the next day. Here the 'next day' was in fact the fateful day the temple was destroyed by fire and the war effectively brought to a close. In other words, the Fort Antonia is documented here standing until the second last day of the battle. Considering that Titus had made the fort his stronghold and the Romans effectively crushed the rebellion the next day, it is evident that the Fort Antonia survived the 70 AD destruction. True, orders were given and the Romans made many attempts to demolish the fort. But all that was before, when the Jews were barricaded inside the fort and the Romans were on the outside trying to take it. Eventually, the Romans did take the fort, and did in fact use it as their stronghold. It is thus that it states that 'Titus retired into the tower of Antonia.'

Even from a military strategist's point of view, it made eminent sense to capture the fort intact and use it as a stronghold to attack the second fortified position of the temple structure itself. Indeed, the temple of Jerusalem doubled as a second stronghold, and after the adjacent Antonia was taken by the Romans, the Jews had moved into the temple proper.

Actually, according to Josephus, the Romans had no intentions to destroy the temple building either. The temple, into which the battle had moved during the last day, was accidentally burnt down by a fire started by the Jews themselves. Titus himself had no desire to burn it and in fact actively tried to stop the conflagration that had gone out of control.

Modern-day scholars however are not inclined to believe Josephus on this issue and accuse him of trying to portray Titus in a favorable light. Flavius Vespasian senior, was after all Josephus' patron. However, what needs to be kept in mind here is that the temple contained large quantities of gold and silver, and burning it certainly was not in Titus' interest. But the fire burnt uncontrollably and Titus himself is said to have engaged in trying to bring it under control. Needless to add, all the gold had melted and run down the cracks and crevices in the floor. The Romans had to dig it out.

To conclude, my reading of Josephus indicates that the Fort Antonia remained largely intact and just the temple was burnt and destroyed. Even here, I doubt if anyone would have taken the trouble of literally 'razing the temple to the ground.'

Moving on, like Josephus who documents the Moriah complex and its destruction by Titus in 70 AD, Strabo too offers a similar view of the complex while describing the earlier attack by Pompey in 63 BC. Here is an extract:

At any rate, when now Judaea was under the rule of tyrants, Alexander was first to declare himself king instead of priest; and both Hyrcanus and Aristobulus were sons of his; and when they were at variance about the empire, Pompey went over and overthrew them and razed their fortifications and in particular took Jerusalem itself by force; for it was a rocky and well-watered fortress; and though well supplied with water inside, its outside territory was wholly without water; and it had a trench cut in rock, sixty feet in depth and two hundred and sixty feet in breadth; and, from the stone that had been hewn out, the wall of the temple was fenced with towers. Pompey seized the city, it is said, after watching for the day of fasting, when the Judaeans were abstaining from all work; he filled up the trench and threw ladders across it; moreover, he gave orders to raze all the walls and, so far as he could, destroyed the haunts of robbers and the treasure-holds of the tyrants. [Strabo, Geography, 16.2.40]

Jerusalem was a 'rocky fortress' which if expanded using the related information presented, would appear to indicate 'situated high upon a rocky mount or ridge.' But what comes next is neither ambiguous nor commonplace, and puts this point of view in perspective. It is an engineering feat that makes one pause in awe. A trench sixty feet in depth and two hundred and sixty feet in breadth was cut into rock. Pompey had had to bridge the trench, 'fill it up, throw ladders across it,' to reach the citadel, which he slyly did on a Sabbath. It appears that this manmade trench separated the mountain ridge (the tail portion) from the parent ridge. This fact is evident from the following extract from Josephus:

It was Agrippa who encompassed the parts added to the old city with this wall, which had been all naked before; for as the city grew more populous, it gradually crept beyond its old limits, and those parts of it that stood northward of the temple, and joined that hill to the city, made it considerably larger, and occasioned that hill, which is in number the fourth, and is called "Bezetha," to be inhabited also. It lies over against the tower Antonia, but is divided from it by a deep valley, which was dug on purpose, and that in order to hinder the foundations of the tower of Antonia from joining to this hill, and thereby affording an opportunity for getting to it with ease, and hindering the security that arose from its superior elevation; for which reason also that depth of the ditch made the elevation of the towers more remarkable. [Josephus, War of the Jews, 5.4.2]

The tail portion of the Moriah ridge was separated from the parent by means of a deep moat or trench. Since the other two sides of the ridge presented inaccessible faces, this exercise of detaching the ridge from the parent, completed the isolation process. The separated tail portion of the ridge now presented itself as a 'wedge' (think 'wedge of cake' sitting on its base) and on top of the wedge was built the fort and the temple.

With Josephus too making mention of the trench, we may consider it a salient feature of the ridge. Josephus goes on to mention that as the city of Jerusalem grew, the parent portion of the ridge, which perhaps was earlier intentionally kept vacant for security reasons, too became inhabited. This parent portion of the Moriah ridge was counted as the fourth mount of Jerusalem (the city, it appears, comprised of four mounts) and was called 'Bezetha.'

Having read just about everything that was about the temple complex and the Fort Antonia, I was confident that if ever the fort and the temple complex ruins were to come into my cone of vision, I would be able to readily identify it. In short, I was ready to examine the Salah ed-Din complex or any other and make a reasonably well-informed judgment.

But before reexamining the Salah ed-Din's Citadel, I decided to take a cursory look at the pile of diagrams of the temple-fort complex that modern-day enthusiasts and scholars had produced, based on textual information derived from ancient world sources such as Josephus and others, in much the same manner that I have gleaned my information. Their Fort Antonia, I noted with satisfaction, was placed to the north of the temple and had square towers. The temple was set on a level platform and the mount itself was clad with stone. This tiresome interpretation of the 'platform' that overwhelmed the mount too was faithfully depicted. Initial inspection revealed that apart from that one flaw and the fact that the buildings were perfectly proportioned, and therefore looking terribly stilted, these diagrams seemed okay to me. It is only later that I became aware of a glaring omission that these depictions shared. None of these diagrams depicted the fosse or trench that separated the Mount Moriah from 'Bezetha,' the parent portion of the ridge.

Why has this trench not been represented? It is by no means an unambiguous detail. Josephus hints at it, Strabo plainly paints it and indeed has Pompey energetically 'filling up the trench, throwing ladders across it' and what not. This is not to say that other scholars have not discerned it or mentioned it. The fosse or trench is in fact a very well known topographical feature of the Mont Moriah complex. Some believe that the trench existed in the currently accepted reconstruction scenario, but is now not discernable for it had been filled up. Whatever the argument, it was missing from these diagrams. I was saddened, for it was precisely this manner of 'reverse engineering,' this compulsion to trim or tuck away textual sources to conform to the modern-day archaeological reconstruction that is the bane of this field of study. 'Alexander went to Siwa' they say. But he never did; he had been to Ammon!

The time was now ripe, I decided, to step up to the Salah ed-Din Citadel and see if it was indeed the Mount Moriah temple-fort complex. I swooped down at it and studied the ruins from every angle, peered at every photograph of it that was available on the net, until I knew its every crumbled corner.

Alarmed by my austerities, the gods finally relented. Seeing my prodigious and pathetic struggle, they were grievously troubled. Gradually, ever so subtly, they began to reveal hidden details of the citadel that I had not noticed before. With increasing astonishment, I gathered a mountain of similarities between the documented picture of Jerusalem and the Salah ed-Din Citadel complex, until one day the firm, unshakable conviction that I was indeed peering down into the sanctum sanctorum of the temple of Jerusalem, took root in my unsullied heart.

It is all there. The high mountain ridge, the valleys on two sides, the deep man-made fosse cut into living rock, which both Josephus and Strabo mention and Pompey had to throws ladders across to breach, the needle column that supported the elevated pathway across the fosse, etc., are all exactly as described.

The Fort Antonia is, as mentioned, situated to the north of the mount and still in good repair; indeed, as Josephus documents, the fort was not destroyed. The single, imposing square tower, larger than the other towers of the fort, the one that was originally built by John Hyrcanus, or even by the Jebusites, too, is easily discernable. The eastern tower that was specifically built for Herod to peer into the temple compound does indeed afford this view. The parameter walls, dungeons, the large cisterns, the steps leading up to the temple, the various gates that are mentioned, are all there and exactly as described.

The temple of course, lies in ruins, although its massive northern wall (that faced the Fort Antonia) and the foundation of the rest of structure still stand. Thanks to its elevated position, the entire complex upon the Mount Moriah appears to stand exactly as it was after the 70 AD destruction, with merely minor deterioration. The only other change is that a minor mosque of relatively recent antiquity has nested within its vacant premises.

A complete list of all the similarities between the Qal'at Salah ed-Din complex and the Jerusalem temple-fort complex is available at the end of this chapter. Photographs and diagrams that will bring home the truth as nothing else can are also given at the end of this chapter. The exact coordinates of Mount Moriah temple-fort complex are:

35.5955 N, 36.0567 E

These coordinates will set you down in midst of a ruined temple, built on top a high ridge in the Jabal an Nusayriyah Mountains, in modern-day Syria. Adjoining to it, on the very same ridge, you will see the still standing citadel and recognize it as the one that is now whimsically called Qal'at Salah ed-Din. This was never a crusaders citadel and Salah ed-Din perhaps never even came anywhere near it. This in truth is the Jerusalem acropolis upon the Mount Moriah. All around, upon the other three mounts that surround it, Opel to the west, Mount of Olives to the east and Bezetha the fourth half-mount to the north, you will see ruins of the city of Jerusalem.

Incredibly and entirely by the mercy of the Supreme Lord, I had managed to unravel this Gordian knot. After a ten-year struggle, that involved far too many steep learning curves, and as many false leads, I was able to steer this uncharted expedition to the shore.

All I needed now was a closure, a heavenly sign to sign off, for I am a religious fool, and do believe is such things. And as I searched for this elusive heavenly sign, I kept repeatedly coming back to the 'glint' that originally led me to the Salah ed-Din. Here indeed it is:

> *Then one comes to Iope, where the seaboard from Aegypt, though at first stretching towards the east, makes a significant bend towards the north. Here it was, according to certain writers of myths, that Andromeda was exposed to the sea-monster; for the place is situated at a rather high elevation—so high, it is said, that Jerusalem, the metropolis of the Judaeans, is visible from it. [Strabo, Geography, 16.2.28]*

The chance glint from the coast of the white-stoned metropolis of Judaeans that was set deep in the Jabal an Nusayriyah Mountains on a high ridge, had registered as a novelty way back in time and the young Strabo dutifully documented it. The year is 40 BC or thereabouts. From the heights of Iope upon the coast, "Jerusalem, the metropolis of the Judaeans, is visible," he wrote. The distance had had to be great, for the citadel could only be seen from this elevated vantage point. Also, this rare sighting was one of those that sent a shiver down the spine. It was, after all, the dreaded den of robbers.

Upon reflection, I realized that it must have been quite a sight to see something situated so far away. Indeed, the distance was about 15 miles! This reverie gave birth to an innocent thought. Perhaps it is true the other way around as well. Perhaps the sea was visible from the Salah ed-Din and this strange vision too was considered a novelty of sorts. This was wistful thinking, of course, but if it was true, it would uniquely confirm my findings and I would gladly accept it as a sign of confirmation and approval.

A glint, a glimmer, a shimmer of the sea from the Salah ed-Din! Surely, oh Jerusalem, this is not too much to ask!

Meanwhile, I impatiently waited for an internet document to open. It was taking abnormally long and finally when it did open, I groaned. Oh no, not again! Indeed, in my rabid search for information, this monster PDF file had repeatedly snagged in my net. It was an ordinary, run-of-the-mill nine-page brochure, documenting the repair works carried in 2000 by the Aga Khan Trust for Culture at the Ayyubid and Mamluk sections of the Salah ed-Din Citadel. It did in fact have a few good pictures of the interior of the citadel. As for the accompanying text, I had glanced at it briefly, but never really read it. This time however, I read the opening lines and stopped short. It read:

> *The Citadel of Salah ed Din is located high in the coastal mountain range, some 24 kilometres east of Lattakia. On a fine day one can see the Mediterranean sparkling in the far distance. [The Citadel of Salah Ed-Din, AKTC brochure]*[5]

"On a fine day one can see the Mediterranean Sea sparkling in the far distance" from a prodigious distance of 24 kilometers! Prompted undoubtedly by destiny, an unknown person, possibly an architect attached to AKTC who had penned the brochure, thought it a novelty grand enough to set it down as the opening lines of this fine brochure!

Ah, Jerusalem had heeded! She gave me her sign of approval, my sparkle, my closure! A hundred or more irrefutable pointers, beginning with Balak's anguished cry to Strabo's lope pointer, have unerringly led me to this spot. This high, ridge-top citadel with the ruins of a temple adjacent to it, along with the surrounding countryside, consisting essentially of four mounts, was, without a shadow of doubt, Jerusalem, the same to which Jesus called out:

> *O Jerusalem, Jerusalem, which killest the prophets and stonest them that are sent unto thee; how often would I have gathered thy children together, as a hen doth gather her brood under her wings and ye would not! [Luke 13:34]*

Jerusalem had heeded even then. She had sent him her finest. Stoic, simple-hearted Jewish men, who were cast in the moulds of Jerusalem, that had for centuries brought forth such men who fully understood the subtle science of God and who were ready for the trials and tribulations that this task demanded. Alas, she also knew—and provided—the fire of adversity that hones, imparts the resilience and strength required to withstand the stratospheric heights that her latest product, her topmost prophet, this Jesus was determined and destined to reach.

Readers, I give you that Jerusalem; I give you the keys to the kingdom!

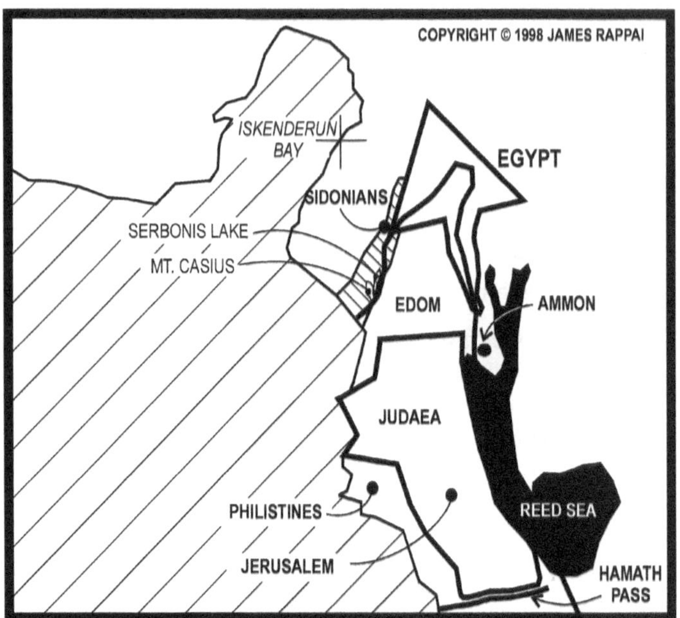

Diagram 20: **Judaea and Jerusalem.** *Judaea and Jerusalem according to my reconstruction. Here Jerusalem is the Salah ed Din's citadel and the immediate area surrounding it. "From Hamath pass (Homs gap) to the River of Egypt (Nile-Orontes from Antakya to sea)" (2 Chronicles 7.8) is how the Bible anchors Israel. This holds true here in my reconstruction.*

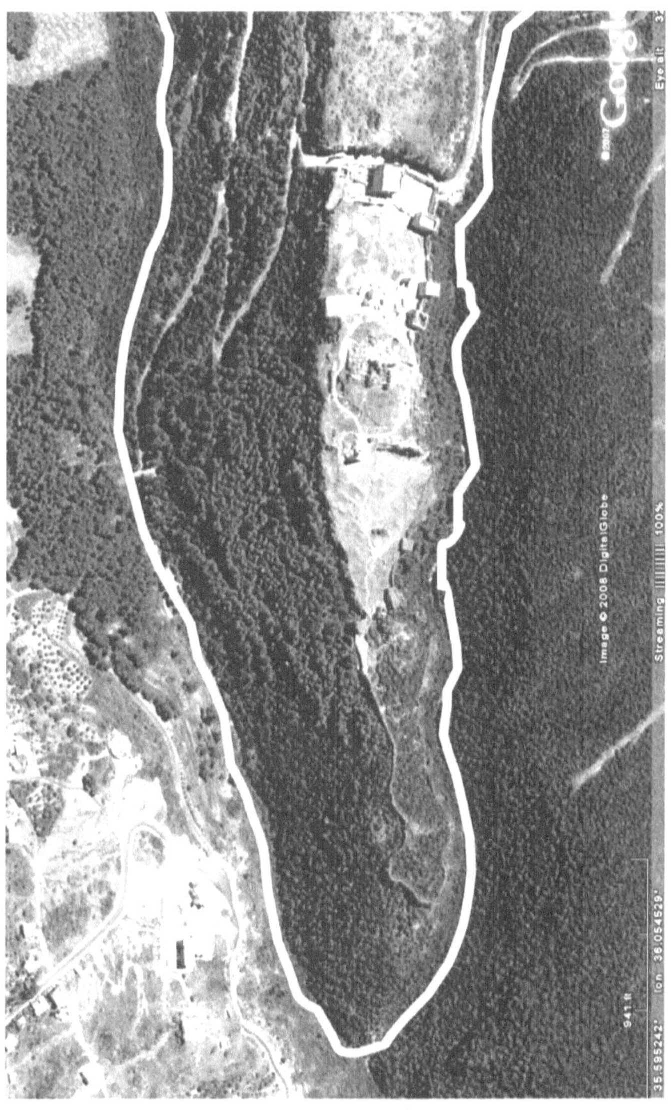

*Diagram 21: **The Temple Mount Ridge.** Satellite view of the Mount Moriah Ridge. Upon it, the fort-temple complex of Jerusalem can be clearly seen. Google Earth coordinates are: 35.5955 N, 36.0567 E. It is erroneously called the Qal'at Salah ed-Din and is situated 15 miles east of Lattakia in Syria.*

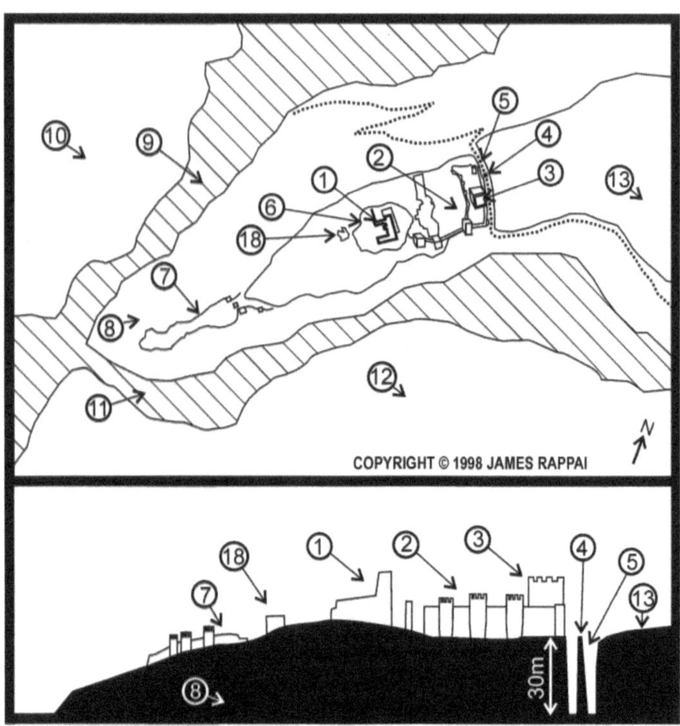

Diagram 22 & 23 (next page): **The Temple Mount.** *Labeled diagram of the of the Mount Moriah complex. The satellite view of the complex on the previous page and the next (close up) may be studied using this diagram.*

1. *Temple* **2.** *Fort Antonia* **3.** *Original Jebusite tower* **4.** *Needle column* **5.** *Fosse (trench) that separates the Moriah ridge from the parent mount, which was called Bezetha.* **6.** *Temple boundary wall* **7.** *Herod's outer parameter wall* **8.** *Mount Moriah Ridge.* **9.** *Tyropoeon Valley* **10.** *Mount Opel* **11.** *Kidron Valley* **12.** *Mount of Olives* **13.** *Bezetha* **14.** *Plinth of old temple?* **15.** *Herod's observation tower* **16.** *New intrusive construction* **17.** *Passageway from fort to temple* **18.** *Solomon's palace?* **20.** *Praetorium?*

4
5
3
20
2
17
16
15
14
1
6
18
266 ft
image © 2008 DigitalGlobe
©2007 Google
COPYRIGHT © 1998 JAMES RAPPAI

*Diagram 24: **The Mount Moriah Complex.** Aerial view. The Fort Antonia (2) is in the foreground, with original Jebusite tower (3) in the centre. The temple (1) is visible in the background. The needle top (4) and trench (5) too are visible.*

Diagram 25: **The Temple.** *The ruins of the temple of Jerusalem upon Mount Moriah. The (insert) should give an idea of its massive size. It is situated south of the fort complex on the ridge, and is on higher ground.*

Photograph 26: **Inside view of Fort Antonia.** The stones used in the original tower (left) are bigger than the rest of the construction. The once covered walkway can be seen to the right.

Photograph 27 &28: **Cistern.** An underground cistern beneath the complex. **River.** (second picture) Water erosion marks in the valleys by the side of the Temple Mount that suggest seasonal streams.

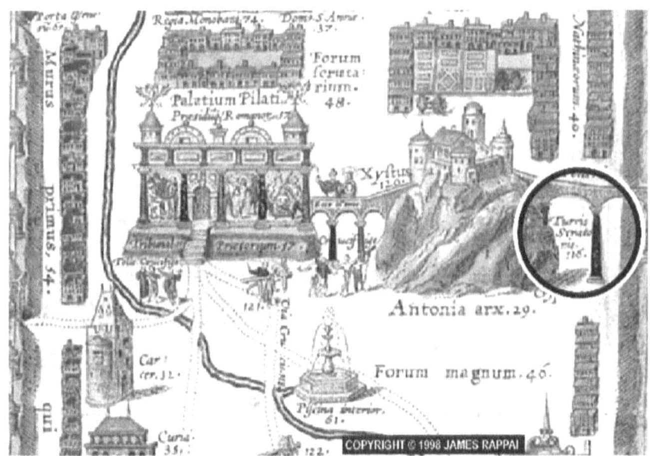

*Diagram 29: **Map of Jerusalem.** Artistic impression of the temple and the Fort Antonia as seen in an old crusader's map. Note the 'needle columns' that support the elevated walkway to and from the Fort Antonia. It surprisingly reflects the real 'needle.'*

*Photograph 30: **The needle column.** It once supported a retractable walkway. 31. **The massive trench:** It separates Mount Moriah from the parent Bezetha Mount*

Qal'at Salah ed-Din Complex	The Jerusalem Acropolis (The Mount Moriah Complex)
Qal'at Salah ed-Din complex sits atop a high mountain ridge in the Mountain ranges of Jabal an Nusayriyah	The temple-fort complex of Jerusalem was built on a high mountain ridge in the mountain ranges of the Amorites
A fortress whose walls meanders and enclose a considerable area of the ridges pinnacle surface is seen atop the ridge. The ruins of an imposing temple is seen in its midst of this fortress	Fort Antonia, as the fort of Jerusalem was called, walls meandered and encircled and enclosed a sizable area of the Mount Moriah pinnacle surface. The temple of Solomon, of grand proportions was within this fort complex
On a clear day, the Mediterranean Sea, which is about 15 miles away, is visible from the Qal'at Salah ed-Din complex	According to Strabo, on a clear day, Jerusalem, which was atop a high ridge in the mountains, was visible from the heights near Iope, a harbor on the coast
Two valleys flank the said mountain ridge. Erosion marks signal that a seasonal river flowed by its sides	Two valleys, the Kidron on the east, and the Tyrepoan on the west flank the Mount Moriah ridge. A river, at times called the Gihon, supplied water to the citadel
Two higher mounts, one to the east and another to the west flanked the ridge upon which Salah ed-Din citadel is built. These two plus the mount ridge itself and the parent portion of the ridge, totaling four separate mounts, appeared to have formed the city proper connected to the Qal'at Salah ed-Din acropolis.	Jerusalem's was a four mounts city. The Mount Moriah was at the centre, Mount Olives to its east, Mount Opel to the west. Bezetha, which was the parent portion of the Moriah ridge, was to the north. From the Mount of Olives, which was higher that Moriah, one could get an excellent view of or into the Temple

A deep trench (92.4 feet deep, 66 feet wide, and 514.8 feet long) cut through living rock, separate the ridge from the rest of the mountain	According to Strabo, a trench (60 feet wide and 260 feet long) protected the Temple Mount complex on the north side. He mentions how Pompey had to 'fill it up, throw ladders across it' to attack the Fort Antonia
A lone 28 m high 'needle' column that supported an elevated pathway still stands in the center of the trench	No mention of a needle column found. However, fosse is mentioned, and Pompey threw ladders across suggesting that a removable pathway complete with needle column did exist
Whitish stones obtained from excavating the fosse have been used to build much of the fort	Strabo mentions that the stones obtained from the trench were used to build the towers on the parameter wall
The Salah ed-Din fort has square towers	The Fort Antonia had 'square' towers
One tower is built of larger stones earlier and is differently proportioned, suggesting an earlier construction	The Baris Tower was built earlier by John Hyrcanus or the Jebusites before him. The rest was built by King Herod at a later date
An awkwardly placed (not equidistant) eastern tower from which one can readily peer into the temple arena exists in this complex	A tower (eastern) close to the temple was built as an afterthought, for Herod to peer into the temple complex
Large cisterns with terracotta pipes lead down into the valley below. Erosion marks of a seasonal river are seen at the base of the temple mount	Large water cisterns were an integral part of the Mount Moriah complex. A water source by the temple was a perquisite
A temple ruin of imposing proportion that seems to be the central edifice of the complex is situated on slightly higher ground in the midst. The fort proper is	The Solomon's temple rebuilt by Herod clearly had immense proportions and was the central theme of the complex. It is documented to have been on higher ground and to the south of

| north of the temple | the Fort Antonia complex |
| Ruins exist further south of the temple compound upon the ridge | Solomon's palace and meeting hall were built south of the temple compound |

CHAPTER 48

THE HYPOTHESIS

Ancient world scholars have shown themselves to be rock-solid dependable. Their information is impeccable and has proved to be one hundred percent accurate. The same goes with the Bible. The Bible can be accepted as a viable historical source, without anyone getting all crabby or pernickety about its reliability.

The Bible was never at fault. Its archaeological evidence has merely become obscured by a fatal mapping error of the core biblical arena. Overzealous peer reviewing with intent to ensure that the mega Egypt reconstruction error never came to light, is the cause of this anomaly.

Needless to add, Egypt too is a make-believe reconstruction. The real Egypt was in the Near Eastern arena in the regions currently occupied by a small portion of modern-day Turkey and largely by modern-day Syria. The people of this region are actually the true descendents of the sophisticated Egyptians, the first citizens of the ancient world!

Now, I realize that my work presents a viable hypothesis that admirably resolves the Biblical enigma and numerous other related anomalies of this region. If I were to encapsulate my hypothesis in a brief sentence, it would state:

Canaan of the Bible and Ethiopia of the ancient world secular scholars are the same. The kingdom of Canaan-Ethiopia was situated in the regions currently occupied by modern-day Syria. Ancient Egypt too was located in the Turkey-Syria region. Ancient Israel (Judaea) was

Actually, this is much more than a hypothesis, for, on its very first test run, this hypothetical model readily proves its viability by promptly pinpointing Jerusalem. This indeed is a discovery of great significance that boldly takes this hypothesis into the realm of a full-fledged archaeological discovery. To the above hypothesis-discovery I attach my name and call it the 'James Rappai Hypothesis-Discovery.' Using my hypothesis-discovery as the key, all the regions connected to these kingdoms and indeed the entire Levantine belt can very easily be reconstructed to their original or real geography.

What then of the ruins we currently call Egypt? Well, the answer to that question may be had from yet another of my books. The book in essence, reveals it to be the ruins of an aberrant and obscure African civilization we currently know very little about.

Would the modern-day scholars agree with my hypothesis-discovery? Well, probably not, for they have far too much to lose. However, considering that in my presentation every point is concurrently established by two or more ancient world sources and that it ultimately finds archaeological evidence for what is unmistakably the Jerusalem complex, it would be unwise, I would think, to disagree. Besides, there are far too many people out there, including a section of biblical scholars, who would be more than willing to support my ideology. Biblical maximalists especially would be glad I am sure, to jump wildly and cheer this behemoth fire-breathing dragon of an ideology that has finally surfaced. Had they not perilously held on to its 'located elsewhere' tail for so long?

Would the lay audience agree? Well, probably yes, especially considering that my reconstruction is derived from corroborative ancient world textual sources, presents a perfect fit, and has ruins too to match. However, if pressed, their vote would swing right back to the modern-day scholars in an absurd show of solidarity, revealing a timid, insincere and immature intellect that results from the stranglehold that science, even quasi-science has on the average person, which is a shame.

Ten conscientious scholars or less is all it will take to acknowledge this as the real reconstruction of the biblical arena. Ten willing to step forward, if for nothing else other than to rescue the Bible from an ignominious exit, willing to giving it back its pitifully gained historicity and thereby its spiritual credibility. Or, ten indeed to appease, for he had once famously said, "I will not destroy it for ten's sake." [Genesis 18.32]

But really, it is an inevitability, a minor detail in the greater scheme of things. The arrow has been shot, the truth has been revealed. That it will strike and strike true is a mathematical certainty.

But oh just look at the glorious marksman chosen! I am "not eloquent... slow of speech and of a slow tongue" [Exodus 4.10] and in so many ways, patently the wrong person for such a grand scholarly adventure. But this too is in keeping!

The Promised Land

The Old Testament narrative contains a number of instances that lend themselves well to deliver a spiritual theme. There is the central theme of a 'Promised Land,' which although definitely a terrestrial enterprise, does admirably serve to drive home the concept of spiritual emancipation and the Kingdom of God. Indeed, by their adherence and devotion to the God of the Old Testament, the Jews gave to the western world its first taste of love of Godhead, the rarest of rare fruits of spiritualism.

From a purely spiritual perspective however, there is perhaps not a grain of true spiritualism in the Old Testament. Never is there a mention of the soul, nor is the concept of emancipation ever mentioned, let alone elaborated. The monotheistic theme that seemingly shines through is unreal and merely attests to the fact that the Jews were loyal to their own oracle. What is more, the God of the Old Testament's perception of death is bewilderingly abrupt and mundane. All he has to offer on the subject is the gruff dismissal, 'go and be gathered amongst your ancestors.' Now, that is hardly an encouraging comment on the subject.

Spiritualism is an endeavor to 'save the soul.' If there is no 'external Kingdom of God' to 'transcend' to, then there is no spiritualism. What we often mistake for spiritualism is propitiation to the gods, demigods or oracles, wherein the aim is to garner immediate and discernable gain in this world, in this lifetime. This form of worship or prayers has, you will appreciate, absolutely nothing to do with the soul and the concept of emancipation. Petitions or prayers for a good job, a good wife, food on the table does not in any way constitute spiritualism.

Unfortunately, most people cannot differentiate between the two, and often mistake one for the other. They pray to a demigod or their favorite oracle for liberation, knowing not that the demigod in question too is in bondage and has no idea what in the world is it that you want. Worst still is, if you pray to the Supreme Lord for material gain. He will, with questionable humor, interpret it as a cry for emancipation and take away what little you have, for material comforts are a hindrance on the path to salvation. Indeed, there is a class of Indians, who, for this very reason, are wary about worshiping the Supreme Lord! Imagine standing up and asking Jesus for material goodies when he is in the midst of a sermon, extolling the congregation to give up 'the good life' and apply oneself to building a future in the Kingdom of God!

Speaking of Jesus Christ, if spiritualism is what you want, then certainly he is your man. Compared to the Old Testament, the New Testament of Jesus Christ is effervescently spiritual. Indeed, his mission statement begins with the bold and explosive declaration: 'My kingdom is not in this world!' Now, here is a refreshingly direct and one hundred percent spiritual presentation! Here is undisguised transcendence from the very first word go! Here is someone who showed utter disregard for a transient or terrestrial kingdom and urged everyone to build assets in the Kingdom of God!

Jesus Christ then goes on to deliver the highest spiritual tenets available to man. The concept of love of Godhead, which is truly the means to deliverance. And the best part is, these are the very same tenets that the Vedic literatures deliver under the theme 'the most confidential knowledge' with the utmost of reluctance in a hush-hush manner, and even then only to the sincerest of seekers. Jesus, on the other hand, distributes it freely, as if he indeed held the Keys to the Kingdom in his hands!

But where did Jesus get his science of God? Does it have precedence? Is there a bona fide school of thought from where the seed of these teachings could have emanated? Since there is no documented proof, I cannot be sure.

However, going by his teachings, it can be said that there is, in India, in the Vedic Literature, a specific subset of teachings called Vaishnava literature. Here you will astonishingly find a similar monotheistic religion with its distinctive goal of emancipation. Vaishnavism is not very popular in India though. The sad fact is, the Indian masses, were never properly initiated into this sublime science and therefore worship the numerous demigods and are smugly content to obtain worldly returns. Very few actually strive for self-realization.

It is this esoteric science, known only to the priestly class of Indians, whose micro-registers we find in the teachings of Jesus Christ.

Now, ordinarily when we see a crossover, the end-product is usually a hybrid derivative. It would contain a smattering of the original teachings, some local beliefs, rounded off with a humanitarian or a social reform theme that invariably compromises its core spiritualism. Surprisingly however, this is not the case with Jesus' teachings. The tenets of the science of self-realization as delineated by the Vedic Vaishnava Literatures are surprisingly intact in his teachings and appear to be expertly transported and translated to this corner of the world! What little has been added in terms of delivery, referring specifically to the parable format, is not deviant, but surprisingly illuminative, and carries the hallmarks of deep understanding.

The parable of the Prodigal Son succinctly delivers the core idea of this religion. A son wanders off from the comforts of his father's home, essentially in search of himself. Initially, he is happy but soon gets embroiled in the world and its web. We find him down and out and in that state, recall the comforts of his father's home, and yearn for it. The father who had all along awaited the return of his son, one who has thankfully been exorcized of his envy, gladly takes him in.

Let us now unfold this parable, elaborate its various elements and try to understand its deep spiritual import. I have here taken the liberty of borrowing a few details from the original Vedic sources to bring clarity to the subject.

We are the sons or 'independent particle spirit soul' component of the Supreme, tainted with envy, and desiring to leave, become masters in our own right. Now, there is nothing wrong with this desire of becoming masters ourselves, and no one is asking us to conform to a subservient mode. However, the fact remains that we are infinitesimal part and particle of the Supreme and our constitutional position is that of his subordinate counterpart. While the Supreme Lord holds the position of the enjoyer, the living entity holds that of the enjoyed exactly as in a male and female relationship. Both parties, you will appreciate, equally enjoy the union, albeit from different perspectives. Now, we are best served if we stay in our constitutional station. Even so, as is often seen, a wife at times, grows envious of her husband and wants to experience the world from his perspective. This is, in essence, is the reason why the Prodigal son walked out from his father's home.

To facilitate our desire, the Supreme Lord places us in a special universe. This universe ensures that our endeavors are properly and impartially rewarded or punished. This special universe is indeed our fiefdom, wherein we can try our hands at becoming the masters of all that we survey.

However, since we are 'infinitesimal' spirit souls and cannot actually move or manipulate matter, everything has to be arranged for us. This is why, in the special universe, everything is carefully stage-managed. Happiness, miseries, conquests and defeats are all thrown in to give the impression that we are indeed wrestling with the elements, moving and shakings things, living life to the fullest, all on our terms. The whole drama is managed end to end by the Supreme Lord who alone can manipulate matter. We cannot do a thing. We merely provide the desire and establish the direction that we would like to go, and there the Supreme Lord arranges to take us.

This special universe is three-tiered. The middle world represents our playing field, and it is here and here alone that we sow the seeds of our actions. We reap in the upper or lower planetary systems, after which we are back to the middle world to sow afresh. Life in the playing field world is followed by one in the hellish or heavenly planets. After a cauterizing trip to a hellish planet or a rewarding one to a heavenly one, depending on how we have acted, we are back once again for another round in the playing field world, to sow afresh.

Multiple planets exist in each tier. Heavenly planets in the upper tier are numerous, where rewards ranging up to that enjoyed by demigods are meted out. Likewise, innumerable hellish planets exist in the lower tier, wherein the full range of retribution is meted out.

Hints to the inner workings of this special world as described above can very easily be discerned. To begin with, the 'infrastructure,' meaning the multitude of planets, is there for all to see. Take a look at the night sky. Some of those cheery bright lights up there are hellish planets! Birth and death provides a hint of the cyclic existence mentioned. Where one is born largely determines ones' future in terms of wealth and position. We can therefore tentatively conclude that we arrives on this planet with a pre-assigned package of happiness and distress and this hints of the retribution and reward that is intrinsically interwoven into the scheme of things. Examples of reward and retribution are available in wholesale to convince even the most diehard atheists that there probably is a well-oiled machinery out there that remorselessly govern these things.

Here, in this special universe, we will spend many lifetimes chasing our dream of becoming masters of our own destiny. We become embroiled in various ways and realize that this business of becoming a master is something for which we are not constitutionally equipped. When we tire at last of this rollercoaster ride, and begin to yearn for the anxiety-free existence of living under someone else's roof, ache for pleasure that is not stained with our sweat or tainted with our blood, and truly hanker to go back, then the Supreme Lord will himself feel the full force of our forlorn and heartfelt cry—and reciprocate, cut a swift path out of the tangle for us.

Incidentally, the abode of the Supreme or the Kingdom of God is a very real place. It is not a terrestrial kingdom, nor is it a state of mind or a philosophical utopian concept. Such a place exists and it lies beyond this special universe. Interestingly, it goes by the appellation, 'Free of Anxiety.' Hundreds and thousands of planets offering an infinitely superior life exist in the spiritual sky, wherein life, completely free of anxiety and everlasting happiness can be had. To put it in perspective, life, as we know it in this world—but in a greatly enhanced form—is available in the spiritual realm. It certainly not the 'drifting in the clouds singing hosannas' kind of drab existence that it is generally made out to be!

The means of reaching the spiritual world is one of purification. In the parable, the son is purged and purified by his situation and by constantly remembering his father, not to mention the comforts of his father's home. Likewise, we too have to recall and meditate on the Supreme Father. There is no harm either in recalling the comforts of His home. In other words, you may well aspire to go to the Kingdom of God simply for the better life it promises.

But how; what is the exact process? As mentioned before, the Supreme Lord is the scouring agent in this sublime cleansing process. Generic titles, names of His prophets, and so on, will not do the trick. The various practical activities by which you can carry out this cleansing process are by remembering, by congregational singing, by hearing, by rendering service, by worshiping, and by genuinely petitioning or praying to the Supreme. Needless to add, to efficiently carry out these processes, it is important to have a clear vision as to who exactly the Supreme Lord is, and what is His name, form and pastimes are. The above process has to be complemented with leading a sinless life. It makes no sense to begin purging at one end and continue to perform actions that bind and bring us back to this world of misery. Find out what these are and steer clear. As can be seen, the parable of the Prodigal son, encodes nearly every element of this enlarged version.

Incidentally, there is yet another popular presentation of the same theme that the world knows quite well. It is Plato's 'Allegory of the Cave.' Plato, however clips its wings of transcendence, territorializes this sublime theme and yokes it to pull a mundane politico-philosophical theme. Sir Thomas More further perverted it and gives it that 'Utopian' coloring and the concept is thus understood today as a speculative, fanciful and unrealizable goal. Indeed, most well-read individuals today would inform you with a smirk that the concept of Kingdom of God and transcendence, is Utopian, fanciful, no more than the mind venting steam. The truth however is that this concept originated from the Vedic Literatures, and has been enshrined in its texts since time immemorial, long before More, Plato or Socrates walked the earth. And this original version verily speaks of a transcendental and very real world.

Put aside therefore, the flickering pleasures of this life and other short-term goals, and go for a permanent solution. Forget about becoming the world's richest or the greatest, work merely to keep body and soul together, and aim to gain the very best treasure that this world can offer. Set your hearts on transmigrating to the Kingdom of God. Pack your back and go. *Go to the real Promised Land!*

ACKNOWLEDGMENTS

Writing this book gave me intense pleasure. I was possessed and invested countless hours of labor, stretching over a number of years, to unravel this mystery. To those who stood by me all along and allowed me to pursue my avocation that increasingly ate into my earning hours ... my wife Mona (whose patience had worn really thin.), and my two sons, I apologize, and offer my sincerest thanks. Mona, who also proofread my text (not without mauling my carefully wrought prose, which she found tortuous in general and unhappily frivolous in places), I thank yet again. I also thank my parents Rappai and Teresa, my brother, sister and other relatives and friends who offered encouragement and support in various ways.

I would also like to thank the modern-day scholars whose work has helped me unravel this mystery. Finally, I would like to express my gratitude to the ancient world secular scholars, especially Herodotus, Strabo and Josephus, upon whose square shoulders I so grandly ride.

James Rappai

The author, James N. Rappai, is a religious (Gaudiya Vaishnava) scholar with strong Christian antecedents. He was born on 28 December 1961 into a Christian family of Kerala, India, that has its roots in the very region on the Malabar Coast, where St. Thomas, the direct disciple of Jesus Christ, established the foundation of his very own church, some two thousand years ago. It is here, as he himself says in awe, that you would find incredibly staunch Christian families, who have sent up to fifty generation of sons into priesthood!

James was attracted to religion right from the very beginning. However, it was in graduate school, while studying Industrial Design that this latent attraction truly and insistently came to the fore. He undertook an intense search for the truth—a journey that took him to various spiritual centers of India. The search led him to many ancient centers of learning, including to one on the bank of the Ganges, to a Vaishnava School of Thought that taught a brand of religion that astonishingly mirrored the very same Christian ideologies with which he was fondly familiar. Here he learnt Indian philosophy for five long years.

James' interest in religion and the Bible eventually spilled over into the field of religious history, archaeology and the mysteries related to it. He was vaguely aware that archaeological evidence for the Bible was missing, and propitiously, at that very juncture, he came across an old Time Magazine article titled, 'Are the Bible's Stories True?' that said as much. Indeed, the article went on to highlight the fact that most Biblical scholars were of the opinion that the Bible had no historicity whatsoever and that much of the archaeological reconstruction of the core biblical arena in modern-day Israel was purely speculative. It ended on an optimistic note and stated that there were still a handful of die-hard scholars who called themselves 'maximalists' around who believed that it was all a huge mistake—possibly a fatal mapping error—and that any day a cache of archaeological evidence could be stumbled upon, at which stage, scholars, even those who currently do not believe in the Bible's historicity, would only be too glad to revise their opinion.

James (naively) took that as his cue and began his research. Fortunately, he made a breakthrough, and 'The Bible Came From Syria' is the outcome. In essence, the book points to a major if not fatal mapping error as being the root cause for the no show. At the same time, it also highlights the follies of authoritarian peer review. Indeed, following the rigid and unforgiving methodology of peer review that is enforced in this field of study, modern-day scholars have gone ahead and stripped the Bible of its historicity and thereby its credibility.

GLOSSARY

Abydos tablet: Limestone slab discovered in 1818 by W. J. Bankes at Abydos ruins. It supposedly contained a rare list of pharaoh names.

Amorite: Generic term found in the Bible that referred to a people who lived in the south country or Canaan.

Ancient world secular scholars: The term used in this book to refer to the body of ancient scholars, especially Greek scholars, such as Plato, Herodotus, Strabo, etc., of classical antiquity who serve here to corroborate the history documented in the Bible.

Asmach: Elite soldiers attached to Pharaoh Psammetichus. The term is only found in Herodotus' history.

Balaam: A popular seer mentioned in the Old Testament.

Bedouin: A nomadic Arab tribe.

Canaan: A name often used in the Bible in a generic sense to refer to the region that lay south of Egypt. It was home to many indigent kingdoms such as Edom, Moab, Ammon, Israel, etc. Originally, perhaps the term may well have referred to specific tribe in this area.

Deserters: The term used by Herodotus to refer to a settlement or kingdom in Ethiopia that was formed by the mercenaries who had deserted Egypt, the king and their families in the reign of Pharaoh Psammetichus.

Diaspora: The term is used here to refer to the Jewish Diaspora. It denotes the historical dispersal of the Israelites from the core biblical arena to Egypt, Assyria and other regions.

Ebers Sothic Calendar: The Egyptian year, it was assumed, was divided into three seasons. Flooding of the Nile, the growing season and the drought season. These three seasons were divided into four 30-day months that totaled up to a 360-day year. To make their calendar synchronous with real cycle of the planets, the Egyptians, it is thought, added five additional days to the year. However, they forgot to add an additional day every 4th year (equivalent to the modern-day calendar's the leap year adjustment) to maintain the synchronicity. This omission resulted in the Egyptian calendar going out of sync by a day every fourth year. It would not make an immediate difference of course but it eventually it would starkly register and especially if you were a stargazer, as the Egyptian apparently were. Indeed, they noted that Sirius the Dog Star, which is the brightest light in the Egyptian celestial sphere and thought to rise on the first day of the flooding, was showing up during the planting season. A correction of one full year at the rate of one day every four (365.25x4) or a period of 1461-years was required to be made if the Dog Star was to rise heliacally on the first day of flooding once again. This 1461-year cycle has become known as the Sothic year. Since it is based on the 1870 find at Thebes, of an artifact that apparently recorded the heliacal rising of the Dog Star on the ninth day of the third month of Shemu, by Georg Ebers, the professor of Egyptology at Leipzig, it came to be known as Ebers Sothic Calendar.

Elephantine: Southern most city of ancient Egypt. Elephantine was Herodotus' last stop on his 'discovery of Egypt' voyage that he had undertaken, upon the waters of the Nile. Beyond Egypt, the land was inhabited by a people referred to the generic name 'Ethiopians.'

Elisha: Jewish Prophet, disciple of Prophet Elijah.

Exodus: The Jewish exodus from Egypt.

Gihon: Gihon is the name of a river mentioned in the Book of Genesis (2:10-14) that is said to have flowed though the entire length of Ethiopia.

Greek academia: My coinage, roughly corresponding to the term 'The Age of Pericles' or 'Golden Age,' used to denote the historical period in Ancient Greece, which lasted roughly from the end of the Persian Wars to the death of Pericles. Pericles (who was a prominent political leader and general of Athens) and his wife Aspasia promoted art and literature and associated with scholars from Greece and outside Greece. Notable amongst these scholars were: Thcydides, Democritus, Anaxagoras, Hippodamus and Herodotus.

Eratosthenes: (276 BC–194 BC) Eratosthenes of Cyrene was a Greek mathematician, poet, athlete, geographer and astronomer. He is noted for devising a system of latitude and longitude and for being the first known to have calculated the circumference of the Earth. He also created a map of the world based on the available geographical knowledge of the era.

Ethiopia: Generic term originally used by Greek scholars of classical antiquity to refer to the conglomerate of city-states located in the region south of Egypt.

Eusebius, Pamphilis: (240-309AD) A philosopher and student of Pamphilis. Eusebius who was from Caesaria, provided 50 Bibles from Alexandria to Constantine. The Bibles of Jerome and that of a succession of Roman scholar's were based upon this version.

Herodotus: Herodotus of Halicarnassus was a Greek historian from Ionia who lived in the 5th century BC and regarded as the 'Father of History.' He is the author of 'The History of Herodotus,' which serves here as the key ancient world secular textual source that corroborates the Bible's documented history.

Homer: Homer is the name given to the purported author of the early Greek poems the Iliad and the Odyssey. Nothing is known of him, though scholars support the idea that Homer was a real person.

Hyksos: 'Shepherd kings' of Asiatic origin who ruled Ancient Egypt. Possibly, they were the Priest of Vulcan kings of Herodotus who is documented to have ruled Egypt for 300 years.

Josephus, Flavius: (37–100AD) Jewish historian. His work include 'Antiquity of the Jews,' and 'History of the Jewish War.' Josephus was a controversial figure who played the role of a negotiator and gained favor of Flavius Vespasian (not to mention, the ire of the Jews) and eventually took his name. He elaborately recorded the destruction of Jerusalem in 70 AD by the Romans led by Flavius Vespasian's son Titus.

Labyrinth: The monument built by the 12 native Egyptian kings who ruled Egypt immediately after Sethos. According to Herodotus, it surpassed the pyramids in grandeur.

Levant: A term generally used by archaeologists to refer to the core biblical arena on the East Mediterranean Sea board.

Libya: The continent west of the Nile. According to ancient world scholars it was roughly triangular in shape.

Manetho: An Egyptian historian and priest who lived during the Ptolemaic era, ca. 3rd century BC. Manetho recorded Aegyptiaca (History of Egypt). His work is often used as evidence for the chronology of the reigns of pharaohs.

Pericles: Pericles (ca. 495–429 BC) was a prominent and influential political leader, orator and general of Athens during the city's Golden Age, specifically, the time between the Persian and Peloponnesian wars.

Pithom and Raamses: Pithom and Raamses are Egyptians store cities mentioned in the Bible, which the Jews help construct.

Plato: Plato (428 BC–348 BC), was a Classical Antiquity Greek philosopher. Together with his teacher, Socrates and his student, Aristotle, Plato helped to lay the philosophical foundations of Western culture.

Psammetichus: According to Herodotus, the Egyptian king who ruled Egypt after the end of the Priest of Vulcan king's reign.

Sea of Reeds: The Reed Sea was the name of a sea or large lake in Egypt, which Moses is said to have cleaved and led the Exodus Jews across to freedom. It was later arbitrarily changed to read 'Red Sea.'

Sesostris: Sesostris, according to Herodotus, was the first of the Priest of Vulcan kings who ruled Egypt for 300 years.

Sethos: According to Herodotus, Sethos was the last of the priest of Vulcan kings who ruled Egypt for 300 years.

Sodom and Gomorrah: Two city-states of a group of five (Sodom, Gomorrah, Admah, Zeboim and Bela) collectively referred to as "the Cities of the Plain" (Genesis 13:12) Sodom and Gomorrah were destroyed by "brimstone and fire from the Lord out of heaven."

Strabo: Strabo was philosopher cum historian cum geographer who was born in Pontus, which had then recently become part of the Roman Empire. He is famous for his 17-volume work entitled, 'Geographica,' which presented a descriptive history of people and places from different regions of the world known to his era.

Tarshish: A favorite port of calling upon a remote and currently unidentifiable coast that belonged to barbaric tribes to which Solomon, the King of Tyre and possibly the Egyptians sent their ships to trade and procure large quantities of jungle produce.

Turin papyrus: An ancient Egyptian map generally considered the oldest surviving map of geographical interest from the ancient world.

Ur of the Chaldees: Ur was an important city in a nation called Chaldea, later called Babylonia. It was the hometown of Abram (Abraham), who became the father of Isaac and the grand patriarch of Israel.

Notes & References

This book contains a number of brand new ideas that are mine and mine alone. Hence, I am unable to provide references for them. All the ideas are however based on ancient world texts. I have provided in-text citations as well as endnotes references for these ancient world texts. Please note that these texts are often presented by modern-day translators in a manner that seems to support or sanction the currently accepted reconstruction or interpretation. Mine however are fresh interpretations. The ancient world textual sources cited in this book are as follows:

1. **'The Bible.'** (King James Version)
2. **'The History of Herodotus.'** Written by Herodotus (c. 490 BC–431 BC). Translated by George Rawlinson
3. **'The Geography.'** Written by Strabo (c.64 BC –24 AD). Translated by H. L. Jones
4. **'Antiquity of the Jews.'** Written by Josephus, Flavius (37–100 AD). Translated by William Whiston
5. **'Wars of the Jews.'** Written by Josephus, Flavius (37–100 AD). Translated by William Whiston

---

Prologue

[1] The Bible (KJV), Numbers 24.5&6

[2] The Bible (KJV), Numbers 24.2

[3] The Bible (KJV), Joshua 24.13

[4] The Bible (KJV), Genesis 17.8

[5] Cultivating 'Love of God' thereby awaking it in ones heart, is the only means of going back to the Kingdom of God. This is the process of obtaining liberation outlined in all the mainstream monotheistic religions the world over. *mayy eva mana adhatsva, mayi buddhim nivesaya, nivasisyasi mayy eva, ata urdhvam na samsayah. Translation:* Just fix your mind upon Me (the Personality of Godhead) and engage all your intelligence in Me. Thus, you will live in Me always, without a doubt [Bhagavad-Gita 12.8]

Introduction

[1] In 1929 Woolley (Sir Charles Leonard Woolley) stirred world-wide interest with a melodramatic telegram, sent to London: We have found the flood! Deep down in the 40-ft. shaft sunk into the mound, Woolley had discovered a stratified layer of river clay almost 10 ft. thick. The deposit, he reasoned, could have come only from a flood of immense dimensions, a disaster of such magnitude that it had without doubt given substance to the Genesis legend of Noah and the Ark. http://www.trivia-library.com/b/major-archaeology-discovery-biblical-ur.htm

[2] Lemonick, Michael D. 'Are the Bible's Stories True?' Time magazine article, December 1995

[3] Ibid

[4] Ibid

[5] Ibid

[6] Williams, Jay. 'The Times and Life of Edward Robinson.' The Bible & Interpretation, 2000, http://www.bibleinterp.com/articles/robinson.htm

Chapter 1

[1] Encyclopedic reference. http://en.wikipedia.org/wiki/JeanFrançois_ Champollion

Chapter 3

[1] Today we have a St. Jude as well as a St. Thomas. However, it is quite likely that they were the same person. A local tradition of eastern Syria identifies Jude with the Apostle Thomas, also known as Jude Thomas or Judas Didymus Thomas. Interestingly, 'Thomas' means twin in Aramaic, as does 'Didymus' in Greek. Wikipedia 2008. What is not generally known is the fact that he was called twin because he looked exactly like Jesus. Ironically, it is the 'twin' appellation that Jude was given that cause the inadvertent duplication

[2] This bit of incidental documentation of the deserters by Herodotus can be considered the original toehold of this hypothesis-discovery

Chapter 4

[1] Herodotus. 'The History of Herodotus,' 2.137,140. Herodotus reports that, "the blind Anysis fled away to the marsh-country… He had lived in the marsh-region the whole time, having formed for himself an island there by a mixture of earth and ashes." Evidence such as the above suggests that disappearing into the marshes or through it was a viable and often used escape route

[2] Herodotus. 'The History of Herodotus,' 2.30

[3] Editorial, 'Critical Chronology And The Exodus,' Concordia Theological Quarterly, Oct 1985, http://www.ctsfw.edu/library/files/pb/ 1450

[4] The idea that the Moses Aaron team were trying to take all the Jews out of Egypt was quite well known to the Pharaoh and his counselors. Exodus 10.7

Chapter 5

[1] Josephus, Flavius. 'Antiquity of the Jews,' 10.2

Chapter 67

[1] The Bible (KJV), Numbers 25.1

[2] The Bible (KJV), Numbers 25.8

[3] Herodotus. 'The History of Herodotus,' 2.30

Chapter 7

[1] The Bible (KJV), 1 Kings 2.5-9. Moreover thou knowest also what Joab the son of Zeruiah did to me, and what he did to the two captains of the hosts of Israel, unto Abner the son of Ner, and unto Amasa the son of Jether, whom he slew, and shed the blood of war in peace, and put the blood of war upon his girdle that was about his loins, and in his shoes that

were on his feet. Do therefore according to thy wisdom, and let not his hoar head go down to the grave in peace. But shew

kindness unto the sons of Barzillai the Gileadite, and let them be of those that eat at thy table: for so they came to me when I fled because of Absalom thy brother. And, behold, thou hast with thee Shimei the son of Gera, a Benjamite of Bahurim, which cursed me with a grievous curse in the day when I went to Mahanaim: but he came down to meet me at Jordan, and I sware to him by the LORD, saying, I will not put thee to death with the sword. Now therefore hold him not guiltless: for thou art a wise man, and knowest what thou oughtest to do unto him; but his hoar head bring thou down to the grave with blood

[2] Saifullah, M S M, et al. 'Qur'anic Accuracy vs. Biblical Error: The Kings & Pharaohs of Egypt.' http://www.islamic-awareness.org/ Quran/Contrad/ External/ josephdetail.html

[3] Encyclopedic reference. Etymology of the term 'Pharaoh.' Wikipedia

[4] David Rohl, 'A Test of Time.' Century Press 1995, p 301-302

[5] Actually, every scholar seems to have a different date. The first dynasty began according to Champollion in 5867 BC, according to Mariette, in 5004 BC, Lepsius in 3892 BC, Breasted 3400 BC, and Wilkinson in 2320 BC.

[6] David Rohl, 'A Test of Time.' Century Press 1995, p 133-203

[7] I am sure Egyptologists have a contrived reason for it, but I see no reason to conjure up separate Pharaohs... one for the oppression and another for the Exodus. The Bible refers to only one Pharaoh (Pharaoh Psammetichus) during this period

Chapter 10

[1] Machines that 'recorded' sound were around for the better part for a century. Yet, it never occurred to the scientists who regularly used them, to run the machines backwards and 'playback' the sound. Edison, it is reported, took one look at the recording, and immediately discerned that a machine that 'ran backwards,' could readily be made to replay the recorded sound. http://en.wikipedia.org/wiki/ Phonograph

Chapter 11

[2] Assuming of course that Lot too had dreamed of establishing a kingdom or two in this choice valley as did Abraham. Considering that he did in fact establish a handful of kingdoms on the Plain of Jordan, and much before Abraham, this would be a safe assumption

Chapter 16

[1] Encyclopedic reference. http://encarta.msn.com/ encyclopedia_76 15562 05 /dead _sea.html

Chapter 27

[1] Herodotus. 'The History of Herodotus,' 3.12

Chapter 28

[1] Encyclopedic reference. http://en.wikipedia.org/wiki/Battle_of_Issus

Chapter 29

[2] http://www.apologeticspress.org/rr/reprints/Ras-Shamra.pdf

[3] Encyclopedic reference. http://www.encyclopedia.com/doc/1P2-17083049.html

[4] Ibid

[5] Encyclopedic reference.
http://en.wikipedia.org/wiki/Mari,_Syria

[6] Encyclopedic reference.
http://www.encyclopedia.com/doc/1P2-17083049.html

Chapter 32

[1] Herodotus. 'The History of Herodotus,' 2.6

[2] The Syrian Casius is the original Mt. Casius. It was located close to Samandagi on the Syrian coastline. At least that is where the earlier generation of modern-day scholar's had placed it. You will have to locate an earlier date publications to find the reference. The current lot of modern-day scholars however, no longer subscribe to this reconstruction

geography and therefore have relocated Mt. Casius in Egypt

[3] Milner, Thomas. 'Geography of the World.' Printwell Publishers 1988, Jaipur

[4] Strabo. 'Geography,'16.2.8

Chapter 33

[1] Herodotus. 'The History of Herodotus,' 2.158

[2] Herodotus. 'The History of Herodotus,' 2.137

[3] Milner, Thomas. 'Geography of the World.' Printwell, 1988. Jaipur

[4] Herodotus. 'The History of Herodotus,' 2.60

Chapter 34

[1] Charles, R. H. 'The Book of Jubilees.' Clarendon Press, 1913
http://www.Pseudo epigrapha.com/jubilees/index.htm

[2] Dr. S. Riehl, 'Late Bronze Age Tell Atchana,'
http://www.urgeschichte.uni-tuebingen.

de/index.php?id=193, Also, http://www. alalakh.org/ project.asp

Chapter 35

[1] Mertens, Richard. 'Deep into the Landscape.' Univ. of Chicago Magazine, Volume 95, Issue 3, Feb 2003. http://magazine. uchicago.edu/ 0302/features/

Chapter 37

[1] Joseph Fitchett & McAdams Deford. 'A River Called Rebel.' Saudi Aramco World, June 1973 http://www. Saudiaramcoworld .com/ issue/ 197303/a.river. called.rebel.htm

Chapter 41

[1] John Lewis Burckhardt. 'Travels in Syria and the Holy Land,' page 146. http://www.gutenberg.org/dirs/etext05/8sria10.txt

Chapter 44

[1] Encyclopedic reference. http://www.britannica.com/EBchecked/topic/ 657111/ ziggurat #ref = ref253473

Chapter 47

[1] Strabo. 'Geography,' 16.2.28.

[2] Meryl Getline, 'Ask the Captain.' http://www.usatoday. com/travel /columnist/ getline/2005-02-21-ask-the-captain_x.htm. At 35,000 feet, you would be able to see about 230 miles. For purposes of comparison, from a 100-meter tower (330 feet high), you could see about 22 miles.

[3] From the footnote in 'Antiquities of the Jews' provided by translator, William Whiston. This fort was first built, as it is

supposed, by John Hyrcanus; see Prid. at the year 107; and called "Baris," the Tower or Citadel. It was afterwards rebuilt, with great improvements, by Herod, under the government of Antonius, and was named from him "the Tower of Antoni;" and about the time when Herod rebuilt the temple, he seems to have put his last hand to it. See Antiq. B. XVIII. ch. 5. sect. 4; Of the War, B. I. ch. 3. sect. 3; ch. 5. sect. 4. It lay on the northwest side of the temple, and was a quarter as large

[4] The Bible, (KJV), Mark 15.16. 'And the soldiers led him away into the hall, called Praetorium; and they call together the whole band'

[5] 'The Citadel of Salah ed-Din.' AKTC brochure on the works carried out in the Ayyubid and Mamluk sections of the Citadel in 1999-2000

Photographs & Diagrams: All the diagrams, maps and charts are by the author.